COMPOSITION AND APPLIED GRAMMAR

THE WRITING PROCESS

7

Miles C. Olson

Daniel R. Kirby

Gale Dugas Hulme

Allyn and Bacon, Inc.

Boston   Rockleigh, N.J.   Atlanta   Dallas   San Jose

London   Sydney   Toronto

The Writing Process—Books 7 through 12

Authors and Consultants

Miles C. Olson, Senior Author—Professor of English Education, University of Colorado at Boulder; Director, Colorado Writing Project.

Allen Berger, Consultant—Professor of Language Communications, University of Pittsburgh; Director, Pittsburgh Reading and Writing Consultants; Editor, *English Education.*

Nancy Tia Brown, Coauthor, Book 12—Project Director in Career Education and Gifted Education, Jefferson County Public Schools, Colorado; former high-school foreign languages teacher.

Warren E. Combs, Coauthor, Book 8—Writing Consultant, Clarke and DeKalb County Schools, Georgia.

Philip DiStefano, Coauthor, Book 11—Professor of English Education and Reading, University of Colorado at Boulder; Co-Director, Colorado Writing Project; Consultant, National Assessment of Educational Progress.

Michael G. Gessner—Research Associate, Center for the Study of Reading and Writing, University of Colorado at Boulder. Contributing Author, Book 11.

Gale Dugas Hulme, Coauthor, Books 7 and 10—Language Arts Consultant for Gwinnett County Public Schools, Lawrenceville, Georgia; former high-school English teacher and department chair.

Sandra Jones—Language Arts Supervisor for the Dougherty County Schools, Albany, Georgia. Contributing Author, Book 7.

Daniel R. Kirby, Coauthor, Books 7 and 10—Professor of English Education, University of Georgia at Athens.

Kathleen Kirby—Instructor, University of Georgia, Athens, Georgia. Contributing Author, Book 10.

Carol B. Kuykendall, Coauthor, Books 9 and 12—Executive Director, English Language Arts, Houston (Texas) Independent School District.

Cherie A. Lyons, Coauthor, Book 12—Project Director in Career Education, Jefferson County Public Schools, Colorado; former high-school English teacher.

Iris M. Tiedt, Coauthor, Book 10—Professor, San Jose State University (California); Director, South Bay Writing Project.

Acknowledgments for material quoted from other sources will be found on page 328 which is an extension of this page.

Senior Editor: Patricia A. Browne
Editor: Faith W. Critchley
Senior Designer: Beverly Fell
Preparation Services Coordinator: Martha E. Ballentine
Production and Art Services by Tonia Noell-Roberts

Library of Congress Catalog Card No. 81-68466

Printed in the United States of America

ISBN 0-205-07540-1

6   7   8   9   89   88   87   86   85

CONTENTS

Unit ONE   **Sharpening the Pencil**   **1**

Chapter 1   Writing About Feelings   3

         2   Telling   17

         3   Opening Your Senses   33

Unit TWO   **Watching and Writing**   **45**

Chapter 4   Tuning In   47

         5   Talking Back to the Tube   63

Unit THREE   **Juggling Words**   **79**

Chapter 6   Sketching a Character   81

         7   Games Poets Play   107

         8   Performing Poetic Feats   129

Unit FOUR   **Searching**   **161**

Chapter 9   Digging in the Decades   163

     10   Sharing Discoveries   183

Unit FIVE   **Writing to Get Things Done**   **199**

Chapter 11   Exploring the Family   201

     12   Reviewing the Family   229

     13   Post Office Power   259

Unit SIX   **Telling Tales**   **287**

Chapter 14   The Wisdom of the People   289

     15   Ghost Writing   309

WRITER'S HANDBOOK   H-1

Index

Sharpening
the
Pencil

l peaceful a

f lonely. I fee

g us. I feel like g

nd starting over and

ussing with my sister

l want to run and

ly being a baby again

Chapter 1

Writing About Feelings

This is a book about writing. Before you say, "So what," look through the book. It may look like an ordinary English book, but we hope you will find it surprisingly different. We hope you will find the activities interesting and even inviting. This book can help you improve as a writer, if you are willing to work at the job.

What Writing Isn't . . .

Writing isn't often easy. Let's face it. Sometimes writing is scary business. If your hand gets sweaty or butterflies in your stomach start zooming around when you think about writing, you are not alone. Even very experienced writers get nervous and frustrated about writing. What is so nerve-racking about writing? Why is it difficult to get all those words in our heads to flow down our arms and onto the page?

Two problems worry most beginning writers: (1) What do I say? and (2) How do I say it correctly? Both problems are important, and this book is designed to help you solve them. Each writing activity in this book begins by helping you think about what you want to say. Ideas come first in good writing, and the activities will help you get your minds working each time you write.

Some of you may be afraid to write because you do not know how to spell every word you want to use. You may not know where all the commas and semicolons go. You may not always know where sentences begin and end. Relax. This book will help you with those problems as you work through the writing activities. Spelling, punctuation, and the other mechanics of writing are important, but you will learn those as you use them in your writing. Right now your job is to concentrate on getting your thoughts and feelings on paper. From the very beginning this book will "accent-u-ate the positive," as Jiminy Cricket once said.

3

What Writing Is . . .

Writing is turning your mind inside out. When we put our thoughts and feelings into words and put those words onto paper, we are writing. Writing is more than that, however. Those thoughts on paper must make sense to someone else—a reader. Writing is communication: communicating thoughts and ideas to another. We judge writing by how well the message gets across.

Communicating with others is usually much easier in person. If we can see people and talk to them, we can usually understand them and they can understand us. Most human beings are good talkers. We learn how to talk as young children by listening to the older people around us. Communicating in writing is different. The reader can't see us. The reader can't ask us questions. The reader has only our words on the page. If the writing is clear, the reader "hears" us and understands our message. If the writing is muddy, the reader is left wondering.

Free Writing

You will be doing many free writings throughout this book. Free writing is a way to get your mind working and your words flowing. When you write freely, write as fast as you can, jotting down whatever crosses your mind. If you get stuck, just write, "I can't think of anything to write," or reread what you've written so that you can pick up the flow of your ideas. The important thing is to keep the words coming. *Don't* worry about spelling or punctuation. If you think of a word you can't spell, just put down the first few letters of the word. Get your thoughts down on paper quickly.

~~~~~~~~~~~~~~~~~~~~~~~~~~~~~~~~~

Getting It Down

Me and Writing

Write for ten minutes about your past experiences with writing. Think about them for a few minutes. You could tell about something you wrote which made you proud, about how you feel when the teacher gives a writing assignment, or how you feel right now as you try to get your thoughts on paper. Remember: Keep writing; keep moving the pen across the page; keep the words coming.

~~~~~~~~~~~~~~~~~~~~~~~~~~~~~~~~~

Free-Writing Checklist

Because you wrote your free writing quickly, it may need a careful second look. Use the following checklist each time you finish a piece of free writing:

1. Reread your free writing quietly to yourself.   Checking
2. Ask yourself these questions: It
    a. Does it sound like me talking?   Out
    b. Is it truthful?
    c. Does it say what I wanted to say?
3. Check carefully for missing words.
4. Fix up any parts which aren't clear.
5. Reread your free writing again.

Put your free writing aside now, and look at these writings by other students:

> When I am asked to write something, everything seems to go
> blank. It's as if someone just cut off my head. There's just
> nothing up there to come out.
>
> *Jacki*

Does this sound like something you have felt before? Jacki gives us a vivid picture. We can see the poor, headless student sitting there without anything to say.

> Some of the things I like about writing are that you can
> express your thoughts by writing them down. You can commu-
> nicate with anyone you want to without talking, and it's a way
> to demuddle your thoughts. I don't like writing when a teacher
> just gives you a sheet of paper and says, "Write something."
>
> *Mindy*

Mindy tells us about things she likes and dislikes. She uses the surprising word *demuddle* which expresses just how she feels. In the last sentence Mindy lets us hear the teacher's voice say, "Write something."

One time I wrote a poem about "wind" and I got it in the newspaper. I felt very proud of myself. My family was proud, too.

Sometimes I write about movies.

Sometimes I get frustrated when I can't spell a word. I get very frustrated when I can't think of anything to write.

I feel good when I let someone read a story I wrote and they say, "That's good."

Matt

Matt shares a proud moment with us and we can feel how pleased he was with his poem. He uses the strong word *frustrated* when he writes about spelling. In the last sentence he writes of sharing his writings with others and we hear them say, "That's good."

Jacki, Mindy, and Matt have all written honest feelings with surprising and vivid words. Read your free writing again. Mark any surprising or vivid words. Mark any parts you think are particularly good. Your teacher may ask you to share some of these parts with the class. Keep all your free writings in a writing folder.

Helping Each Other

Learning to write need not be a painful and embarrassing experience. Writing comes easily for some people. Others struggle to get even a few words on paper. Some writers can spell any words; some have a terrible time with spelling. In a writing class, "We're all in this together." The teacher is your best resource, but he or she cannot give each of you as much individual help as you may need. That means writers must help each other. You may find it difficult to share something you have written with other students, at first. This next activity is designed to help you find out more about yourself and the other students in the class. Sharing information about yourself will make it easier for you to work with other students.

~~~~~~

Getting It Down

Personal-Interest Inventory

Write the answer to each of the following survey questions on a separate sheet of paper. Complete this survey as honestly as you can. Your teacher may ask you to share some of your answers.

1. What is your name?
2. What is your nickname, if you have one? How did you get your nickname?
3. What is your birthdate and astrological sign?
4. List some places where you have lived.
5. Which place where you lived feels or felt most like home? Why?
6. What was the best birthday you ever had? Explain.
7. List your favorite in each of the following categories:
   TV show
   Recording group
   Movie
   Book
   Sports team
8. Name someone you really respect and look up to. Why do you respect this person so much?
9. What is your favorite subject in school? Why do you like that subject?
10. What is the best thing you've ever done at school?

SPOTLIGHT

Writing About Yourself

Have you ever sat down somewhere in a quiet place and tried to sort out your thoughts and feelings about yourself and who you are? Sometimes writing down your jumbled thoughts and feelings can help your untangle them and make sense of them.

Read this excerpt from the novel *Very Far Away from Anywhere Else* by Ursula K. LeGuin. A boy named Owen talks about school and how he sees himself:

I am always the youngest person in my class. And the youngest person in my family, being the only child. They let me into school early because I was such a bright little jerk. I have always been bright for my age. Who knows, at forty-five I may still be bright for my age. That is partly what this thing I'm telling, this story, is about. About being a bright little jerk.

It's OK, you know, up to about the sixth grade. Nobody really cares, least of all yourself. The teachers are mostly pretty nice to you, because you're easy to teach. Some of them love you for it, and give you neat books for extra reading. Some of them resent it, but they're too busy with the Behavior Problem types to have time to really make you feel lousy for being ahead of the others in math and reading. And there's always a few other kids, usually girls, who are as smart as you are, or smarter, and you and they write the class skits, and make lists for the teacher, and so on. And besides, for all the talk about how cruel little kids are, they haven't got a patch on older people for cruelty. Little kids are just dumb, the smart ones and the slow ones. They do dumb things. They say what they think. They haven't learned enough yet to say what they don't really think. That comes later, when kids begin to turn into people and find out that they are alone.

I think what you mostly do when you find you really are alone is panic. You rush to the opposite extreme and pack yourself into groups—clubs, teams, societies, types. You suddenly start dressing exactly like others. It's a way of being invisible. The way you sew the patches on the holes in your blue jeans becomes incredibly important. If you do it wrong you're not with it. You have to be with it. That's a peculiar phrase, you know? With it. With what? With them. With the others. All together. Safety in numbers. I'm not me. I'm a basketball letter. I'm a popular kid. I'm my friends' friend. I'm a black leather growth on a Honda. I'm a member. I'm a teen-ager. You can't see me, all you can see is us. We're safe.

1. Owen calls himself a "bright little jerk." How do you think he feels about himself? How would you summarize who you are in three words?

2. Owen says little kids are dumb because "they say what they think. They haven't learned enough yet to say what they don't really think." "Saying what you think" is being honest. How often do you say what you think? Does that ever get you into trouble? When do people say "what they don't think"?

3. In the last paragraph Owen talks about the fear of being alone. Notice two strong verbs in the second sentence: *rush* and *pack*. What else is unusual about this paragraph? Look at the short two-word sentences. Notice how he repeats "I'm a . . ." Can you hear Owen's voice? Does it sound like a real person talking?

Read this next selection from the novel *The Real Me* by Betty Miles. This is a story about Barbara. She talks about herself quite honestly.

I'm not exactly fat, but I am what you might call "plump" or "chubby" if you are the kind of person who uses those words.

Naturally, I would like to be slender and attractive. I always read those ads about losing weight that have long stories, with Before and After pictures. First the person confesses how big she was, "I was married to a cowboy, but I was as big as a horse," and then she tells how she discovered delicious candies that killed her appetite and she lost 100 pounds and went from Hips 40 to Hips 34. If I lost 100 pounds I would be dead, but I wouldn't mind losing three or four.

My mother says the only reducing aid I need is a closed mouth. She says if I would be more careful about snacks I would certainly lose weight, and that anyway I will lose my fat stomach when I get older, and have a nice figure. It's funny not to know how you are going to look in the future. I keep watching the eighth-grade girls. They act so sure of themselves, as if they know they are real teen-agers, and not this dumb age I am, which people call "pre-teen" or "young junior" when they want to sell you clothes. It's awful to have to go to one of those departments and hunt for something that fits, and have the salesladies try to sell you "Little Princess" underwear and call you "dear."

1. Barbara is conscious of her appearance, but she keeps her sense of humor. What funny lines do you see in this excerpt?
2. She mentions being at a "dumb" age. Do you ever feel you are at that "dumb" age? What are some "dumb" things you do that drive other people crazy?

It's your turn now to write about yourself. To help you think of some words to get you started, borrow from the following "word bank." The words in this word bank have been used by other students in their feelings writings. Use any of these words if they fit your feelings. Your teacher may ask you to brainstorm more words for the bank.

| frustrated | scared | proud | idiotic |
| excited | satisfied | tired | gigantic |

bored	apprehensive	guilty	out–of–place
confused	anxious	helpless	uneasy
lonely	terrified	powerful	useless
peaceful	stupid	clumsy	lost
	curious	energetic	

~~~~~~

Feelings About Me

Getting It Down

Use the word bank and any other words in your head to write about yourself. Write for ten minutes. Do not worry about punctuation or spelling. Choose honest words. Don't stop writing.

~~~~~~

Checking It Out

Use your free-writing checklist on page 5 as you read over your feelings writing.

Following is a sample feelings writing by another student:

I feel peaceful, and I feel sort of lonely. I feel afraid to grow up. I feel like going back and starting over and never fussing with my sister again. I want to run and start over by being a baby again. I just feel a little clammed up and frustrated with myself. I don't know why. But, I am feeling better because I'm letting out what was inside of me.

Janet

Janet's opening sentence is powerful. She shares two different kinds of feelings: "peaceful" and "lonely." Her wish to start over is vivid because she mentions wanting to be a baby again. "Clammed up" is another expression which gives the reader a picture of her feelings. Janet's writing is moving because she shares real feelings so honestly.

Read your free writing again. Circle any vivid words or sentences. Mark any parts you think others would like to hear. Your teacher may ask you to share some of these parts with your class. Put this writing in your writing folder.

~~~~~~

SPOTLIGHT

Writing Truthfully

You have been writing and thinking about your feelings. Describing your feelings is a good way to start writing because you are an expert on your own feelings. Good writers write about things they know, and they speak truthfully. You can be a better writer if you use the words *inside your* own head. Sometimes beginning writers try to use somebody else's words. Their writing may sound phony or untruthful. The words *inside your* head are the best words to describe your feelings. Use them fearlessly, and your writing will have the ring of truth.

Let's look at some examples of truthful writing from other students:

> I am so mad! Mrs. Brooks gave Karen a discipline notice just because she laughed in class. I know Brooks warned her, but I still don't think it's fair. Karen was sitting in the office crying when I went by.
>
> *Cinda*

Cinda is "mad" and she lets us know it. There are no phony words in that writing.

> I am worried because my Dad is real sick. His blood pressure is sky high and he is overweight. The doctor said if he doesn't lose weight and if his blood pressure doesn't come down, he will die. Mom, my brother, and I have tried to get him to take care of himself. "If you won't do it for yourself, do it for us," we said. We beg him every night not to eat so much. He won't listen to us. Oh I hope he doesn't die.
>
> *Beth*

Beth shares an honest concern about her father. We can hear how worried she is because she uses her own words to express feelings.

Writing About Someone Else

Most of us have someone in our life we look up to. Sometimes that person is a parent or a teacher. Sometimes it is an older brother or sister. Sometimes it is a friend our own age. Think for a minute: Who is someone you really respect and admire? While you are thinking, read this short excerpt from a short story called, "Someone Special." David tells about a teacher in his past for whom he had special feelings.

You know what happened to me in the fourth grade? I fell in love. Man, did I fall in love. Her name was Miss Simpson, my teacher. She was really somethin' else. Miss Simpson was tall and smooth, with black shiny eyes and beautiful black skin, just about the same color as mine. Her hair was always up on a big afro, and she wore the greatest clothes I ever saw. All kinds of fancy colors and styles. Sometimes she wore dashikis and stuff, that's African clothes, and all kind of beads and bracelets. She was a flash dancer, too. She used to show us African dances, and breathing exercises, like yogi stuff from India.

David

1. Notice how David begins by describing what Miss Simpson looked like. Which of these describing words do you like best?
2. Notice how specific David's writing is. He doesn't just tell us Miss Simpson is pretty, a fancy dresser, and a good dancer. Instead he *shows* us these things by using words. Point to some of these good, concrete, specific words.

Read this example of writing about a friend from A *Taste of Wild Blackberries* by Doris Buchanan Smith:

That Jamie. For my best friend he surely did aggravate me sometimes. I mean, if we got to pretending—circus dogs, for instance—he didn't know when to quit. You could get tired and want to do something else, but that stupid Jamie would crawl around barking all afternoon. Sometimes it was funny. Sometimes it was just plain tiresome.

1. How is this writing different from David's?
2. How does the author give us a picture of Jamie without describing him?

Feelings About a Person

Getting It Down

Have you thought of a person who means something to you? Think of *specific* reasons why you like him or her. Write the name of that person at the top of a sheet of paper. Then do either of the following: (1) Jot down a list of things that person does or doesn't do. Be specific. (2) List some words which describe that person. Use concrete words. Write for ten minutes about your person, using some of the words in your list.

Checking It Out

Use your free-writing checklist on page 5 to check your writing. Mark any parts of your writing that you like. Circle any surprising or vivid words.

Your teacher may ask you to share some of these parts with your classmates.

Writer's Workbench 1

Strong Verbs

A verb is the heart of a sentence. Strong verbs capture the reader's eye. Strong verbs add power to your writing and give a punch to your sentence. Look at this example:

The tired, old man (walked) down the street.

Walked is the heart of the sentence. It tells us what the old man did: he *walked*.

Walked is a tired verb. It is a word we use all the time. Good writers work to use fresh, strong verbs.

Walked is not a strong verb. We do not know *how* he walked. Strong verbs would help the reader *see* the old man. Strong verbs would provide the reader with a mental picture.

Think of some strong verbs to replace *walked*.

The tired, old man (♡) down the street.

How about *stumbled* or *shuffled* or *limped* or *wandered*?

These four examples are strong verbs because they give the reader a more vivid picture of the old man.

Form small groups. Each member of your group should choose one of the following sentences. Working individually, brainstorm as many strong verbs as you can for the tired verb in the heart. Write them on a sheet of paper. After five minutes, share your list with other members of the group and add any of their suggestions to your list. Following is an example:

The tired, old man (walked) down the street.
paced
trudged
stumbled
skipped

1. The big jet (flew) into the sky.

2. The dancers (moved) in the bright lights.

3. Our scout troup (walked) up the mountain.

4. The flag (moved) in the breeze.

5. The red car (drove) out of the parking lot.

6. The uncertain skier (skied) down the slope.

Writer's Workbench 2

Revision

Good writers revise and rework their writings many times before they are satisfied. The books and stories you read may have been rewritten many times before you see them. The free writings in your folder are *first drafts*. You wrote them quickly without worrying about precise wording or the mechanics of spelling and punctuation.

Look back over your free writings. Choose the one you like best or the one you think has the most potential. If you can't decide, ask your teacher or a friend for advice.

Use the following checklist to revise and rework the writing you have selected:

Editing

1. Read your writing aloud carefully. Have you left out any words? Does your writing make sense?
2. Look at the verb in each sentence. Can you think of a stronger verb?
3. Have you used vivid words to help the reader "see" your writing?

Proofing

This is the final step in finishing a piece of writing. You may need some help here. Don't be afraid to ask for it.

1. Check to see that each sentence begins with a capital letter and ends with a period, a question mark, or an exclamation point.
2. Double-check any questionable spelling.
3. Recopy the writing very carefully.
4. Exchange papers with a friend and read each other's papers carefully.
5. Smile. You have just *finished* a piece of writing.

Chapter 2

Telling

Long ago, before human beings could read and write, they communicated their histories by telling them to each other. Older people told the young about past wars and celebrations and traditions. Fathers explained to their sons about providing food and shelter for their families. Mothers told their daughters about gathering and preparing food and raising children. People learned about life events and roles by listening to someone tell about them.

Before television and before magazines and newspapers, people depended on telling not only for important information, but also for entertainment. Storytellers, people who had developed a flair for telling, were welcome guests around the hearth fires.

Life is not as simple as it used to be. Mothers work; fathers work. Mothers and fathers share the responsibilities for raising children and maintaining a home. Many rely on television and other electronic media to do much of their telling.

The art of storytelling is all but lost in the electronic, instant information world in which we live. Good storytellers are harder to find. Is there someone in your family—a grandparent, an uncle, an aunt—who is good at telling stories about what life was like in the "old days"? Can you remember a favorite family story? Ask one of your older friends or relatives to tell you a family story.

Hundreds of years ago medieval knights wore fancy embroidered coats of arms. These colorful shields told of the knight's bravery and strength. The shield was a picture story telling about the knight's accomplishments.

You may not have any heroic exploits to advertise, but you do have interests and abilities which you could tell to someone else. In the following activity you will first *draw* your story and then tell someone else about the pictures. You don't have to be a great artist. For this shield you will sketch a picture of some things *you* find meaningful. Sometimes stick figures will work. Other times you may want to draw something in more detail. Whatever you decide, remember that your effort is more important than your artistic talent.

Coat of Arms

Getting It Down

Use the shield your teacher has given you or draw one of your own. Divide the shield into six parts, similar to the following:

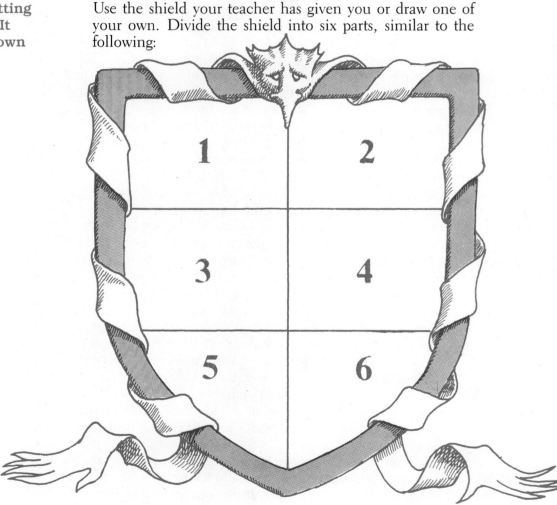

In *space 1* draw *two things* you do well. Think of two activities you do well and draw pictures to illustrate them. Maybe you play soccer, or the oboe. Maybe you write stories. Maybe you are a good babysitter. Maybe you sleep well.

In *space 2* draw a picture of the place where you feel most at home. It may be a tree house in your back yard or a hideout by the river or your own bedroom or the couch in front of the television. Draw the place where you feel most comfortable.

In *space 3* draw your greatest success. Maybe you learned how to swim or you got straight A's or you wrote a story which appeared in the newspaper or you trained your dog to do some tricks. Draw something which made you feel very successful.

In *space 4* draw three people who have been most important in your life. Think about parents, relatives, teachers, members of the clergy, friends, or pets who have contributed to your life, and draw three of them.

In *space 5* draw a picture of what you want to be doing in ten years. How old will you be in ten years? What do you think you will be doing—working, traveling, playing? Draw it.

In *space 6* draw a picture of what you would do if you had a holiday and you could spend it any way you wished. Maybe you would take a trip to Mexico or fix up your bike or read books or ski down a mountain.

Across the bottom, write three words you would like others to say about you. This is your motto.

Share your coat of arms with someone else and tell him or her what the pictures mean. Your teacher may want to post your shields around the room.

Checking It Out

Writer's Workbench 1

Sentences, Sentence Parts, and Non-sentences

So far you have been learning to write by practicing writing. The free writings, the strong verbs practice, and the revision work you have done in the first chapter are important steps in becoming a better writer. In this chapter and throughout the remainder of the book you will also practice building and combining sentences. Sentence-combining exercises are based on knowledge about writing which is already in your head. The exercises are designed to give you more options in your writing style so that you can vary your sentence length and surprise the reader.

As with any new activity, there are some basic definitions you need to know:

Sentence: A sentence is a string of words that makes sense and is complete.
Example: I like to write stories.

Sentence Part: A sentence part is a string of words that makes sense but is not complete.
Example: Some of the boys

Non-sentence: A non-sentence is a string of words that does not make sense.
Example: girl that I strange

● For more information about sentences, sentence parts, and non-sentences, see page H-63 in the Writer's Handbook at the back of this text. Check to see whether you understand these definitions by doing the following activity:

Number from 1 to 10 on a sheet of paper. Write S if the string of words is a sentence. Write SP if the string of words is a sentence part. Write NS if the string of words is a non-sentence.

1. Hoping it wouldn't rain.
2. Soccer is a tough sport.
3. After we finished the ice cream.
4. Yellow of table stop to.
5. A little-known rock group called the "French Fries."
6. I was paid a dollar for that story.
7. Saturday and paid tennis in bad.

8. Dropping from the airplane and hoping for a soft landing.
9. She didn't mention the alligators.
10. Here before I mountain buffalo.

Make up three examples of your own for each definition: sentence, sentence part, and non-sentence.

Good storytellers do not always stick to the truth. Sometimes they exaggerate the facts to make a good story. Remember the Paul Bunyan legends and that huge blue ox, Babe? Sometimes storytellers rearrange the facts to make the story more interesting. Sometimes storytellers invent characters and events which are believable, but not true. What kind of storyteller are you? To help you find out, do the following activity.

True and False Stories

Tell a story to your classmates. The story may be either true or false. It should be about something that has or might have happened to you. For example, it might be a story about the second grade. ("When I was in second grade, I won the school spelling contest.") It might be a story about when you were a baby. ("I won a contest for the best-looking baby in Texas.") It might be a story about your father or mother. ("My father was an Olympic swimmer." "My mother went to school with the First Lady.")

After you have told your story, your classmates will guess whether it is true or false. The object is to fool them.

Getting It Started

Group Story

Now that you've practiced storytelling, try writing a story as a group. Your teacher will divide you into groups of four. Following are four story-starters. Each member of your group will write a paragraph in each of the four stories. When your group is finished, you will have four stories.

Getting It Down

1. When I was much younger I was very interested in animals. Our house looked like a zoo. I had animal cages everywhere . . .

2. Over the years I've had a number of strange friends. Let me share some of these characters with you . . .
3. Every day is an adventure in my life. The first thing I do each morning . . .
4. One time I really worried my parents. I'm usually pretty good, but once I . . .

~~~~~~

Checking It Out

Read your group stories to each other.

~~~~~~

SPOTLIGHT

Childhood Memories

One of the joys of growing older is collecting memories. Sometimes, young people think of old age as an awful, lonely period of sitting around doing nothing. Many older people say that they enjoy the time to sit and replay old memories and laugh and relive the good times from the past.

Even though you are young, you also have a storehouse of memories from your early years. Remember the trip to Disneyworld or the summer you spent with your grandmother or the dog who always slept on your bed? Of course, not all memories are pleasant, but one of the curious characteristics of human beings is that they tend to remember good times and forget bad times. Read the following memory about good and bad times from the book *Temple of Gold* by William Goldman:

> Giving credit where it's due, I freely admit that had it not been for my mother, I never would have gotten him in the first place, as my father was against it from the start, mainly because he didn't like dogs. You couldn't help liking Baxter though, since he was far and away the greatest animal ever to walk on four feet, a thoroughbred cocker spaniel, small and golden brown. Once I got Baxter—which happens to be my father's middle name, proving I was no moron even then—I

was almost never home, but rather out in the ravine or running around the neighborhood or down at the beach.

All of which secretly suited my mother, I think, because she was at that time challenging for the lead in the faculty wives' league and the local PTA. There were always meetings going on at my house, three and more per week. My father took to coming home later than usual.

The day it happened there was a big PTA meeting at our house, so I obviously planned to be absent. Which I was. I went down to the beach and skipped stones awhile. Then I threw sticks for Baxter to fetch, trying to fake him out by

pointing one direction and throwing in the other. I didn't fool him once, since he was smarter probably than I was, even though I was more than eight at the time. Finally, I got bored and he was panting some, so we headed for town, and right when we crossed the main street, with me watching it all, Baxter was run over and killed by a big gray car.

At first I didn't believe it but just stood there as the car ground to a stop and the driver got out. He came back and looked down at Baxter. Then he prodded him with his shoe. When I saw that I let out a yell and went tearing up, not caring about the people gathering around or the honks from the other cars stymied there on the main street of town. I was screaming blue murder and nothing anybody could do would make me stop, so finally they all stepped back. I bent over Baxter, picked him up, cradling him in my arms, the blood from his body slopping onto my clothes.

Then I started home. Because I was crying, the trees, the grass, the sky, everything melted together and I saw mostly the color green, a long tunnel of green with me in the middle, walking through it, going home. I kept expecting Baxter to come to, so I shook him every so often. We were both drenched with blood and my stomach ached from crying and that walk is the closest I ever expect to come to the march on Calvary.

Kicking the front door open, I went into the living room. It was set up like an auditorium, with rows of wooden, stiff-backed chairs, an aisle down the middle, and a speaker at the front—who happened to be my mother. When she saw me, she stopped talking and stared. All the others did the same, turning, watching me as I stood there holding Baxter, the both of us covered with blood.

"Baxter's been murdered," I said, and right away the room was full of buzz-buzz-buzz. But nobody moved. "Baxter is dead," I said again, staring straight at my mother.

She just stood there. I was looking right into her eyes, the both of us like statues, and in her eyes I could see it, that she was ashamed. Of me.

I turned and made for the door when I heard Mrs. O'Brien saying: "You go on with the meeting. I'll take care of Raymond," and then she had an arm around me, not caring about the blood. She was a fine woman, Mrs. O'Brien; built kind of like a cube, but fine nonetheless.

She talked to me awhile, saying that probably we ought to bury Baxter, seeing as how he was dead. I nodded, and went to get the shovel from the garage. Then we both walked into the ravine. Putting Baxter down gently, I started to dig. When the hole was large enough, I set him inside and began covering him. While I was doing that my mother came down and told me how sorry she was.

1. Raymond tells us about a very sad moment from his childhood. Have you ever been through an experience such as this? What was it? Could you write about it?
2. Look at the paragraph in which Raymond talks about starting home (page 24). He says, "the trees, the grass, the sky, everything melted together, and I saw mostly the color green, a long tunnel of green with me in the middle. . . ." Notice how he captures the feeling of walking and crying: "a long tunnel of green."
3. Look at the strong verbs the author uses. List ten good verbs that put the reader at the scene.

Jot List

Have you been thinking about some memories from your childhood? List three or four vivid memories on a sheet of paper. Share these memories with a partner and explain why they are memorable.

Select the memory which is most vivid. Ask your partner to help you make the choice.

Now jot down, as fast as you can, anything which comes to mind as you think about that memory. Make a list. Record sights, sounds, any details. Play that memory over in your head, and write down any words or phrases you can think of. Don't stop too soon. Keep that list going. How did you feel when it happened? What was the weather like? What did other people do? What details can you remember? Keep working on your list.

Reread your list and circle the most vivid details. These are details you will want to be sure to include in your memory writing.

Getting
It
Started

Writer's Workbench 2

Sentence-Combining

In this exercise you will use cues to combine three sentences into one longer sentence. In the following example, the cues (,) and (, and) tell you how to combine the sentences. Move each cue in parentheses to the front of the sentence it follows as the arrows indicate. Cross out any repeated words.

Uncle Arnold slowed his truck.

, Uncle Arnold wheeled into the Crown Station.   (,)

,and Uncle Arnold filled the gas tank.   (, and)

The combined sentence is:

Uncle Arnold slowed his truck, wheeled into the Crown Station, and filled the gas tank.

Combine the following sentences on a separate sheet of paper. Use the preceding example as a guide.

1. The excited horse threw his rider.
    The excited horse bolted for the fence.   (,)
    The excited horse headed for the woods.   (, and)

2. The pilot swooped low over the field.
    The pilot dipped his wing tip.   (,)
    The pilot smiled at the crowd.   (, and)

3. Magic Johnson ripped off the rebound.
    Magic Johnson flipped an outlet pass.   (,)
    Magic Johnson headed up court.   (, and)

4. The teacher smiled at Mike.
    The teacher winked at Marie.   (,)
    The teacher patted Joey on the head.   (, and)

5. Please don't fold this page.
    Please don't crumple it.   (,)
    Please don't tear it.   (, or)

6. The hungry trucker munched his burger.
   The hungry trucker gulped his coffee.   (,)
   The hungry trucker asked for more coffee.   (, and)

7. The kite soared.
   The kite dove.   (,)
   The kite zoomed crazily in the wind.   (, and)

8. You can call me Ray.
   You can call me Jay.   (,)
   You can call me Ray-Jay.   (, and)

9. Stop at the tracks.
   Look for trains.   (,)
   Listen for the whistle.   (, and)

10. Put two dollars in an envelope.
    Address it to me.   (,)
    Seal it with a kiss.   (, and)

Invent two exercises of your own using the same rules.

Childhood Memory

Take out your childhood memory jot list. Read it over, thinking about your memory. Now free write about that memory as vividly and completely as you can. Tell the little details about the experience. Use as many details from your jot list as possible. Don't stop writing until you have told the whole story.

Getting It Down

Use the free-writing checklist in Chapter 1 as you reread your free writing.

Checking It Out

Writer's Workbench 3

Beginnings

Take a look at the beginning of your memory writing. How did you start your story? Following are three ways good writers begin stories. See if one might work for your story.

"Once Upon a Time"

Remember all those fairy tales you used to like when you were a child? Most of them began with "Once upon a time." Many good stories begin by taking the reader back to the very beginning. They have opening sentences such as:

"I'll never forget that day . . ."

or

"I was only eight years old then . . ."

or

"It's been ten years but I still remember . . ."

All of these beginnings use time as a way of getting the reader into the story. Write an opening for your story using time as a reference.

In the Middle

Another effective way to begin a story is to start in the middle, maybe at the most exciting or vivid point in the story. That excitement catches the reader's eye, and then you backtrack in your story to fill in the details. In Raymond's story, for instance (page 22), the author might have begun with, "As we crossed the main street, with me watching it all, Baxter was run over and killed by a big gray car."

When you begin your story in the middle, you ask the reader to jump into the story. Find the most important point in your story and write a beginning paragraph from that point.

At the End

Some stories begin at the end. The reader knows how the story ends as soon as he or she reads the first paragraph. Good writers sometimes tell the ending first to get the reader curious about how it all happened.

> "It really hurt to lose that game. We had practiced so long and so hard."
>
> or
>
> "I learned a valuable lesson that day and I never forgot it."
>
> or
>
> "People say I'm a good skater, but it wasn't always this way. I remember my first time on skates . . ."

Take a look at your memory writing. Write a beginning paragraph that tells the end of your story.

You should have three possible beginnings for your memory writing. Read each one over carefully. Decide which works best. Ask the advice of a classmate or two.

CHECKPOINT

Your teacher will use Checkpoint 1 on page 31 to evaluate your childhood memory paper.

Your score will be computed by multiplying the appropriate number from 1 to 5 (listed across the top of the scale) by the number next to each category. For example, if your score in *Strong Verbs* is not 1 ("Use verbs that paint a picture."), but not quite 3 ("I see you've been working at it."), your teacher will judge it to be a 2, multiplying 2 by 4 for a score of 8 in *Strong Verbs*. If you have no errors in *First Word Capitalization and End Punctuation*, your teacher will multiply 2 by 5, for a total of 10 in that category. Each category is scored in this way. A paper that is perfect in each category rates 100. This kind of scoring enables you to see where you excel and where you need to improve.

Use the following checklist to revise and rework your writing:

Editing

1. Read your paper aloud.
2. Check for strong verbs and vivid details.
3. Reread your beginning. Be sure it gets the reader into your story quickly.

4. Check to be sure that all of your sentences are *complete*. Don't leave any *sentence parts* lying around in your writing.
5. Could any sentences be restructured by combining them with other sentences?

Proofing

1. Check all sentences. Do they begin with capitals and end with a period, question mark, or exclamation point?
2. Check that spelling. If you're not sure, ask or look up the word.
3. Recopy your paper carefully.
4. Exchange papers with a friend for a last double check.

CHECKPOINT 1

	1	2	3	4	5

Honest Writing   ×4=

Try again. Write fast. Use the words in your own head.

You're moving. Keep working.

Yes! Fresh honest language. Good!

Vivid, Concrete Detail   ×4=

Try again. Your writing is bare. Add more specific detail.

Some good detail in your writing. Add more specifics. Stay away from generalizations.

Surprising words. Concrete word pictures. Good!

Strong Verbs   ×4=

Try again. Use verbs that paint a picture. See Writer's Workbench 1 in Chapter 1.

I see you've been working at it.

Good. I like those verbs!

First Word Capitalization and End Punctuation   ×2=

Many sentences do not begin with capitals. Many sentences do not end with appropriate punctuation. See me for help.

Some errors. Proofread carefully.

All sentences begin with capital letters and end with appropriate punctuation.

Overall Impression   ×6=

You really haven't given this assignment a fair shot. Spend more time developing ideas for writing.

Yes. I see potential. Keep working.

I was touched by your writing. You connected with your audience.

Chapter **3**

Opening Your Senses

As human beings, most of us are blessed with five senses. We use our *sight* to read the Sunday comics, to watch a favorite TV show, and to look at a flock of birds flying overhead. We use our *hearing* to listen on the phone, to hear a baby cry, and to listen to music. We use our sense of *smell* to catch the first signs of good food in the kitchen, to enjoy the sweet fragrance of the honeysuckle in the spring, and to notice that after-a-rain fresh smell. We use our sense of *taste* to savor the last crumb of a fresh brownie, to judge whether the gravy needs salt, and to tell whether the lemonade is too tart. We use our sense of *touch* to find a light switch in the dark, to ruffle a kitten's fur, and to enjoy holding the hand of someone we love.

Many people who do not have all five senses say they get along well because they have learned to rely on the ones they have. Blind people, for instance, rely on their hearing: little sounds we might ignore mean something to them. Blind people also learn to use their hands for eyes by reading books in Braille. Have you ever thought about how much you rely on your five senses?

Take out a sheet of paper. Divide into two columns labeled *Things I See* and *Things I Hear*. Close your eyes for a few seconds. Open them and write down all things you can see. Look around the room. See little things: a crack in the ceiling, a scuff mark on the floor. See big things: the teacher's new bulletin board, the teacher's desk. See and write. Make a list.

Now close your eyes again and keep them closed. Listen quietly. What do you hear? Hear something close: your own breathing, the tick of your watch. Hear something far away: voices in the hall, an airplane far overhead. Keep your eyes closed and listen. Make a mental list of what you heard. Now open your eyes and write a list of the things you heard. Did you hear more with your eyes closed? Why?

Because your senses work automatically without your thinking about them, it is easy to ignore them. Good writers work to include words in their writing which will appeal to the reader's senses. In this chapter you will learn to awaken your senses so you, too, can use sensory language in your writings.

Writer's Notebook

You are going to begin keeping a Writer's Notebook in this chapter and you will use it in the next two chapters as well. Your Writer's Notebook is simply a place to keep thoughts, ideas, and reactions which you might use for writing. The writing in your Writer's Notebook is your own and you can feel free to record whatever you wish. This chapter will provide some specific assignments for your Writer's Notebook, but there will also be time for you to write about any thoughts and feelings you may have. Keeping a Writer's Notebook is a relaxed way to practice writing.

Beginning Your Writer's Notebook

Getting It Started

As a way of beginning your Writer's Notebook and warming up your pen or pencil, complete the following sentences. Copy each sentence part into your Writer's Notebook and write as much as you wish about each topic. Relax and write freely and honestly. Your Writer's Notebook is your own place to record thoughts and feelings.
1. I'm most happy . . .
2. Sometimes I wish I were . . .
3. When I get home from school . . .
4. The most important thing to me is . . .
5. I'm pretty good at . . .

Which Sense?

Getting It Down

You've been using your senses to see and hear things. If you could have only one of the five senses, which one would you choose? What are some experiences you would miss if you had only one sense? Respond to these questions in your Writer's Notebook. Take some time to think about what it would be like to do without four of your five senses.

Recording Sensations

Keep a record in your Writer's Notebook of unusual things you hear, see, touch, smell, and taste during the next twenty-four hours. Keep your Writer's Notebook handy. See how many interesting sensations you can notice. For example, smell some spices in your kitchen. Listen to some "night sounds." Eat a different fruit or vegetable. List the first smell that hits you as you walk into your home after school. Feel something carefully with your eyes closed. Record as many sensations as you can.

Getting It Down

Writer's Workbench 1

Sentence-Combining: Subordinating Conjunctions

To combine the sentences in this exercise, move each cue in parentheses to the front of the sentence it follows. Then combine the sentences. Following is an example:

A⊳ Maria walked past the bakery.   (As)

, She smelled the fresh bread.   (,)

The combined sentence is:
As Maria walked past the bakery, she smelled the fresh bread.

In the preceding combined sentence, the word *As* is a subordinating conjunction. It connects the adverb clause *As Maria walked past the bakery* to the rest of the sentence. ● For more information about subordinating conjunctions, see the Handbook, page 67.

Now combine the following sentences. Write them on a separate sheet of paper.

1. Sandy felt the cool sea breeze on her face.
   She walked toward the beach.   (as)

2. Miguel ate his Brussels sprouts.   (After)
   He made a terrible face.   (,)

3. The old man ran his fingers over the piano keys.   (As)
   The room came alive with music.   (,)

4. The fire crackled and popped.
   The campers huddled close for warmth.   (as)

5. The birds are already chattering restlessly.
   The sun comes up.   (before)

6. The train rumbled noisily past.   (After)
   The commuters hurried to their homes.   (,)

7. The snow had melted.   (When)
   The daffodils popped up to take a look.   (,)

8. I smelled the popcorn.
   I heard it popping.   (before)

9. The skiers returned from the slopes.   (After)
   They talked excitedly in front of the fire.   (,)

10. You can have that strawberry shortcake.   (Before)
    You must eat all of your squash casserole.   (,)

Create three sentence-combining examples of your own using the rule you have just practiced.

~~~~~~

Sensory Tour

Getting It Down

Your teacher may plan a tour for you or you can take your own tour around your neighborhood. All you need for the tour is a pencil or pen and your Writer's Notebook. Make the following observations as you walk around on your tour:

1. See something smaller than your hand.
2. See something bigger than you are.
3. Hear something far away.
4. Hear something very close.

5. Feel something soft.
6. Feel something rough.
7. See something old.
8. Smell something manufactured.
9. Smell something natural.
10. Taste something you like.

Write each observation in your Writer's Notebook. Describe your observations with specific and vivid words. Enjoy your tour.

SPOTLIGHT

Now read the following example of sensory writing from *I Am the Cheese* by Robert Cormier:

The rain begins without warning, slashing at my face, pelting my body. Clouds had gathered as I pedaled along toward Carver but they hadn't concerned me because the sun and the clouds had played disappearing games since my departure this morning. Then a sudden torrent greets me as I pump along a narrow section of Route 119. Mud kicks at my legs because the front tire has no fender, nothing to prevent the mud from splashing. The rain slants toward me and the bicycle. I am driving into the storm.

I draw up at the side of the highway and ponder the situation. Squinting, I see a house about a quarter of a mile away, but I don't want to get mixed up with people. Trees offer the only shelter and I push the bike toward a large maple, heavy with branches. The rain showers leaves down as I approach and I realize the tree won't offer much protection because most of the leaves have already fallen. I lean against the tree trunk in disgust. The rain is really coming down now, in wavering sheets, tossed by the wind. The cold enters my clothes, seeps into my skin and into my bones. My father's package is soaked and the road map is ruined. I pull my father's package off the bike and hug it to me, slipping it inside the jacket. The package is wet but I don't mind. The rain continues. I watch the map dissolving. And I am suddenly hungry, ravenous. I am starved. I can't ever remember being as hungry as this.

Cormier has captured a picture with words. The reader can feel and hear and see the rain and the bicycle rider.

1. List some words from this selection which let you feel the rain.
2. List some words which let you hear the rain.
3. List some words which let you see the rain.

Notice how the author uses sentences of different lengths effectively. Find an effective long sentence. Find an effective short sentence. How does he use the short sentences in his writing?

Word Pictures

Getting It Down

Your eye is the camera; your words are the print. Find yourself a place to sit where you can observe quietly, perhaps a street corner downtown or a parked car at a shopping center, or a fast food restaurant. Or you might choose a less hectic place, perhaps a quiet pasture, a city park, a doctor's office.

Observe quietly for ten minutes, recording as many specific sights and sounds as you can in your Writer's Notebook. Look and listen carefully. Notice even tiny things. Use your eyes as a camera; use your words to make a print.

Selecting Details

Creating vivid and forceful word pictures is a matter of choosing just the right details. The choice is difficult because our senses take in so many details that we cannot begin to include in our writing. A good writer has a feel for selecting details and putting them together to form a picture for the reader.

How would you describe your class to someone who does not attend your school? What details would you select? Make a list first of things you might describe for that person. List big things first and then list small things.

Write a summary sentence about your class such as "Our class is the friendliest place in the school" or "Our class is the most active class in the school" or "Something bizarre is always happening in our class." Now select some of the details from your list which illustrate your summary sentence. Following is an example:

Our class is the most comfortable place in the school. We have a talking corner in the back with a soft couch and a bright orange carpet. Near the window a spider plant and a philodendron drop leafy arms. Our desks form a half circle around the teacher's cluttered desk. A picture of a space ship hangs next to the dusty American flag. Kids are happy in this room.

Gwen

Notice how this writer has begun her paragraph with a summary sentence. Next she selects some concrete details: talking corner, soft couch, orange rug. She arranges the details to create a picture of a comfortable room. She ends her piece with a short summary sentence: "Kids are happy in this room."

Now write your summary sentence and select details to illustrate your point. You do not have to begin as Gwen did. Do it your way, but create a vivid picture.

Descriptive Details

For each of the following summary sentences, make a list of as many descriptive details as you can think of. Brainstorm your lists, thinking of big and small details.

1. The school cafeteria was packed with noisy students.
2. I felt as though I was the only person alive as I sat by the quiet lake.

3. The kids were excited as they entered the gates of the amusement park.
4. My bedroom is my special room.
5. The table was loaded with food for Sunday dinner and my family members were ready to eat.

Choose one of the summary sentences which stirs up a picture in your mind or write one of your own. Use the list you have brainstormed to select the most concrete and vivid details. Write one or two paragraphs in your Writer's Notebook using those details.

Writer's Workbench 2

Sentence-Combining: Descriptive Words

This Workbench will help you practice selecting details and remind you about using commas in the correct places. When you use more than one word to describe something, you will need to remember to separate the descriptive words with commas. Read the following sentence:

The convertible chugged into the service station.

Chugged is a good, strong verb, but we need a better description of the convertible to "see" it in our minds. What are some words that

might describe the car? How about *faded, blue, ancient, rusty, noisy, battered, tired, faithful, scarred*? Let's choose three of those descriptive words to improve the sentence.

> The ancient, battered, and scarred convertible chugged into the service station.

Notice that the descriptive words create a better picture of the convertible and that commas separate the descriptive words. • (See the Handbook, pages H-13–15, for more information about using commas to separate words in a series.)

This same sentence could be written as a sentence-combining problem:

> The convertible chugged into the service station.
> The convertible was <u>ancient</u>.
> The convertible was <u>battered</u>.   (,)
> The convertible was <u>scarred</u>.   (, and)

Notice that only the underlined parts of the sentences are included in the combined sentence:

> The ancient, battered, and scarred convertible chugged into the service station.

Now do the following exercises on a sheet of paper.

1. A man rested on the park bench.
   The man was <u>tired</u>.
   The man was <u>old</u>.   (,)

2. Footprints covered the carpet.
   The footprints were <u>tiny</u>.
   The footprints were <u>muddy</u>.   (,)
   The footprints belonged to a <u>dog</u>.   (,)

3. The rainbow arched a track across the sky.
   The track was <u>golden</u>.
   The track was <u>green</u>.   (,)
   The track was <u>purple</u>.   (,)
   The sky was <u>grey</u>.   (, and)

4. The child cried softly.
   Choose from these descriptive words: lost, small, frightened, lonely, dirty, shy.

The child was (your word).
The child was (your word).   (,)
The child was (your word).   (, and)

5. A cobweb sparkled in the sunlight.

>   Descriptive words: fragile, delicate, moist, thin, intricate.

The cobweb was (your word).
The cobweb was (your word).   (,)

6. The kids were afraid to go into the house.

>   Brainstorm words to describe the house. Complete the exercise:

The house was (your word).
The house was (your word).

7. The dog greeted me at the door.

>   Brainstorm words to describe the dog.
>   Complete the exercise:

The dog was (your word).
The dog was (your word).

SPOTLIGHT

The following excerpt from John Steinbeck's suspenseful story "Flight" is full of vivid sights and sounds:

> Pepé rode on through the pass. His little eyes were nearly closed with weariness, but his face was stern, relentless and manly. The high mountain wind coasted sighing through the pass and whistled on the edges of the big blocks of broken granite. In the air, a red-tailed hawk sailed over close to the ridge and screamed angrily. Pepé went slowly through the broken jagged pass and looked down on the other side.
>   The trail dropped quickly, staggering among broken rock. At the bottom of the slope there was a dark crease, thick with brush, and on the other side of the crease a little flat, in which a grove of oak trees grew. A scar of green grass cut across the flat. And behind the flat another mountain rose,

desolate with dead rocks and starving little black bushes. Pepé
drank from the bag again for the air was so dry that it
encrusted his nostrils and burned his lips. He put the horse
down the trail. The hooves slipped and struggled on the steep
way, starting little stones that rolled off into the brush. The
sun was gone behind the westward mountain now, but still it
glowed brilliantly on the oaks and on the grassy flat. The rocks
and the hillsides still sent up waves of the heat they had
gathered from the day's sun.

1. Find some words the author uses to picture this lonely, isolated
   trail.
2. Notice how Steinbeck repeats words to create strong pictures.
3. Find some words which tell you how Pepé feels.
4. Find some strong verbs which capture the feeling of the trail.
5. Use some of Steinbeck's words to describe a place or a person
   you know well.

Writer's Notebook Check

Look back over the Writer's Notebook entries you wrote for this
chapter. Be sure you have all six activities numbered and in your
Writer's Notebook. Select one entry you particularly like. Draw a
star beside it and indicate why you like it. Your teacher may provide
time for Writer's Notebook sharing in class. Share that best writing
with other members of your class if you wish.

Watching
and
Writing

Tuning In

These next two chapters are about television. If you are like most young people, you are an expert on the subject of television because you spend some time each day watching the tube. In these chapters you will be using your viewing time to do your homework for this class. The purpose of Chapter 4 is to involve you in analyzing your television viewing habits. You will use your Writer's Notebook again to record the programs you watch and your reactions to them. You will also conduct an opinion survey and talk about commercials. Group projects at the end of the chapter will help you share what you have learned. Watching, reacting, and discussing should help you become more aware of the place of television in your life. If television viewing is not a part of your daily routine, alternate activities will help you learn more about advertising and leisure activities.

TV in Your Life

If television viewing is part of your life style, use your Writer's Notebook to respond to the questions in section A. Add anything you wish about you and your television viewing habits.

If television viewing is not a part of your life style, respond to the questions in section B.

Getting
It
Down

A

1. On the average, how much time do you spend watching television each week?
2. On what day or night do you spend more time than usual watching television?
3. Are meals or bedtimes planned around TV in your family?

4. Do you plan your watching each evening or do you watch whatever comes on the screen?
5. Do you and your family ever disagree on what shows to watch? How do you work it out?
6. What types of shows are viewed by adults in your family only? By only you? By the entire family?
7. Does anyone set rules for your television viewing time? For the types of programs you watch?

B

1. What is your *general* opinion of programs on television?
2. What are TV's good points? Bad points?
3. In your opinion, do your friends spend too much time watching TV?
4. Name some of the activities you enjoy instead of watching television.
5. What effect, if any, has your "nonviewing" habit had on the amount of time you spend reading? Writing letters? Talking with your family? Doing schoolwork?

Television Ratings

As you know, TV shows come and go. Each year in the fall, the networks introduce a "new season." This new season is usually a package of shows, some new, some old, with new characters in new settings. Soon after the new season begins, however, the new shows begin to disappear or they are moved to new time slots. The missing shows have been cancelled by the network because too few people were watching them. Have you ever had a favorite show cancelled? Did you wonder why and who did it?

Networks decide which shows to cancel largely on the basis of the shows' *ratings*. Independent rating companies survey thousands of television viewers, asking them which shows they watch. When too few people are watching a show, its ratings are low. Low ratings make sponsors unhappy because not enough people are seeing their commercial messages. So no matter how much you may love a television show, if millions of other viewers do not share your opinion, the show will not remain on the air.

One of the most famous examples of a popular show being cancelled was *Star Trek*. This science fiction show had a small but enthusiastic audience. After the show was cancelled, its fans kept the show alive by organizing into fan clubs and sharing their favorite *Star Trek* stories. They called themselves "Trekies" and their devotion to their show eventually convinced movie-makers to produce a *Star Trek* movie.

Ratings are gathered in several ways, but one of the most important rating systems is the Nielsen Rating. The A. C. Nielsen company asks selected families to keep a television viewing diary. Members of the family keep a careful record of the shows they watch week by week. The Nielsen company collects and summarizes the diaries and gives each show a rating. The rating is the percent of the television audience watching that show. These ratings are very important to a show's success, and shows with very low ratings disappear quickly.

Television Viewing Diary

For the next four days keep a Nielsen-type diary of your television viewing habits. At the end of the week, the class will compile these diaries and publish a class rating summary.

Keep your notebook on top of the TV set so you won't forget to record what you watch. Use the following sample page as a model for your diary. If you do not watch television in your home, keep a diary of your activities, using a form similar to that of the TV viewers.

Getting
It
Down

TUESDAY, MAY 5
  4:00—Set off
  4:30—Set on—not watching
  5:00—Six Million Dollar Man
  5:30—Six Million Dollar Man
  6:00—Dinner—set off
  6:30—Dinner—set off
  7:00—NBC Nightly News
  7:30—Family Feud
  8:00—Happy Days
  8:30—LaVerne and Shirley
  9:00—WKRP
  9:30—Mash
10:00—Bedtime

Comments and reactions:

(Write about anything unusual on television: a presidential news conference, a severe weather briefing, a special program, a power failure.)

Reminders for Your Diary

1. Keep your diary by half-hours beginning at 4:00 P.M. each day.
2. Keep the diary for four consecutive days.
3. Record each show you watched even if you only watched part of it.
4. Indicate when the TV set was off or when you were not watching.
5. Keep each day on a separate page to be turned in later.
6. Keep a careful record; don't forget.

Writer's Workbench

Sentence-Combining

The words *Because, If, Although,* and *Unless* frequently begin sentences. We use these words to indicate that one part of the sentence is a consequence of the other part, as in this example:

>   If you do not do your work in this class, you will not pass.

What will be the consequence of not doing your work? You will not pass. Following is another example:

>   Because she watched the late show, Susan was sleepy this morning.

Why was Susan sleepy? Because she watched the late show. In both of these examples, the sentence parts are related by cause and effect. That is, one fact is caused by the other.

Solve the following sentence-combining problems using the rule you have used earlier in this book: move the word or punctuation mark in parentheses to the front of the sentence it follows. Use the following example as a guide:

>   You do not watch television.   (If)
>   You will miss all the new shows.   (,)

If you do not watch television, you will miss all the new shows.

Write each combined sentence on a sheet of paper. Read it aloud calling out the comma as you read.

1. You do your homework first.   (Unless)
   You cannot watch television.   (,)

2. The weather forecast predicts sunny skies.   (If)
   It will probably rain.   (,)

3. The movie lasted until eleven.   (Because)
   I did not see the ending.   (,)

4. Some television commercials are outrageous.   (Although)
   They influence many people.   (,)

5. That show is a rerun.   (If)
   I won't watch it.   (,)

6. I practice the piano faithfully.   (Unless)
   I cannot go skating tonight.   (,)

7. The players believe in themselves.   (If)
   They will play better.   (,)

8. There is a shortage of fuel.   (Although)
   Some people continue to waste it.   (,)

9. Learning French is not easy.   (Because)
   You must study every night.   (,)

10. You remember the comma in this sentence.   (Unless)
    You will not get it right.   (,)

Notice that a comma always follows the sentence parts introduced with *Because, If, Although, Unless* ● For further information about the comma see the Handbook, pages H-13–20.

Create three sentence-combining problems of your own using the rule you have just learned.

Survey of TV Viewing Habits

In the previous activities you examined your own viewing habits. In this activity you will investigate the kind and amount of television viewing of other people you know. Survey three people, someone older than you, someone younger than you, and someone your own age. If you watch TV regularly, do section A of this activity. Keep the results of your survey. Later in this chapter a group of students will tally and report them to the class. If you watch little or no TV, find three people whose leisure-time habits are similar to yours, and do section B.

A

1. Name
2. Age
3. On the average how many hours do you spend watching television each week?
4. What kinds of shows do you prefer to watch? Sit/Com, Soap Opera, Game Show, Sports, Drama, News.
5. What is the one show you always watch?
6. What is the best *new* show on TV?
7. What is the *worst* show on TV?
8. What is the best soap opera on TV?
9. Which channel has the best evening news?
10. What television commercial is most memorable?
11. What would you like to see more of on television?

B

Talk with three people who watch little or no TV. Ask them their reason for their "nonviewing" habit. Be the detached reporter. Keep your views to yourself. Now go to your Writer's Notebook and summarize your findings. Did you hear the same reasons more than once? Did anyone offer an unusual reason? How did their reasons compare with yours?

Television Advertising

Television advertising is a major influence on what we buy and where we buy it. Advertisers spend four billion dollars a year on TV commercials selling us soap and soup, flea collars and floor wax, dog food and deodorant. Our clothing styles, life styles, and even our language are strongly affected by our favorite characters on television. Who is the most popular character on TV right now? What influences has he or she had on your language or dress?

Television advertising is sometimes criticized because it is so irresistible. Sometimes we buy things we don't need because the product looks good on television. Advertisers have also been criticized because they may present a one-sided view of their product or make false claims for its effectiveness.

SPOTLIGHT

Television ads for sugar-coated cereals, for example, have come under fire recently. The heavy number of ads on children's programs and the ads' effectiveness alarmed parents and public-interest groups. In 1977 the sugar controversy peaked. Each side had a different point of view. Each side wanted to *persuade* the public to its side. Read these three points of view.

Broadcasters

The FTC says young children tend to want anything they see advertised. Of course they do. They always have, and probably always will—including things in the supermarket and toy store which haven't been advertised.

It will take a lot more than a ban on television advertising to curb a child's sweet tooth.

Sugar is great. It tastes good. Many parents offer a chocolate bar as a reward. I don't think sugar will ever be considered anything but a delicious treat—with or without advertising.

Broadcasters are parents, too. The National Association of Broadcasters' Television Code includes strict guidelines for advertising toys and food products to children.

Vincent T. Wasilewski

General Mills

An advertising ban would be a step backward in the cause of good nutrition. All General Mills cereals include 25 percent of the U.S. government recommended daily allowance of at least seven important vitamins and iron. In addition, breakfast cereals are low in fat and low in calories.

The staff of the FTC contends pre-sweetened cereals should not be advertised to children because they may cause dental caries. In doing so, they ignored the results of three separate dental research studies, all of which show that pre-sweetened cereals do not contribute to an increase in dental caries. The results of these studies are not surprising, since 95 percent of all cereals are consumed with milk and during meals. Further, only two percent of a child's annual sugar consumption comes from pre-sweetened cereals. There is more sugar in a 6 ounce glass of orange juice or a banana than there is in a serving of pre-sweetened cereal.

Arthur R. Schulze

The FTC

The average television-watching child sees approximately 20,000 TV commercials per year.

By age 11, that child will have been exposed to $2.6 billion worth of TV impressions (7,000 per year) for sugary cereals, sticky, chewy candy bars and the like.

Should children be protected against such advertising until they are old enough to understand it? Should an advertiser who sells children sugar also tell them the facts about good nutrition?

The FTC proposals could help create an environment of relative "freedom," in which parents can educate their children about dental care and nutrition without having to fight 7,000 sugar ads a year.

The broadcasters' own regulations haven't seemed to work. The National Association of Broadcasters Code, for example, allows the broadcast of more ads to children in some periods (12 minutes per hour in after-school programming) than to adults (9½ minutes per hour in prime time).

Dee Pridgen

Whose point of view do you find most convincing? Write your own reaction to the sugared-cereals controversy.

What Do You Think?

Not all advertising is bad, of course. Some commercials and advertisements are humorous or artistic or creative. Respond to the following questions in your Writer's Notebook:

1. What is your favorite television commercial or magazine advertisement? Why do you like it?
2. What is your least favorite commercial or advertisement? Why do you dislike it?
3. What makes a commercial or advertisement effective?

Television advertising is big business. When companies spend money on advertising, they expect results. Most commercials are written and produced by advertising agencies who work under pressure to produce these results.

With all of this money being spent on commercials, television advertising has become highly sophisticated. Careful market surveys are taken to find out what kind of commercial appeals to the potential buyers of a particular product. Think for a minute. If you were an advertiser who wanted to sell bubble gum, what type of commercial would you use? You probably would not picture a school teacher saying, "I always chew Dandy Bubble." School teachers are not important buyers of bubble gum. How might the makers of Dandy Bubble make the product attractive to potential buyers?

Have you ever noticed how similar many commercials are? Advertisers use a number of stock appeals to influence their audience. Following are some of the standard appeals advertisers use. Can you think of others?

Factual: A no-nonsense business-like appeal.
"Our automobile gets 47 MPG."
or
"This milk contains only 2% butterfat."

Comparison: Comparing one product with another.
"Our product has more peanuts than the leading brand."
                                        or
"Our soap gets out greasy dirt better than brands B and C."

Testimonial: Famous and not-so-famous people give glowing reports about the product.
Famous baseball player says, "I always chew Dandy Bubble during a tough game."
                                        or
On a hidden camera, Mrs. Swartz of West Covina, California, says, "I tried this sink cleaner for two weeks and it worked wonders."

Clever production: Dazzles the audience with fanfare or dramatics.
Beautiful girls tap dancing on huge broadway stage singing, "Dandy, Dandy, Dandy Bubble."
                                        or
Mrs. Swartz looking on in amazement as a giant green man cleans her sink sparkling clean.

Bargains: Appeals to the bargain hunter in all of us.
"For two weeks only, buy one package of Dandy Bubble, and get one free."
                                        or
"Our prices have never been lower during our 25% off sale."

Integrity: Emphasizes honesty and character.
"We've been in the business forty years, and we care about you."
                                        or
"Service is our only product. We're working to keep you happy."

Soft sell: Charms the viewers or uses reverse psychology.
A baby sits on the floor playing with facial

tissue. A voice says sweetly, "Now that's softness."

or

"We know you're tired of claims and high pressure ads."

Popularity: Appeals to our desire to be one of the bunch. Scenes which show that *everybody* has the product.

or

"We're number one in sales."

There are many other appeals, and many commercials are combinations of these. Keep your eyes and ears open. See if you can use these appeals to analyze commercials in the following activity.

~~~~~~

Getting It Down

Audience Appeal

Through careful surveys advertisers know the age, sex, and buying habits of TV viewers. Advertisers plan their commercials to appeal to a specific audience. Commercials on daytime programs are different from commercials on weekend or prime time shows. Using the following guide, watch and analyze in writing three daytime commercials, three prime time commercials, three Saturday morning commercials, and three Sunday afternoon commercials. If you do not watch television regularly, do Section B of this activity.

A
Guide for Commercial Watching

1. Day and time
2. Product advertised (Include brand name.)
3. Briefly describe the situation.
   Example: Women smells neighbor's coffee and comes over to investigate.
4. To whom does the commercial appeal?
   Example: Housewives, young children, parents, young couples, fathers.
5. Which of the appeals on pages 56–58 does the advertiser use to persuade the viewer to buy the product?

B

Find three advertisements in magazines or newspapers. In your Writer's Notebook describe the advertisements and write the kinds of appeals the advertisers use to persuade the reader to buy the product.

Then imagine you are an ad writer and have been asked to market the Dandy Bubblegum product. Choose three of the audience appeals described on pages 56–58, and write three different ads for Dandy Bubblegum that would persuade people to buy that product.

Group Projects

Your teacher will assign you to a group and ask you to choose one of the following projects.

Project 1

Collect all the television-viewing diaries that your classmates prepared for Getting It Down, page 49. Your group project is to analyze and tally the diaries, rating shows to discover which were the most-watched ones. To do this project well, you need to organize yourselves carefully. Work in pairs with one person reading the diaries and one person marking a tally sheet. As an example, suppose you and your partner are tallying Tuesday. Make yourself a tally sheet like this:

4:00	Show A	5
	Show B	3
	Show C	7
	Not watching	11

When you have finished the tallying job, go back and give each show a rating. The rating is the percentage of people watching that show. In the preceding example, twenty-six students recorded their viewing at 4:00.

		Number	Percent
4:00	Show A	5	19.2
	Show B	3	11.5
	Show C	7	26.9
	Not watching	11	
		26	TOTAL POTENTIAL AUDIENCE

Find Show A's rating by solving this problem: 5 is what percent of 26? Divide the number (5) by the total potential audience (26).

$$26\overline{)5.0} \quad .192$$

Multiply by 100 to get the percent: .192 × 100 = 19.2
Show A's rating is 19.2.

Practice on B and C to be sure you understand the process. Use a pocket calculator if one is available. Continue this procedure until you have given all the shows on Tuesday a rating.

Select the top-ten rated shows from your list. Compare their ratings with other shows on other days.

Meet as a group to select the top-ten rated shows in your class.

Put the results on a poster and display them. Your teacher may ask your group to explain your findings to the class.

Project 2
With members of your group collect all the survey sheets from Getting It Started, page 52. Tally the following items:

1. On the average, how many hours do people spend watching television? Figure separate averages for children and adults.
2. Best *new* show on TV.
3. Worst show on TV.
4. Best soap opera.
5. Best evening news.
6. Best commercial.

Summarize your findings. Make a chart illustrating your findings or give awards for the various categories. Your teacher may ask you to share your findings.

Project 3

Create your own television commercial with members of your group. First decide on a product. Analyze who the potential buyers of that product might be. Choose the appeal which might be most effective. Write a script for a 60-second television commercial for that product. Time your commercial carefully. Be able to defend your choice of appeal.

Your teacher may ask you to act out your script for the class.

Project 4

With your group select an imaginary product and design a magazine advertisement for that product. Use one of the appeals on pages 56–58 or create your own special advertising strategy.

Chapter 5

Talking Back to the Tube

In the preceding chapter, you investigated the television viewing habits of people you know. In this chapter you will apply some of the information you have gathered to look at television critically. You will be using your Writer's Notebook again to record reactions and take notes for writing assignments.

Television is so much a part of our culture it is difficult to imagine life without it. Most of us rely on our television sets to provide news, information, and entertainment daily. During an average evening in this country at 8:30, at least 75 million people are watching their television sets. Because of this large audience, television is a powerful medium for both helpful and harmful influences on all of us. In this chapter we will discuss this powerful medium and write about some of its influences.

Television and Your Life

In several experiments conducted in this country, families voluntarily unplugged their television sets. Researchers found that when the television set was off for an extended period of at least a month, children read more, helped around the house more, played together more, interacted with adults more, and missed their favorite programs.

What do you suppose your home would be like if you unplugged the television set? Write a short piece in your Writer's Notebook about how your life would change without television. What would you do in the evening? On weekends? What would you lose? What would you gain?

If you do not watch television, write about what your life would be like if the TV set were plugged in. What changes would occur in your home?

Getting
It
Down

In a small group, share any parts of your Writer's Notebook entry you wish to. Compare different'ways your lives would change if you suddenly had to live without, or with, television.

People have disagreed for years about the effects of television watching on young people. Marie Winn, in her book *The Plug-In Drug*, likens TV watching to drug addiction. She says little children have become a generation of "television zombies." They sit in trance-like states addicted to that flickering light on the screen. Marie Winn and other critics believe that it is not what we watch on TV that is harmful to us. It is the act of sitting in front of TV sets hour after hour that does the harm. Some critics have called people who watch TV all day "videots."

Other groups of parents and educators are concerned about the kinds of programs we watch on television. These groups believe television shows are too violent. They believe that watching violent shows may be a harmful influence on young children. These concerned people do not see television watching as bad. They just want children to watch television shows without fighting, shootings, and murders. The television networks have responded to this criticism by presenting a "family hour" each evening. During this time when most young children are watching, the networks are being more careful about the kinds of shows they present.

Violence on Television

Can TV be held responsible for a crime? Can seeing violent acts lead to violent actions in young viewers? A fifteen-year-old boy shot and robbed his 82-year-old neighbor. The case was unusual. The boy's attorney blamed TV violence for the crime. He charged that the boy's viewing hours (6–8 hours each day) of TV violence from an early age caused the tragedy. The jury found the boy guilty.

What do you think? Do you believe the boy's attorney? How do you feel about violence on TV? Should violent shows have time restrictions? Should they be banned altogether? What show do you feel is the most violent on TV? Do you watch it? How does your family feel about your watching violence on TV? Think about these questions and respond in your Writer's Notebook.

Still other groups are more concerned about the effects of television on family life. Families do not talk or interact with each other during TV watching. Marie Winn says, "More than violence, I am interested in the things that take place in normal families because the set is on, and families are often watching in separate rooms. They are separated from each other by their TV sets."

A fourth group of people believe TV is just one more medium of communication. A medium is a means of exchanging messages between people. A telephone is a medium; a letter is a medium; a bumper sticker is a medium; television is a medium. This group believes it isn't television that harms people. It is what TV watchers do with the medium. If television is dull or disgusting, then people need to demand that it become better. "People control television," they say. "It is only an electronic gadget. If you don't like a program, turn it off." In an article called "How to Fight Bad TV," Ralph Nader explains, "You *can* do something about what comes into your home. But to become more effective as a public citizen, you must first become more educated as a private viewer."

Confused by all the different opinions? There are many sides to the television controversy. One thing is certain. Television will continue to be an important part of our lives and an important topic of discussion among various critics.

Who's in Control?

Where do you stand in the television debate? Does television control people or do people control television? What are some good things and bad things about television? How can people become more educated private viewers? Respond to these questions in your Writer's Notebook.

Getting
It
Down

**Getting
It
Down**

Taking a Closer Look

Later in this chapter you will be writing an opinion paper about television. This activity will prepare you for that writing assignment by asking you to take a closer look at two TV shows.

Think a minute. Is there a show on TV you really like? Have you ever thought about why you like it? How about a show you dislike? Choose one show you like and one you dislike. Be sure you have strong feelings about these shows. Watch these shows very carefully this week using the Reaction Questions as a guide.

If you do not watch TV, create an "ideal" show in your imagination. It can be an educational or entertaining show. Then create one you would consider too "dumb" for anyone to watch. Briefly describe each show in writing. Then apply the Reaction Questions to your shows. You may want to leave out question 3.

Reaction Questions

1. What is the name of the show?

2. When is it on?

3. How often do you watch it? (never miss it, always miss it, etc.)

4. What type of show is it? (situation comedy, game show, drama, soap, sports, news/documentary)

5. Who are the main characters on the show?

6. What type of people are they? (male/female, old/young, average American working people, artists, police officers, housewives, doctors, etc.)

7. List the things you like or dislike about the show.

Writer's Workbench 1
Language of Persuasion

Learning to express your opinion convincingly is an important part of writing a good opinion paper. The words you choose should be clear and forceful so the reader knows exactly how you feel. Compare these two opinions:

1. That show left me cold. The characters are simply not believable.
2. I don't really like that show very much. It just seems like the characters don't act right.

Which opinion is stated more forcefully? Example 1 is direct, clear, and forceful. Example 2 voices the same opinion, but not as forcefully. How are these two examples different?

Weasel Words

Example 2 has a number of weak words which we often use by habit in our informal writing. These words can be called "weasel

words" because writers use them to "weasel" or weaken their statements. Good opinion papers avoid weasel words.

Can you find the WW's in example 2? (*really, very, seem*) These words weaken example 2 and leave the reader with a lukewarm feeling. Other weasel words are *rather, kind of, a lot*, and *too*.

Write an opinion statement about soap operas. Use as many weasel words in it as you can. Now rework the sentence to state your opinion directly and forcefully. Remember: When you state an opinion in writing, avoid weaselry.

Writer's Workbench 2

Sentence-Combining

Practice combining the sentences in this Workbench using the cues (that), (the fact that), (JOIN), and SOMETHING. The words in all capital letters, (JOIN) and SOMETHING, are new cues. (JOIN) simply means put the two sentences together to form one. SOMETHING shows you where to join them. SOMETHING and (JOIN) should not appear in your combined sentence. The following examples show how to use these cues:

> Sarah heard SOMETHING.
> Her favorite television show had been cancelled.   (that)
>
> Sarah heard that her favorite television show had been cancelled.
>
> I know SOMETHING.
> I must finish my homework.   (JOIN)
>
> I know I must finish my homework.

Now do these sentence-combining problems on a separate sheet of paper:

1. I knew SOMETHING.
    My mother would not let me watch the late show.   (that)

2. I believe SOMETHING.
    Television programs can be improved.   (JOIN)

3. Carmen hopes SOMETHING.
    Her opinion paper will be good.   (that)

4. Ralph heard SOMETHING.
    "Romeo and Juliet" is on television tonight.   (that)

5. Children watch television frequently.   (The fact that)
    SOMETHING is a concern to some people.

6. Sally hopes SOMETHING.
    She can have a telephone in her room.   (that)

7. Allen knows SOMETHING.
    He will make the soccer team.   (JOIN)

8. The principal called Steve to the office.   (The fact that)
    SOMETHING does not mean Steve is in trouble.

9. Joanne heard SOMETHING.
    Lisa is giving a Halloween party.   (that)

10. The entire class felt SOMETHING.
    The test was very difficult.   (that)

Sharing an Opinion

Most of us have opinions about many things:
> "I don't like that color."
> "She has pretty eyes."
> "That band has such a good sound!"
> "The evening was a disaster."

When someone disagrees with or challenges our opinion, we may try to persuade him or her to see our side of the issue. Read this discussion:

Cindy: I didn't like that movie at all.
Sharon: Oh, I thought it was great. Why didn't you like it?

> Cindy: Well, for one thing, the music was too loud, and the ending just left me wondering. I don't think it really ended at all. I guess I like movies with happy endings. I didn't pay $3.00 to go see a movie and feel strange when it's over.

In this short excerpt, Cindy offers specific reasons for her opinion. These reasons are sometimes called *evidence*. Cindy offers specific evidence to support her opinion.

Specific Evidence

Getting It Started

When you write an opinion paper, it is important to support your opinion with specific evidence. In a small group brainstorm specific reasons or evidence for the following opinions:

1. **Opinion:**   School should be held year round without a summer vacation.
   Evidence: a. Students could finish school earlier.
   b. Taxpayers would save money because buildings would not sit empty.
   c. (Can you think of another?)

2. **Opinion:**   Students should decide the menu for the school cafeteria.
   Evidence: (Brainstorm your own.)

3. **Opinion:**   Bike paths should be provided on all main streets to encourage bike riders.
   Evidence: (Brainstorm your own.)

Always brainstorm for ideas for good evidence before you write an opinion paper. You will not be able to use all of your ideas, but you can choose the most convincing ones from your list. Good opinion papers usually offer three or four examples of specific evidence.

SPOTLIGHT

Read and discuss the following opinion papers written by students:

> I think television commercials should be banned. Commercials constantly interrupt my programs. Every fifteen minutes during a movie there are five minutes of commercials.
>
> Most commercials are not truthful. Take dog food commercials, for instance. I know companies want more people to buy their product, but really, most people don't care. Dog food is dog food! My dog will eat any kind of dog food, and his health is the same as it always was. Besides my dog doesn't even watch the commercials.
>
> Television would be more enjoyable if there were no commercials. Come to think of it, though, when would I get to get a snack?
>
> *Greg*

Use the following questions to discuss Greg's attack on television commercials:

1. Is Greg's opinion stated clearly? Explain.
2. What evidence does he offer to support his opinion?
3. Is his evidence *specific* and *convincing*?
4. Do you like his humorous ending? Does it strengthen his opinion paper?
5. What other evidence might Greg have used to support his opinion?

> I hate television shows that have crimes and killing. There are too many of these on TV. These shows influence people and cause people to commit crimes.
>
> Television has turned little kids to violence. When I look around now, I see little kids with guns in their hands playing cops and robbers and cowboys. They have learned this from television.
>
> Crime shows and police shows sometimes make bad guys look good. The criminal doesn't always get caught and sometimes the police look dumb.

I think violent shows should not be on TV. There is
enough violence in the world now.

Pam

1. What three points of evidence does Pam use in her paper?
2. Does she need more *specific* evidence? Brainstorm other ideas
   she might use.
3. Think about Pam's ending. Does she state it strongly? How
   could she give it more clout?

Writer's Workbench 3

Adding to Your Word Bank

Some new or unusual words are used throughout this chapter.
These special words are often used to talk about TV. You may want
to use these words in your opinion paper to make your writing more
specific.

videots	media	televise	addicted
medium	influence	electronic	dramatic

Add these words to your word bank. First, find each word in the
chapter. Then copy the sentence containing the word in your
Writer's Notebook. Underline the word in the sentence.

As the following list indicates, each of these words is a
particular part of speech. ● If you need definitions of noun, verb, or
adjective, see the Handbook, pages H-65–66.

1. <u>videots.</u>   This invented word is a noun. What two words have
   been combined to create this new word?
2. <u>medium and media.</u>   These words are nouns. A *medium* is a
   means of communication. Television is a *medium*. The
   word *media* is the plural form. The electronic *media* are
   radio, television, and movies. Notice that the word *media*
   takes a plural verb (are).
3. <u>influence.</u>   This word can be a noun or a verb.
   (Noun) Television is a powerful *influence* on people.
   (Verb) How does television *influence* you?
4. <u>televise.</u>   The word *television* is a noun. You can make it a
   verb by changing it to *televise*.

(Noun) The game will be on *television* Sunday.

(Verb) Will they *televise* the game Sunday?

5. electronic.   This word is an adjective. It describes any device that uses electricity. How many *electronic* devices can you think of?

6. addicted.   This word is a verb. It means to be hooked on something. What are some things people are *addicted* to?

7. dramatic.   This word is an adjective. It comes from the word *drama*. Sherry uses the word in her writing to describe soap operas. She feels the acting is exaggerated. ". . . they seem so *dramatic*." (page 75) *Dramatic* shows are usually serious. Can you think of some examples of *dramatic* shows?

In your Writer's Notebook write a short paragraph using at least four of your new words.

Opinion Paper

Your assignment is to write an opinion paper about television. Is it basically a helpful or harmful medium? Follow these steps to write your paper:

1. Where do you stand? Is television harmful or helpful? Don't be wishy-washy. Choose one side. Take a stand.
2. What are some reasons for your feelings about television? Opinions need support. Brainstorm a little. Look at your Writer's Notebook entries about television. Make a jot list of as many good reasons as you can.
3. Look over your list. Choose three or four of the strongest and most concrete reasons. Circle these.
4. Now you are ready to begin your paper.
5. Start by stating your opinion.
6. Now develop each of your reasons (evidence) in a separate paragraph. Remember you are trying to convince other students. Use evidence and examples they would know and understand.
7. Wrap up your paper with clout! Restate your opinion strongly, or use a story or illustration, or call your audience to action by suggesting they *do* something.

Getting
It
Down

8. Experiment a bit with form. You do not have to use the same form Greg used. Invent your own approach to the paper, if you wish.

~~~~~~

SPOTLIGHT

Read the following opinion paper:

Everytime I get a chance, I watch soap operas. My favorite is "The Young and the Restless." Actually most of the shows are all alike, but I like that one best. They all have people with family problems, people having nervous breakdowns, death, and kids running away; just the everyday, typical disasters of living.

The problem with watching a soap opera is, it's habit-forming. Once you start, you can't stop. For example, about two years ago I used to make fun of Helena for watching her favorite soap opera, but after watching a couple of shows, I was addicted. I'd come home from school, turn on the set, and watch it. After a while that show started sickening me. All in all, I guess you could rate soap operas as raunchy, but, I do have to keep up with some of them.

The way the writers get you to watch a show is to stop the story right when something exciting is about to happen! So you say, "Well, I'll watch tomorrow, just to see what happens." And poof, you're glued! The writers know how to keep you coming back for more.

When you're watching a soap, they seem so dramatic. The actors just overdo it. For example, on "The Young and the Restless" the day before yesterday, Ms. Chancelor died; she committed suicide. I missed the one yesterday, but someone revived her, so today she is back home, fine and dandy. I don't know why I watch the show. I'm just hooked I guess.

Sherry

1. Does Sherry state her opinion clearly? What is it?
2. Does she give at least three good reasons why she likes "The Young and the Restless"? What are her reasons?
3. Does Sherry give specific examples from the show to support her reasons? If so, what are they?
4. Can you think of any other reasons she might have to support her opinion?
5. How can Sherry revise this opinion paper to make it more clear and forceful?

CHECKPOINT

Your teacher will use Checkpoint 2 on page 77 to evaluate your opinion paper. Rework your paper carefully using the following checklist. Take time to read your paper aloud to a small group of classmates before you begin revision work.

1. <u>Evidence.</u>   Look again at the reasons (evidence) you have given for your opinion. Are there at least three solid ones? Can

you think of any better ones? Have you used specific examples to illustrate your reasons?

2. <u>Arrangement.</u>   Think about how you have ordered your paper. Did you put your strongest evidence first? Last? Move your evidence around to see if this strengthens the paper. Be sure each reason is in a separate paragraph.

3. <u>Language.</u>   Have you expressed your opinion clearly? Do you hear your voice in the paper? Do you use forceful language? Do you avoid weasel words?

4. <u>Punctuation and Spelling.</u>   Check that spelling. Look up any words you are unsure about. Check for end punctuation for each sentence. Check to be sure you have used commas after introductory elements.

5. <u>Reread.</u>   Reread your paper one final time. Are you pleased with it? Does it sound convincing? Is it a neat, clean copy? Relax . . . you are finished.

CHECKPOINT 2

1	2	3	4	5

Evidence   ×4=

Your ideas are unsupported. Rethink your reasons. Back to brainstorming.

At least one of your pieces of evidence is strong. Support more completely.

Yes, good solid support. Fresh, convincing.

Arrangement   ×4=

Be sure you have each bit of evidence in a separate paragraph. Experiment with order.

Check your conclusion or beginning. You can find a stronger arrangement.

Yes, I like the way you have ordered the paragraphs. Your arguments build to your conclusions.

Language   ×4=

Watch those weasel words. Use more forceful language. See Writer's Workbench 1.

Remember your audience. Use words they will understand.

Good, strong concrete words.

Punctuation and Spelling   ×2=

Proofread carefully. Still too many errors. See me for help.

Still have a few errors. Check and double check.

Good job. Careful proofreading pays off.

Effectivness of Your Opinion Paper   ×6=

I'm not convinced. Develop your paper more completely. Use good evidence.

Yes. You are making progress; keep working.

I'm convinced. Good support. Solid paper.

Juggling Words

Chapter 6

Sketching a Character

Will I remember
    how I looked
    and what I did
    When I was young
    (When I am old)?
Will I remember what I wondered?
When I am old,
    Who will I be,
    Still me?

Richard J. Margolis, Age 15

Have you ever had thoughts like Richard's? Have you ever wondered what you will be like as you grow older? Have you ever looked at an older person and tried to imagine yourself at that age? When we are young, we are frequently impatient to become older. If you could choose another age to be right now, what age would you choose? Sixteen—so you could have your driver's license? Eighteen—so you could graduate from school? Twenty-one—so you could be an adult and on your own? Write a short poem beginning with the line "If I were older. . . ."

As people grow older, they sometimes begin to worry about their age. What age comes to mind when you hear someone say, "She's an old woman"? How old is "old," and what words and phrases do you think of when you hear the word "old"?

Old: Positive and Negative

Form small groups. Brainstorm a list of words and phrases commonly associated with older people by following these steps:

Getting It Started

1. Appoint a recorder for your group. The recorder will write the word "old" on a sheet of paper and write down all of your suggestions.
2. Follow these rules for brainstorming:
   Accept everyone's ideas.
   Try for as many ideas as you can. *Quantity* is the goal.
   Encourage *all* kinds of ideas.
   Piggy-back on each other's ideas.
   Don't stop too soon. Keep thinking and suggesting ideas.
   Stay on track.
3. When your group's list is finished, study it carefully. Look for all the words and phrases which make positive statements about the old. Count these. Now look for those words and phrases which create negative pictures of the old. Are there more negative words on your list than positive? If so, what does this tell you about being old in our society?

~~~~~~~~~~~~~~~~~~~~~~~~~~~~~~~~~~~~~

Getting It Down

Using your list of negative words and phrases, write a paragraph describing old people. Use as many negative words and phrases as you can.

~~~~~~~~~~~~~~~~~~~~~~~~~~~~~~~~~~~~~

Checking It Out

Share your negative paragraphs with members of your group.

~~~~~~~~~~~~~~~~~~~~~~~~~~~~~~~~~~~~~

Stereotypes

Your negative paragraph about old people is a *stereotype*. A *stereotype* is an untrue or oversimplified statement about an entire group of people. Many older people have become concerned about the way young people stereotype them. These older people feel young people do not understand that all old people are not helpless and feeble. The stereotype that old people cannot contribute to society is a prejudice called *ageism*. Old people are forming groups to fight ageism. They are trying to inform younger people about the contributions of older people. Many older people are trying to strengthen "Grey Power" in our society in order to focus more attention on their needs and abilities.

Grey Power People

Grandma Moses was painting at 100.
George Bernard Shaw wrote a play at 93.
Golda Meir was the Prime Minister of Israel in her 70s.
Pablo Picasso was an active artist in his 90s.
Coco Chanel was head of her own international design firm at 85.
Larry Lewis ran the 100-yard dash in 17.8 seconds. He was 101.

Grey Power Facts

In many countries old people continue to live with their families, taking an active role in the household.
Approximately ten percent of the total U.S. population is over 65.
By the year 2000, one-third of the U.S. population will be over 65. One-half will be over 60. That will be 50% of the total U.S. population.

SPOTLIGHT

Of course, not all young people look upon older people as useless and helpless. Some young people have special relationships with older people. Read the following selections:

The Mittens My Grandmother Made

My grandmother made me some mittens
knowing I like them better than gloves,
knowing I like the way all four fingers
keep each other warm, the way
they can huddle together into a fist
and the isolated thumb
abandoning his own sweater
to join the rest of the crowd.

And as I wear these mittens
I think of my grandmother,
her hands working like cricket legs all night
and the rocking chair thumping like a dog's tail,
and I think of my grandmother, thinking of me
trudging through the winter,
bundled up like a bear,
my feet buried in Eskimo boots
and my hands in her mittens.

Laura Gilpin

1. What kind of relationship do the grandmother and speaker of the poem share? How do you know?
2. What do the grandmother and speaker have in common?
3. How does the content of the poem relate or not relate to your own life?

That Sunday Jenny and Grandpa found themselves alone in the house, and Jenny was delighted. Mr. and Mrs. Pennoyer had gone for a ride with Ethel and Gail. Vince and Valerie were visiting friends, and despite the rain Frankie was out running. There was no one to complain about Grandpa doing this or Grandpa not doing that. Jenny was sick of hearing the family grievances about Grandpa. She could recite them all, backward, forward, and inside out. She got out their deck of cards, made a pot of tea for Grandpa, and opened a bottle of soda for herself. Outside, cars sloshed by, headlights on to penetrate the gloomy rain. Sitting at the table across from Grandpa, Jenny thought it was almost like so many other afternoons they'd spent together—the standing lamp casting a sheen over the bare dark wood of the table, rain smearing the windowpanes, and the cards flick, flick, flicking in the silence.

"Ha, ha! Gin!" Grandpa rubbed his hands together. He was dressed today, wearing baggy trousers, an undershirt, and the new cardigan Mrs. Pennoyer had bought him. The sweater seemed to irritate him and he twisted his shoulders uncomfortably every few minutes.

"Let's play another hand," she said. "I'll be reckless. Penny a point."

"Profligate with your money, my girl. All right. Watch yourself now. I'm out for blood."

Time passed so pleasantly that Jenny was surprised when

she heard the front door swing open. Mrs. Pennoyer came in, took off her scarf, and shook raindrops off her coat. "You two still at it? Better clear the table, Jenny, it's nearly suppertime. Grandpa, you want to eat with us tonight? I've got a roast in the oven."

Norma Fox Mazer

1. How do you know Jenny has a special relationship with Grandpa?
2. In what ways are they alike?
3. In what ways are they different?

Writer's Workbench 1

Sentence-Combining: Paragraphing

In the preceding selection you learned about the good times Jenny and her grandfather share. They obviously enjoy each other's company. This sentence-combining activity tells about another relationship between a grandchild and a grandfather. The sentence-combining cues will guide you in rewriting the selection in paragraph form.

Paragraphing is a way of organizing your writing so a reader can follow your thoughts. Each paragraph contains sentences about one main idea. Each new paragraph will be signaled by an asterisk (*). Begin a new paragraph by indenting that sentence when you see the asterisk (*).

* 1. I remember lying in the feather bed.
  I remember thinking of my grandfather.   (,)
  I remember listening to the ticking of his pocket watch.
     (, and)
  The watch was in the next room.

2. I felt scared.   (If)
  I would listen for the sound of that watch in the dark.   (,)

3. The watch was wonderful.
  The watch was round.
  The watch was gold.   (,)
  The watch was scarred.   (, and)

4. It was never without him.   (Because)
   The watch was my constant reminder he was there.   (,)

* 5. I remember grandfather drove a vegetable truck.
     I remember grandfather <u>swore.</u>   (,)
     I remember grandfather <u>was cross.</u>   (, and)

6. He would not let me sit on his lap.
   He would not let me <u>hug him.</u>   (or)

7. He could not express his love openly.   (Although)
   He showed it in quiet ways.   (,)

8. My grandfather's love was scarred like his watch.
   My grandfather's love was <u>distant.</u>   (,)
   My grandfather's love was <u>powerful.</u>   (,)
   My grandfather's love was <u>constant.</u>   (, and)

9. My grandfather gave me that watch.   (When)
   I knew he loved me.   (,)

Reread these two paragraphs. Look over the selection on pages 84–85. How is this grandfather different from Jenny's grandfather? How is he similar? Would you say that the grandfather and writer in this selection have a special relationship, too? Explain. Why does the writer describe the grandfather's love as "scarred like his watch"?

SPOTLIGHT

The Chinese Checker Players

When I was six years old
I played Chinese checkers with a woman
who was ninety-three years old.
She lived by herself
in an apartment down the hall from ours.
We played Chinese checkers
every Monday and Thursday nights.
While we played she usually talked
about her husband
who had been dead for seventy years,
and we drank tea and ate cookies
and cheated.

Richard Brautigan

1. What did the six-year-old child and the ninety-three-year-old woman share together?
2. How do you know they had a special relationship?
3. What does the word "cheated" in the last line tell you?

A Special Older Person

Think about an older person you have known. Write a short piece describing that person, and telling about something you did together. Write freely, letting words and ideas come to you as you move the pen across the paper. Try to capture the *feeling* you have for that older person. When you have finished your piece, use the free-writing checklist on page 5 to rework your writing.

Getting
It
Down

~~~~~~

**Checking
It
Out**

Share your writing with your classmates.

~~~~~~

**Getting
It
Right**

Revise and rework your writing. You may want to give it to that special older person.

~~~~~~

So far you have been thinking and discussing and writing about older people. Your next assignments in this chapter will prepare you to write a longer piece of writing about an older person. Before you do the writing, however, you will interview an older person to gather information for your paper. Be thinking about an older person you might like to interview. Maybe you have a neighbor you know well or maybe you could spend some time with a grandparent or other relative.

Before you wander off to ask questions, however, there are some important things to know about the process of interviewing.

Writer's Workbench 2

Asking Questions

Interviews look easy, right? All you do is ask questions, and the other person does the work. Well, as you will see, interviewing is more complicated than that. The kinds of questions you ask are the key to good interviewing. Good questions take careful planning and should be written in advance.

Some questions do not work very well in a personal interview. Here are some examples of questions to avoid as you plan your interview:

Yes/No Questions

If you use only questions which can be answered with a simple "yes" or "no," your interview will be short and provide you with very little information. For example, if an interviewer asked you, "Do you like school?", what would be your answer? "Yes," "No,"

"Yuk," or "Are you kidding?" The "Do you like school?" question would not give you much of a chance to develop a longer answer.

How could you change that question to a better one? How about "What are some things you like or dislike about school?" Such a question invites the interviewee to *tell* things and give a more complete response. Yes/No questions are not always bad. They provide information quickly and give you ideas for other questions. In your interview, however, use more carefully thought-out questions. Just for practice, change these yes/no questions into questions which ask the interviewee for a more complete answer:

1. Do you like your age?
2. Are you happy?
3. Are you worried about the future?
4. Do you have a job?

Loaded Questions

Some questions are worded in such a way that the response is almost automatic. Have you ever tried to sell greeting cards or candy door to door? How well did you do? If you were successful, you probably did not begin by saying, "You wouldn't want to buy any candy, would you?" It's too easy for someone to answer no to that question. That is a loaded question.

"You don't like school very much, do you?" is also a loaded question. The questioner has already decided what the answer should be. Think of some other examples of loaded questions. Try to avoid asking loaded questions.

Nosey Questions

Most of us do not wish to share all the details of our lives. We like our privacy, and we don't want people asking us nosey questions.

"How often do you brush your teeth?" is a nosey question.

What are some nosey questions you wouldn't want people to ask you?

Obvious Questions

Don't ask questions to which you already know the answer. The person may become bored with the interview or impatient with your questions.

"What school do you go to?" is an obvious question if the person is sitting next to you in English class.

What are some obvious questions which should not be asked?

We have discussed questions which don't work very well. Following are some tips for writing good questions. Good questions should be *invitations* to the person being interviewed. Good questions make the person *think*. Good questions *build* on one another. Good questions sometimes *surprise* the person being interviewed.

Invitations

Most people are willing to talk about things they like and dislike:
>"What do you like to do on the weekends?"
>"What do you like best about being your age?"
>"What three books would you take with you if you were stranded on an island?"

Many people like to talk about their hobbies and leisure-time activities:
>"What do you like to do after school?"
>"Do you collect anything?" "What?"
>"How will you spend the holiday?"
>"What is your favorite music group?"
>"What is your astrological sign?"
>"Do you believe in UFO's?" "Why?"

Think Questions

Some questions ask the person to think hard about something they know or feel:
>"What makes a good friend?"
>"How have you changed most in the past year?"
>"What is something that makes you proud?"
>"What the world needs now is . . ."

If Questions

Most of us daydream once in awhile and think about how life would be if things were different:
>"If you could be older or younger than you are now, which would you be?" "Why?"
>"If you could change your name, what new name would you choose?"
>"If you could become a famous person, who would it be?" "Why?"
>"If someone gave you $100, how would you spend it?"

Surprise Questions

A few wacky questions can spice up an interview:
"What animal is most like you?" "Why?"
"What is one thing you would never do?"
"What TV character is most like you?"

Look back over the sample questions in this Workbench. Choose two that interest you. Write the questions in your Writer's Notebook and answer them.

Practice Interview

Before you make your debut as an interviewer, you may need a little practice. Your teacher will assign you a practice interview partner. Follow these steps:

Getting
It
Down

1. Write five questions to ask your partner. Keep in mind the suggestions for writing good questions.
2. Take turns interviewing each other. Write down your partner's answers to your questions.
3. Share some of your questions and answers with the class.

How did the practice interview go? What problems did you have? Did you have trouble taking notes? Practice your note-taking skills by doing the following Workbench:

Writer's Workbench 3

Note-taking

Taking good notes as you talk to your interviewee will result in a successful interview. News reporters who must rely on absolutely accurate notes often use a tape recorder to simplify their job. If you have a cassette tape recorder, you might consider using it during your interview.

Even if you have a tape recorder, you need to develop your own shorthand for note-taking. One way to take notes is to listen and write down *key words*.

> **Question:** What do you think of the younger generation today?
>
> **Response:** Young people are not really aware of how good it is to be young. They take good health for granted, and they sometimes complain about trivial things. But, I like young people. I like their energy and enthusiasm and fun-loving spirit.

Some possible key words from this response are *not aware of, good health, complain, likes energy and spirit.* Could you remember what the interviewee said by looking at those key words?

Your teacher will read the response to the following question. Jot down the key words without looking in your book.

> **Question:** What is something you would change about yourself if you could?
>
> **Response:** I'm not sure . . . I think I like the way things are. Oh maybe my name. Yes, I would change my name to Kristy, and I would have long, fluffy hair and real big, round, brown eyes. Hmm. I guess I thought of some changes. Didn't I?

Do you have your key words? Try rewriting the response without looking at it. How did you do?

Note-taking is not easy at first. It takes practice. Try interviewing your partner again. Jot down *key words*.

Conversation with an Older Person

The following activities will take several days of preparation and planning and require you to do some work outside of class. You will write interview questions and conduct an interview with an older person. You will take notes during your interview and write up your interview in a paper entitled "Conversation with an Older Person."

The Questions

The first step in this assignment is to write some good questions which you can ask an older person. The purpose of your paper will be to capture a feeling about that person using his or her own words. Write questions which will give you that information. Think about subjects older people might be especially interested in talking about: "love is important," "friends are special people," "holidays are happy times." Think about subjects older people might have strong opinions about: rock music, the importance of sports, the future, the past.

Refer to Writer's Workbench 2 for suggestions for writing good questions. You may wish to use some of the following questions during your interview:

What is special about being your age?

What thoughts about the future do you have?

What does your family mean to you?

Is there anything that frustrates you about being your age?

Who are some special people in your life? Why are they special?

What do you think of today's music?

The Interview

Choose an older person to interview. Use the following interview tips as a checklist to be sure the interview goes smoothly. Good luck.

1. <u>Be prepared.</u>   Take two pens or pencils and a notebook.
2. <u>Plan ahead.</u>   Have your questions written out. Leave space under each question to jot down the key words in the person's answer.
3. <u>Warm up.</u>   Take some time before you begin the interview to help the person feel at ease.
4. <u>Be attentive.</u>   Once the interview begins, listen carefully. It's easy to begin thinking about your next question and miss some of what the person says.

5. <u>Take your time.</u>   Don't ask your questions too quickly. Be sure the person has completed the answer.

6. <u>Restate.</u>   If you're uncertain about an answer or if you want the person to give you more information, ask the person to clarify the answer.

Making a Collage

This activity asks you to look at life styles—your own and your older person's. As a way of beginning, make two columns in your Writer's Notebook: one labeled "alike," one labeled "different." Decide how a younger person and an older person are alike and different. Use your knowledge of yourself to think about the life style of a young person. Use the information in your interview notes to help you think about your older person's life style.

More than anyone else, you know what makes this older person special to you. Maybe you have shared a special moment. Maybe you have a common interest. You may have experienced the same feelings about each other or about a subject. Whatever the explanation, you can see a

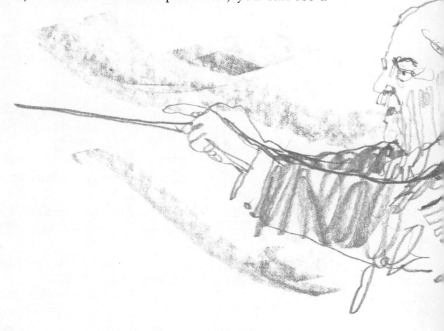

similarity between the two of you. In this activity you will make a *collage* based on the similarities between young and old.

A piece of writing communicates a message with words. A collage communicates a message using words and pictures cut from magazines, newspapers, and other sources. A collage can contain other things, too. Some people use yarn, string, wire, empty spools, or even raw spaghetti to make their collages more interesting. The main idea is to communicate a message visually.

1. Meet with your brainstorming group (Getting It Started, page 81).
2. As a group, think of a statement that makes an honest point about the young and old, such as "Both young and old people enjoy good times."
3. Gather the materials your group will need: old newspapers and magazines, bottles of glue, several pairs of scissors, poster board, a magic marker.
4. Have everyone search for and cut out as many words and pictures as possible. The brainstorming rules apply here, too. Welcome everyone's words and pictures. Look at each other's words and pictures to help you think of ideas.
5. When you have completed your search, spread out your collection on a large sheet of poster board. Examine your collection.
6. Reread your statement about the young and old. As a group, select those words and pictures that best support or reinforce your statement. Remember that this is group work. Be prepared to make some compromises.
7. After your group has made its choices, look at your final selections. Let the words and pictures themselves suggest an arrangement. Do certain words stand out? Are there certain pictures that seem especially effective? Shuffle the words and pictures around until you find an arrangement you like.
8. Glue your words and pictures into place on the poster board.
9. Proofread your statement about the young and old. Print the statement on a small strip of poster board.
10. Display your collage and statement together so that you

can share your non-stereotypic message about the young and old.

~~~~~~

Reviewing Your Notes

Checking
It
Out

Go back to your interview notes and look them over. Were you able to jot down key words and phrases? Can you remember what your interviewee said by reading your notes? Note-taking is a convenient way of getting down information fast. Your notes should help jog your memory. If your notes are patchy or hard to read or left in a drawer for a month, they may not be helpful. Fill in any gaps now while the interview is still fresh in your mind. Recover any words or phrases that are difficult to read. In the following Workbench, you will need an accurate set of notes.

Writer's Workbench 4

Direct Quotations

How people think and feel tells us about them. They often say things that help us know them better. Good reporters realize this. That is why good reporters often let interviewees speak to us directly. Television reporters often conduct on-the-spot interviews. In newspapers and magazines, reporters share interviewees' exact words, too. They do this by using direct quotations, as in this example:

> I asked Mr. Plantt for his views on aging. He said, "You are only old if you think old." He added cheerfully, "My grandchildren keep me young."

In this example Mr. Plantt's exact words are:

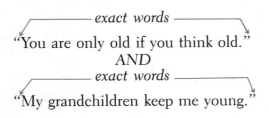

"You are only old if you think old."
AND
"My grandchildren keep me young."

Direct quotations can help the reader get to know your older person better. Look over your interview notes. Find exact comments you would like to share when you write your "Conversation with an Older Person." Circle two or three comments to include in your final paper.

You are using a direct quotation when you use a person's *exact* words. As a writer, you need to let your reader know that you are using the interviewee's exact words. It would be awkward to announce, "Okay, now I'm going to use my interviewee's exact words," every time you wanted to quote your interviewee. Instead you can use signals. These signals are called quotation marks ("   "). Here are some examples:

Uncle José admitted, "Being older has its advantages."

Aunt Hertha insisted, "Playing tennis twice a week keeps you young."

Ms. McDonald revealed, "If I had $100, I would buy a plane ticket to Los Angeles."

There are certain points to remember about using quotation marks. Quotation marks enclose the interviewee's exact words *only*. They show where the interviewee's exact words begin and where they end. In the preceding examples, what are the exact words being quoted?

Quotation marks are like shoes and socks. They are always used in pairs. Notice that there are two quotation marks in each example, one at the beginning of the quotation and one at the end.

You know that the first word of a sentence begins with a capital letter. The same rule applies to using a direct quotation. The first word of a direct quotation begins with a capital letter:

Mr. Grant said, "A real friend is someone who offers you her last piece of gum."

Ms. Ho beamed, "Sunday is my favorite day because my daughter calls from Milwaukee."

Direct quotations often have *quotation stems*. Quotation stems tell the reader *whose* exact words are being used. In the preceding examples, the quotation stems are *Mr. Grant said* and *Ms. Ho beamed*.

In these examples the quotation stems come at the beginning.

This is one pattern for writing direct quotations. When the quotation stem precedes the direct quotation, a comma separates it from the direct quotation:

quotation stem *exact words*

Aunt Lucille admitted, "I'm not used to being old yet."

So far, you've seen examples of direct quotations that *begin* with a quotation stem. Here are some points that apply when using this pattern:

1. Separate the introductory quotation stem from the direct quotation with a comma.
2. Place the appropriate end mark for the direct quotation *inside* the last set of quotation marks.

There are other patterns for using direct quotations, too. For variety, you can place the quotation stem in the *middle* of the quotation or at the *end* of the quotation. Following is the same direct quotation written in these three different patterns:

Pattern 1:   Quotation stem at the *beginning* of direct quotation

quotation stem

Mrs. Murphy said, "My grandchildren are my treasures."

Pattern 2:   Quotation stem in the *middle* of direct quotation

quotation stem

"My grandchildren," Mrs. Murphy said, "are my treasures."

Pattern 3:   Quotation stem at the *end* of direct quotation

quotation stem

"My grandchildren are my treasures," Mrs. Murphy said.

You may want to try more than one pattern for writing direct quotations in your "Conversation with an Older Person." For practice, select one of your circled comments in your interview notes and do the following:

1. Rewrite the comment *exactly* as your interviewee said it.

2. Write a quotation stem. Use a strong verb in your quotation stem. The verb in a quotation stem usually should reveal *how* the interviewee made the comment.
3. Rewrite your direct quotation using each of the three patterns introduced in this Workbench. Use the examples given to help you punctuate each pattern.

● If you need help with using direct quotations, check your Handbook, pages H-29–31, or ask your teacher.

Writing Your Portrait

You are now ready to transform your interview notes into a portrait of that special older person.

〰〰〰〰〰〰〰〰〰〰〰〰〰〰〰〰

Getting It Started

Before you plan your writing, try a free writing about your person. Write as quickly as you can about whatever comes to mind from your interview. Keep writing for at least ten minutes.

〰〰〰〰〰〰〰〰〰〰〰〰〰〰〰〰

The Hook

Getting It Down

Have you found an interesting way to begin your writing? Writers sometimes refer to a good beginning as a *hook*. A good beginning *hooks* the reader and makes him or her want to read more. Look through your interview notes and your free writing for a good beginning line. Let that sentence be your hook. Maybe your hook could be the words of your older person:

"I'm happy with my life now. I live near my grandchildren, and I have time to spend with them," she said with a smile, her eyes crinkling at the corners.

Maybe your *hook* could be a description of the person:

Grandpa sat there in his favorite chair. His eyes were tired; his old rough hands were folded in his lap. "Well, what are you going to ask me?" he said a bit gruffly.

"I wanted to ask you about being old," I said.

Maybe your *hook* could be a feeling about your older person:

I knew she would find the time to talk to me. Even though she works hard at the hospital and comes home tired to cook dinner, she always has time for me. We are very close friends.

Look back through your notes and your free writing for a hook. Keep looking until you find something you think your readers will like.

~~~~~~~~~~~~~~~~~~~~~~~~~~~~~~~~~~~~~~~

Quotations

Use the exact words of your older person as often as you can in your writing. Capture the sound of that person talking in your paper. Select at least three direct quotations to use. Work the quotations in smoothly using description and quotation stems. Look at Writer's Workbench 4, pages 97–100, to solve any punctuation problems.

Getting It Down

~~~~~~~~~~~~~~~~~~~~~~~~~~~~~~~~~~~~~~~

Endings

Experiment with some different endings for your conversation. One of the marks of a well-written piece of writing is a thoughtful ending. Sometimes a quotation works well for an ending:

Getting It Down

Grandmother summed up the interview with a smile. "Well, now you know more about me than anyone else in the world."

Sometimes a feeling works well for an ending:

I feel closer to Mr. Sullivan now. He is not just the old man who lives next door. I wish I had talked to him before.

Sometimes a summary statement works well for an ending:

I learned something from this interview. Older people like to talk to younger people. They are just waiting for the chance to share their memories with someone.

Try two or three different endings. Read them to a classmate. Decide which one you like best. Spend some time working on that ending!

~~~~~~~~~~~~~~~~~~~~~~~~~~~~~~~~

The Write-up

Getting It Down

Now that you have decided what quotations to include in your paper and how you will begin and end it, write your portrait of your special older person. Look back over your interview notes and mark information you want to be sure to include in your portrait. Create a life-like picture. Describe the person. Tell things about him or her. Replay the words that were spoken in the interview so that readers can hear the person talk. Your writing should be a natural conversation with the person you interviewed.

~~~~~~~~~~~~~~~~~~~~~~~~~~~~~~~~

CHECKPOINT

Your teacher will use Checkpoint 3 on page 105 to evaluate your portrait. Read your paper aloud to a classmate to hear how it sounds. Use this checklist to double-check and revise your paper before you hand it in:

1. Have you worked on the opening? Does it give the reader a *feeling* for your person? Does it *hook* the reader?
2. Have you used at least three direct quotations by your older person?
3. Have you punctuated your quotations correctly? Check Writer's Workbench 4, if you need to.
4. Have you included some description of your person's physical features?
5. Are you satisfied with how your "conversation" ends? Did you end with a quotation, feeling, or summary statement?

Writer's Workbench 5

Adding to Your Word Bank

The following ten words were used in this chapter. Read each word and its definition. (The definition tells the meaning of the word as it was used in this chapter. You may find additional definitions in a dictionary.) Then turn to the page indicated and find the sentence in which the word is used. Read the sentence several times to fix the word in your mind. Refer to the definition again as you need to.

1. accurate (page 91)   precise or exact

2. ageism (page 82)   the stereotyping of older people as being helpless

3. collage (page 94)   a visual composition in which pieces of objects such as newspaper and cloth are pasted together on a surface

4. debut (page 91)   a first appearance

5. hook (page 100)   a device writers use to capture the reader's attention

6. impatient (page 81)   quickly annoyed

7. profligate (page 84)   wildly extravagant

8. stereotype (page 82)   an untrue or oversimplified statement about an entire group of people

9. transform (page 100)   to change something

10. trivial (page 92)   small or unimportant

Now that you have reviewed these words and their definitions and have found the sentence in which each word appears, check yourself by completing the sentences that follow. Choose a word which makes sense in the sentence. You will not use all of the words. Write the completed sentence in your Writer's Notebook.

1. A(n) ___ makes the reader want to read on.
2. ___ people are reckless with money.
3. A(n) ___ is an effective medium because it communicates its message visually.
4. The ___ interviewer rushed through the questions.
5. Writing good questions for interviewing is not a(n) ___ matter.
6. ___ notes are helpful to the interviewer.
7. The young lawyer made her ___ before Judge Murray.
8. I would ___ the pumpkin into a beautiful carriage if I had a magic wand.

CHECKPOINT 3

	1	2	3	4	5

Beginning   ×4=

Think about your opening again. Can you find a more interesting beginning?

I see you've been working on the hook.

Good hook! You got me into the paper quickly.

Direct Quotations   ×4=

What happened? You didn't use three quotations. Look back over your interview notes.

Introduce your quotations carefully. Try to get the person's *exact* words.

Yes! You used your quotations very well. I can hear the person talking.

Punctuation   ×2=

Whoops! Better reread Writer's Workbench 4. You will need practice with all those marks.

You made a good effort. Check all of your quotation punctuation carefully. There are a few mistakes.

Good. You were very careful to capitalize and to keep the commas and end marks in the right places.

Ending   ×4=

What ending? Did you forget to try several different endings?

Your ending needs work. Maybe you could find a more effective wrap-up.

A very effective ending. Good work.

A Feeling for the Person   ×6=

Your paper is just too sketchy. Not enough detail and description. I couldn't hear your person talking.

Good effort. You are beginning to get the feeling of good writing. Spend more time reworking and polishing your piece.

Yes. You captured your person on paper. I felt as if I were there during your interview.

Chapter 7

Games Poets Play

Words and more words. Writers love words. They stack them up and spread them out. They steal them and they make them up. Writers and words are very close. They need each other. For the past six chapters you have been wrestling with words, trying to make them do what you want them to. They have not always been your friends.

You have used free writing to let the words spill out of your head, and then worried over the mess trying to make something good of it. You have tried to choose strong verbs and vivid words. You have listened for the sound of your own voice in your words. You have tried to capture the attention of readers and make them listen to your words. You have learned some of the tricks of a writer's mind. You're getting better as a writer. You're ready to experiment with new ways to arrange words and express feelings.

These next two chapters will be a change from what you have been doing. You will have both more freedom and less freedom as a writer. You will be free to invent, combine, and redefine words. You will be free to form words in new patterns—with and without complete sentences—with and without punctuation and capitalization. You will be free to play with words.

But you will have less freedom as well. You will learn new rules for words. You will learn new forms for groups of words. You will choose your words more carefully because you will choose far fewer of them. In short you will be working as a poet. Poets are special people. If writers love words, poets have a mystical relationship with words. Poets have a special touch. Sometimes they are gentle, sometimes harsh, sometimes frivolous, and sometimes deadly serious. Poets choose to send their messages to their readers in short, compact verses. Poets see common things in uncommon ways. Poets express feelings in tightly tied little packages. Poets delight in form and sound.

In these next two chapters you will have many opportunities to use words as poets do. You will find that you enjoy playing the games poets play and, who knows, you may be an undiscovered poet.

Before you plunge into your life as a poet, read and listen to some poems and talk about how poets work. Reading and listening to poetry are good ways to learn about poets.

How Poets Work

First and foremost, poets *play* with language. They use common words in unusual ways and strange words in unexpected places. They have fun with language. Ogden Nash has long been recognized as a humorous poet. Listen to your teacher read this poem aloud:

Away from It All

I wish I were a Tibetan monk
Living in a monastery.
I would unpack my trunk
And store it in a tronastery.
I would collect all my junk
And send it to a jonastery;
I would try to reform a drunk
And pay his expenses at a dronastery.
And if my income shrunk
I would send it to a shronastery.

Ogden Nash

What is funny about this poem? Where did the words *tronastery, jonastery, dronastery,* and *shronastery* come from? Make up some more lines to this poem using Nash's formula.

Some poets like to use sounds in their poems. They begin words with the same letters or they repeat letters. Poems sound better when they are read aloud. Poets play tricks to catch the reader's ear.

Read these sound poems aloud:

Ping-Pong

Chitchat   crisscross
wigwag   flip-flop
rickrack   ding-dong
zigzag   tiptop

Knickknack   singsong
gewgaw   mishmash
riffraff   King Kong
seesaw   bong.

Eve Merriam

How well has the poet captured the sound of a ping-pong game?
Can you think of other sound words she might have used? Which
words do you think sound most like a ping-pong game? What
happened in the last two lines?

Many poets use rhyme to catch a reader's ear. Rhyming is fun.
You may remember enjoying the singsong of the nursery rhymes
you heard as a child. Read aloud these Mother Goose nursery
rhymes:

Jack Sprat could eat no fat,
His wife could eat no lean:
And so, betwixt them both,
They licked the platter clean.

Pease-pudding hot,
Pease-pudding cold,
Pease-pudding in the pot,
Nine days old.
Some like it hot,
Some like it cold,
Some like it in the pot,
Nine days old.

Creating strong poems with good rhymes is more difficult than it
looks. Sometimes beginning poets write better poems if they don't

worry about rhyme. Playing with language, using sounds in special ways, and creating rhymes are just a few ways poets work. Now it's your turn to work as a poet.

~~~~~~

Ego-Tripping

Getting It Down

For this activity you need your Writer's Notebook, a partner, and a split personality. One side of you is poet, the other partner. You will be shifting back and forth between these roles.

Write the letters of your name in a column. Use both your first and last name if you like a challenge or if your name is short. Cal Dean's name looks like this:

C
A
L

D
E
A
N

Using words that begin with the letters of your name, write an Ego-Tripper that describes you. Play with words until the poem looks, sounds, and feels right for you. Consult your partner for feedback. Here are Ego-Trippers by Elizabeth and Cal:

Earnest   Cantankerous
Lean   And
Incredibly   Lovable
Zany   Devilish
Also   Eager
Bright   Astounding
Exact   Nut
Thin
Healthy

〜〜〜〜〜〜〜〜〜〜〜〜〜〜〜〜〜〜〜〜〜〜〜〜〜〜〜〜〜〜

The Name Game

Try a variation of Ego-Tripping. The Name Game tells a mini-story. Print the letters of your name vertically down the left column in your Writer's Notebook.

Tell a mini-story about yourself or just write about yourself. The first word of each line begins with the letter on that line.

Getting
It
Down

〜〜〜〜〜〜〜〜〜〜〜〜〜〜〜〜〜〜〜〜〜〜〜〜〜〜〜〜〜〜

In the following poem Saul shares a part of himself:

Sometimes I pretend I am
A lazy lion or a sleepy King
Up in my brother's tree house
Lying with my back against the cold planks.
> *Saul*

What do you learn about Saul from reading his poem? What kind of experience does he share? Have you had a similar experience?

Going Public

Look over your Ego-Trippers and Name Games. Get your partner's opinion, too. Together choose your best poem. Choose carefully because you will be making your debut as a poet. You and your poem are going public.

You and your partner will work together on this publication effort. Going public will require these materials: one chair, one overhead projector (or other light source), pencils, thin-tipped magic markers, several pairs of sturdy scissors, glue, 4″ × 6″ index cards, and one large sheet of heavy construction paper for each person in the class. Follow these directions:

1. Place a chair in front of a bare wall. One side of the chair should be close to, but not touching, the wall. A semi-dark room works best.
2. Post a large sheet of construction paper on the wall behind the chair. The construction paper should "frame" your head and shoulders when you sit down.

3. Position the light source 5–6 feet from the chair. When turned on, the light will shine directly toward the chair's side. Turn off the light.
4. Sit in the chair with your feet directly in front of you. One side of your body faces the wall. One side faces the light.
5. Close your eyes. Your partner will turn on the light. A silhouette will be projected onto the construction paper. Your partner can move the light closer or farther away until a clear silhouette is projected.
6. Have your partner trace your profile in pencil onto the construction paper. This may take a few minutes.
7. Swap places. Put up a new sheet of construction paper. Trace your partner's silhouette. Move to another area to cut your silhouettes so the next pair can work.
8. Cut out your silhouette. Neatly recopy your name poem onto a large index card. Have your partner double-check your spelling. Glue the index card onto the center of your silhouette. Post the silhouettes around the room.

SPOTLIGHT

Poetry often celebrates people. It praises the known and the unknown, the famous and the not-so-famous. Through poetry, people are applauded for just being themselves.

Spring Fever

Danny dawdles
Sally shilly—shallies
Lloyd loiters
Guy gambols
Sylvia saunters
Peter procrastinates
Amanda meanders
Leonard lingers
Samuel ambles
Dorothy dallies
Harry tarries
and Molly lolls.
Eve Merriam

Eve Merriam's poem is tight. She describes each person in only two words. The entire poem celebrates not only the individuals but the entire group. What do you learn about each individual from the way he or she moves? What can you guess about the group? How do you feel about the title Eve Merriam chose?

Look around you. You and those around you make your class different from all the other classes at school. Your personalities blend to make your class extraordinary rather than ordinary. Celebrate your class in a group-written poem.

~~~~~~~~~~~~~~~~~~~~~~~~~~~~~~~~~~~~~~~

Class Celebration

Write your first name on each of the first few lines of a sheet of paper:

Getting
It
Down

> Sally
> Sally
> Sally
> Sally
> Sally

Now think of a strong verb that captures your spirit, applauds a quirk, or communicates one of your mannerisms. Write it on the first line after your name. Think of some more. Write them down, too. Experiment with your name and several strong verbs. Try a verb that starts with the same letter or has the same sound or contains the same number of syllables as your name. Look at all the possibilities.

> Sally clowns
> Sally shines
> Sally blasts
> Sally shouts
> Sally slams
> Sally shrieks
> Sally sashays
> Sally struts
> Sally cavorts
> Sally shimmers

Say them to yourself. How do they sound? How do they

look? How do they feel? Your contribution to the group poem will be limited to two words. Choose the combination that unmistakably pinpoints the real you. Sally chose this one:

> Sally shimmers

What do you think of her choice? What kind of person do you imagine Sally to be? What makes you think so?

Look at your list. Which combination best describes you? Circle your choice. Now you are ready to celebrate your class in a group-written poem.

Choose a recorder. He or she will need magic markers and a long sheet of butcher paper. The recorder should leave space at the top to add a title later. When the recorder calls on you, give your two-word contribution. The recorder will write the word *and* before the last person's name and put a period at the end of the poem. Use Eve Merriam's "Spring Fever" as a guide.

Have someone read the completed poem to the class. Take a minute to talk about what a stranger might learn about your class after reading your poem. Brainstorm for a title that seems to fit your class personality. Write the title at the top of the paper. Post your class celebration.

～～～～～～～～～～～～～～～～～～～～～～～～～

I Wish . . .

**Getting
It
Down**

Before you go wandering off on your own to write great poems, write another class poem. The teacher who first used this activity called this a *collaborative* poem. Collaborative means "working together." You are to work together to build a class poem. Each of you will share the responsibility by writing one line of the poem. To make sure the lines will fit together, you need some rules:

1. Begin your line with the words *I wish.*
2. Use the name of an entertainer or super hero, a color, and a place in your line:
    > I wish Donna Summer would sing electric blue in my dreams.
3. Use butcher paper to publish your collaborative poem.

Try writing several other collaborative poems. Change the rules. Use different beginning lines.

SPOTLIGHT

Imagine yourself strolling down the street in your neighborhood. You take in the scenery like a sponge absorbing water. You happen to glance at a window as you pass a nearby house. A slight motion (a figure, a hand?) in the window catches your eye. Without slowing down, you look again. Nothing is at the window. Perhaps you saw something. Perhaps not.

Spring is like a perhaps hand

Spring is like a perhaps hand
(which comes carefully
out of Nowhere) arranging
a window, into which people look (while
people stare
arranging and changing placing
carefully there a strange
thing and a known thing here) and

changing everything carefully
spring is like a perhaps
Hand in a window
(carefully to
and fro moving New and
Old things, while
people stare carefully
moving a perhaps
fraction of flower here and placing
an inch of air there) and

without breaking anything
                    E.E. Cummings

This poem compares spring to a hand. Not just any hand—a perhaps hand. Think of another word, a synonym, that means the same thing as perhaps. Substitute the synonym for the word *perhaps*. The first line may now read: Spring is like a *maybe* hand. Which word—maybe or perhaps—sounds more poetic? How would a perhaps hand behave? Would it be certain or uncertain, confident or unsure? Would it be a reality or an illusion? As a class, talk about this unusual poem.

Poets are fond of comparisons. They especially like unexpected comparisons. Like the perhaps hand of this poem, poets often place "carefully there a strange thing and a known thing here." Poets make these unexpected comparisons because they want us to look at the familiar in fresh, new ways. Poets want to s-t-r-e-t-c-h our imaginations like salt water taffy.

Spring Is Like . . .

In your Writer's Notebook, copy the phrase: Spring is like. . . . Close your eyes and drift to spring. Spring is like . . . what? Open your eyes and complete the phrase with a noun or a noun and a descriptive phrase. Write several endings if you wish. Stretch your imagination like a rubber band.

Read over your *Spring is like* list. Some of your comparisons probably touch your past or dreamed-about experiences. Some are probably wacky. Turn your responses into a class poem just as you did with your *Class Celebration* and your *I Wish* poems. Be sure to get at least one response from everyone. Use the chalkboard to publish your poem.

Getting
It
Down

SPOTLIGHT

Spring Is Like

a clothespin
a bike race
a belly dancer
a groundhog looking at its shadow
an afternoon shower
bare feet running through green fields
a wriggling worm
a just cleaned garage
the smell of fresh paint
a skinned heart
my uncle's garden
a tennis racket
trout in a mountain stream
a stuck window
hopscotch
nothing else
fresh paint

short sleeve shirts and cut-offs
a soda and a pack of peanuts
goose bumps on a windy day
winter without the sting
strawberries with whipped cream
Spring is like a game of hide-and-seek. It peeks over
winter's shoulder
teasing me to tag it in sweet-smelling fields of clover

Pete

Look over your class poem and the preceding one. Which comparisons are fresh and unexpected? Which comparisons cause you to draw on your personal storehouse of memories? Decide which comparisons caused you to think about spring in a new or unusual way. For example, talk about *how* spring is like a clothespin or a belly dancer or a skinned heart. Choose three or four powerful comparisons from the two poems. What in these three or four comparisons grabs you?

Writer's Workbench

Similes

Poets are like magicians. They astonish us with the unexpected. They surprise us by having words meet each other for the first time. Such uncommon meetings can bedazzle us by showing us new ways of viewing the world. But even magicians need help sometimes. They use magic hats or trick cards or illusion to assist them. Poets depend on their imaginations for unusual comparisons. They sometimes get help in connecting comparisons. The words *like* and *as* are the assistants. To connect their comparisons poets might say, "Spring is *like* a skinned heart," or "Spring is *as* warm *as* daffodils basking in the sun." Comparisons that use the words *like* and *as* are called *similes*. In this Workbench you will practice writing similes —comparisons using the words *like* and *as*.

Form small groups. Take out your Writer's Notebook and a pencil.

Comparisons Using As

Powerful similes grab you. They avoid worn-out comparisons. Worn-out or trite comparisons were once fresh, but because they have been used over and over, they are now tired. In your Writer's Notebook complete these phrases using tired, worn-out comparisons:

busy as
pretty as
fat as
skinny as

Chances are you wrote comparisons that look and sound dull and lifeless such as "busy as a bee." Here are some examples of fresh and surprising comparisons:

busy as popcorn popping
busy as a dog's wagging tail
busy as a suit of checks, stripes, and plaids
busy as a hummingbird's wings

As a group, brainstorm for comparisons that are fresh and surprising by completing the following phrases. Be zany. Be weird. Let your imagination flow. Record your fresh similes in your Writer's Notebook.

alive as	savage as	brave as
slimy as	stiff as	gentle as
tight as	uncertain as	bright as
deep as	restful as	sticky as
mean as	quiet as	spooky as
cool as	crawly as	loud as
plain as	quick as	busy as
flat as	sharp as	pretty as
tough as	fierce as	fat as
stubborn as	precious as	skinny as

Comparisons Using *Like*

Nature is all around us in the form of wind, rain, sunshine, sleet, and moonbeams. People sometimes take nature for granted. This offers a challenge to you as a poet. Think of similes using the word *like* that will startle readers into taking notice. Be outlandish. Be subtle. Make powerful comparisons.

Try word-shaking to help you get started. To shake out words, answer questions such as those that follow. Apply the questions to sleet, frost, a mud puddle, a moonbeam, a tree, a shooting star, a mountain, and a valley. Have one person record your words on butcher paper.

How large is it? How small is it? How tall? How short? What shape is it? Can you pick it up? How heavy or light is it? Heavy as a city? Light as an eyelash? Where would you hide it? Where would you show it off? What sound does it have? Does it yodel? Does it hum? Is it loud? Does it boom? Crash? Is it quiet? Does it whisper? Murmur? What instrument in an orchestra reminds you of it? How does it taste? What food tastes like it? What dance moves like it? What jewel shines like it? How does it feel? Squishy? Lumpy? Solid? What kind of friend would it be? What kind of enemy would it be? What emotion does it have? Rage? Love? Jealousy?

Use your word-shaking responses to help you complete these similes. Write each simile in your Writer's Notebook. Share your responses.

Sleet is like ——.
Frost is like ——.
A mud puddle is like ——.
A moonbeam is like ——.
A tree is like ——.
A shooting star is like ——.
A mountain is like ——.
A valley is like ——.

Read this poem written by a fourteen-year-old boy:

I Am Waiting

I am waiting
    for love
I am waiting
    for happiness
I am waiting
    for a person to call my own
I am waiting, waiting
    for a fantasy
    a world of things unknown to man

Yes
I am waiting
    for things that can never be fulfilled
    never
I am waiting for a wallet as fat as the president's

Someday yes someday
    before I die.

Yes, I am poor and unworthy
    but I can dream.

Michael Goode

What are some things you can learn about Michael from reading
his poem? What are some things you are waiting for?

~~~~~~

I Am Waiting

Write your own "I Am Waiting" poem. Brainstorm a list of
things you are waiting for. Select the four most important
ones. Write the first four lines of your poem just as Michael
has done. Look at Michael's last line. End your poem on
the fifth line using Michael's "Yes . . . but . . . form."

**Getting
It
Down**

~~~~~~

Share your five-line poem with other members of the class.
Keep a copy in your Writer's Notebook.

**Checking
It
Out**

~~~~~~

taste me,
    I am the wind
touch me,
    I am the lean gray deer
running on the edge of the rainbow.
        Leslie Marmon Silko

~~~~~~

Wander through your memories of rainbows. Let rainbows
wrap around your mind. Gently prod your imagination by
answering the following questions. Your teacher will record
your responses on the chalkboard.

**Getting
It
Started**

What shape is a rainbow? What other wonders in nature have the same shape? A waterfall? Are there others? What architectural structures remind you of a rainbow? Do any animals resemble a rainbow? Close your eyes and imagine a rainbow. A rainbow is multi-colored. What colors do you see? Are there more precise words for the colors of a rainbow? What color blue do you see? What color red? If you could paint a rainbow, what colors would it be? What would you wrap in a rainbow? How would a rainbow taste? If a rainbow were ice cream, what flavors would it be? What other foods are like a rainbow? Do you like music? What musical instrument reminds you of a rainbow? How would a rainbow feel? What texture would it be? When does a rainbow appear? Describe what the weather is like. What does the sun look like when there is a rainbow? The sky? What feeling does a rainbow give you? Misty?

Hopeful? Subdued? If you could dance on a rainbow, what kind of dance would you do? If a rainbow were a precious stone, what kind would it be? Can you think of other things that remind you of a rainbow? Fill the board with rainbow words and images.

Poets love words. One way to discover good words is to shake them out of your own head—the way you just did. The person who created this technique called it "word-shaking." Word-shaking lets words tumble out. In the following activity you will write about rainbows. Read the words on the board to spark an idea for a rainbow writing. Use these words or others in your writing.

Before you begin your rainbow creation, read this poem:

Rainbow Striping

If I could be a painter
I'd stripe the world in rainbows.
I'd swirl a kelly blue
A tiger orange
A pulsing yellow.
I'd stripe ants
And doorstops
And polar bears.
I'd wrap the world in crayons
And never be sad.

Gale

What feeling do rainbows give the poet? Why do you think she mentions ants, doorstops, and polar bears as things she would paint? What other items would you want to stripe?

The Pretty Poem

Write a poem or free write about rainbows. Use the words on the board or any words that somersault onto your paper. Form is not important right now. See what tumbles down.

Getting
It
Down

~~~~~~

Form groups of 3–5. Share your poems and free writings. Let each person read once uninterrupted. Listen carefully. Listen for the best part of that writing. Be selective.

Ask the writer to read the piece a second time. When you hear words or phrases that surprise you, say so. Do certain words sound good together? Mention that. Do you hear words or phrases that paint pictures in your mind? Listen for mind pictures that strike you. Point them out to the writer.

As a group, help each writer recognize the good parts. These have possibilities. Point to the possibilities. File this piece in your Writer's Notebook for now. Put it on the back burner of your mind. Let it simmer.

~~~~~~

Poets have an obligation to help readers. Often this means going beyond creating scenes. It often means *re*creating scenes. It is the poet's job to let readers see scenes through the eyes of the poet. To do this, poets rely on description. By using description, poets let readers look over their shoulders. Poets recreate the mood and feeling of a scene by carefully selecting words. They describe sights and odors and sounds just as they see and smell and hear them. They describe emotions just as they feel them. Only then can poets be sure readers experience scenes as they do.

You've been writing about beautiful rainbows, your wishes, and your dreams. Poets also describe the unpretty side of life. What do these pictures bring to mind?

> buzzards hovering over a dead carcass
> the aftermath of a tornado
> your room after a spend-the-night party
> the face of an enraged orangutan
> garbage cans oozing foul-smelling debris
> a polluted stream

Poets have a knack for describing things, both beautiful and ugly. They practice their craft to keep their descriptive skills sharp. This activity will give you a chance to practice your skills. You will use descriptions to let readers see through your eyes.

The Ugly Poem

For this activity you will describe eight items—one description per line. You can write your descriptions in a word or phrase. The trick is to avoid naming the thing you describe. The only exception to this rule is in line three. In line three you may use the name of the color you describe. Keep your readers in mind as you write. For this poem your classmates will be your readers. Remember that you want to make them feel just as you feel about what you describe. Like any good poet, you want to show off your knack for description.

Line 1   Think of the ugliest animal in the world. Vividly describe the animal or its peculiar habits. Do not use the animal's name.

Line 2   Describe how you feel inside when you are mad.

Line 3   Describe a color you intensely dislike. You may use the name of the color, but be sure to use descriptors that show why you feel as you do.

Line 4   Describe the foulest smell you can think of. Do not name the source of the odor.

Line 5   Describe a garbage dump. Describe how it looks or smells.

Line 6   Describe music that sets your teeth on edge. Describe it so your reader will understand why you dislike it.

Line 7   Describe the texture or taste of a food you try to avoid eating. Compare the food to something else if it helps communicate your feelings. Try using a simile.

Line 8   Describe some scene of violence—a fist fight, a riot, a war. Choose a phrase or two that *re*creates the scene for your readers.

~~~~~~

Checking It Out

Reread your eight-line poem. Be sure you did not use the names of things you described, except in line three. Title your poem "Anger."

~~~~~~

Getting It Right

Now reword your poem until you are satisfied that a reader will sense the emotion of anger. Change words, add others, take some out. Shuffle lines around until they suit you. Add another line or take one out if you think doing so will recreate the emotion of anger in your readers' minds.

~~~~~~

SPOTLIGHT

Here is an original and revised anger poem written by Misty:

Original

ANGER

a sharp beak; shoulders hunched,
smouldering knots
screaming orange that blinds
putrid toe curling, disgusting
slimy lettuce leaves; moldy milk cartons
high pitched sounds of glass breaking
slippery like mush on ice
flash of a steely knife; hearts breaking

Revision
a razor sharp beak; dark shoulders hunched
smouldering knots
a screaming, blinding orange

toes curl in disgust.
slimy lettuce leaves on moldy milk cartons
high pitched sounds of glass breaking
slippery like mush on mirrors
a steely knife flashes as hearts break.

Find a partner and discuss these questions: What changes did Misty
make in revising her poem? How did those changes create a
stronger feeling of anger?

Look at the poems you wrote. What changes did you make?
Point out words or phrases that make you feel the emotion of anger.

Chapter 8

Performing Poetic Feats

Trying to keep poets and words apart, as you discovered in Chapter 7, is practically impossible. Poets and words are irresistibly attracted. Like magnets they are drawn together. Theirs is a wonderful relationship.

As much as poets love words, there is one thing even dearer to them, and that one thing is creating poems from words. Poets are not content to simply be surrounded by words. They have to do something with words. Poets are compelled to communicate.

In a Moment

For just one moment
Pretend
To close your eyes.
What do you see?
Take your time,
You may make notes
Or draw images
Of what you see—
(If you see images)
Use the air
That surrounds you
Now
That is, where you have found yourself
(You may name the place)
Does this air
Have a color, is it warm
Or cool, what is its taste?

If you have imagined
This place
Which is entirely yours—
It belongs to you
(Now)
You have become nothing less
Than one poem
And if this is so
Then what is this
That you are reading
Now?
Have your eyes
Really been closed
Or have you imagined
They were closed?
Does this make a difference
Now?
Go back
To where you began.
Has the air changed?
If so, describe it now
In the same way
As before
If this is possible
Now.

Michael Gessner

The poet urges you to experience life first hand. What is the effect of his short, telegraphic lines? Were you tempted to follow the poet's instructions? Did this form make his message seem compelling?

Form

Poets mold their communications into forms—forms of all shapes and sizes. In this chapter you will discover some of the forms poetry can take. There are all sorts of forms—some short, some long, some simple, some complex, some serious, some zany. As you explore various forms, your experience as a poet will come in handy.

Poets use form to express ideas. By shaping words into form, poets transform ideas into poetry.

My Mother and the Hummingbird

As the green-winged hummingbird
    darts sideways into the
      leaves of our baby apricot tree
Suspended, taking sugar with his
    quivering bill
I move in around the palm tree
    to have a better look
But my mother pushes open
    the window and says
      right now write a poem.
          David Kherdian

What advice does the mother give? Do you think she gave her son good advice? Read the poem aloud. Can you hear its conversational tone? Notice how the poet has arranged his lines to capture his idea in a poem.

Ideas and forms and words are all important, but poetry is more than these. Real poetry is feeling and that feeling is magic.

To the Snake

Green Snake, When I hung you round my neck
and stroked your cold, pulsing throat
    as you hissed to me, glinting
arrowy gold scales, and I felt
    the weight of you on my shoulders,
and the whispering silver of your dryness
    sounded close at my ears—
Green Snake—I swore to my companions that certainly
    you were harmless! But truly
I had no certainty, and no hope, only desiring
    to hold you, for that joy,
          which left
a long wake of pleasure, as the leaves moved
and you faded into the pattern
of grass and shadows, and I returned
smiling and haunted, to a dark morning.
          Denise Levertov

The speaker in this poem feels the weight of the snake on her shoulders. But she feels much more. Describe her feelings as she held the snake. How did she feel when he slithered off?

The magic of poetry depends on expressing feelings with wire-tight precision. This magic happens when reality and imagination are carefully balanced. Form—the way the poet arranges the words on the page—plays an important part in this performance. Such a delicate balancing act can be risky. Poet Lawrence Ferlinghetti explains:

Constantly Risking Absurdity

Constantly risking absurdity
                        and death
            whenever he performs
                        above the heads
                                    of his audience
        the poet like an acrobat
                    climbs on rime
                        to a high wire of his own making
        and balancing on eyebeams
                    above a sea of faces
            paces his way
                    to the other side of day
            performing entrechats
                        and sleight-of-foot tricks
        and other high theatrics
                        and all without mistaking
                any thing
                        for what it may not be
            For he's the super realist
                        who must perforce perceive
                taut truth
                        before the taking of each stance or step
    in his supposed advance
                        toward that still higher perch
    where Beauty stands and waits
                        with gravity
                                    to start her death-defying leap
    And he
            a little charleychaplin man

> who may or may not catch
> her fair eternal form
> spreadeagled in the empty air
> of existence
>
> *Lawrence Ferlinghetti*

The poet describes his craft as being risky. Why do poets take risks?
Look at the way the poet has arranged the lines of this poem. Has
he taken a risk? Explain. Think of a poem in which you took a risk.
Explain what you did and how you felt.

Poets are like nimble circus performers. They have much in
common with tightrope walkers. Tightrope walkers make every step
count. Poets make every word count. In spite of the risks, poets get
a kick out of performing the magic of poetry. They like to juggle
ideas and words and forms without dropping a line.

Try making words count in this next Workbench.

Writer's Workbench 1

Personification and Metaphor

Have you ever watched people work on a crossword puzzle? They
mutter to themselves, eyes glued to the puzzle. They scratch their
head and rub their chin. They chew on their pencil as they stare
into space searching for an unknown word.

People enjoy mind-stretching games. They like to exercise their
minds as well as their bodies. They like to puzzle over brain teasers
and word games. They enjoy figuring out riddles and puns. Poets
know this. They know people enjoy word play. They provide plenty
of exercise for our imagination.

In Chapter 7 you practiced using similes to compare unlike
things. In this Workbench you will practice using two other
methods of comparing things, personification and metaphor. Read
these two poems:

> For the performance the entertainer
> Gathered all the necessary props:
> Swords of fire, flaming batons,
> Plates that spin on wooden sticks

Then stretched his invisible canopy
Across the sky like a circus tent
And when the crowd arrived, Night spun
Carnivals of bright stars, hurled
Meteors and tossed high the white plate of the moon.
The celestial juggler performed until exhausted
And when morning came, Night slept.

Anonymous

The Night

The night
    creeps in
    around my head
    and snuggles down
    upon the bed
    and makes lace pictures
    on the wall
    but doesn't say a word at all.
        Myra Cohn Livingston

In both poems the poets have compared night to a human being. They have given night human characteristics. When poets give human characteristics to something that is not human, they are using *personification*. What kind of person is night in the first poem? What words tell you this? What kind of person is night in the second poem? Which personality of night do you like better?

With your classmates brainstorm for other human characteristics of night, such as:

Night is a silent thief.
Night is a mysterious stranger.
Night is a gloved hand.

Choose one of the preceding lines or one that you brainstormed. Add lines telling what night does as a thief or mysterious stranger. Arrange your lines into a short poem.

What are some other things you could dress up as people—the wind, rain, love, anger . . . ?

When poets compare unlike things without using the word *like* or *as* they are using *metaphor*. In this poem, the poet compares the sea to a hungry dog:

The Sea

The sea is a hungry dog,
Giant and grey.
He rolls on the beach all day.
With his clashing teeth and shaggy jaws
Hour upon hour he gnaws
The rumbling, tumbling stones,
And 'Bones, bones, bones, bones!'
The giant sea-dog moans,
Licking his greasy paws.

And when the night wind roars
And the moon rocks in the stormy cloud,
He bounds to his feet and snuffs and sniffs,
Shaking his wet sides over the cliffs,
And howls and hollows long and loud.

But on quiet days in May or June,
When even the grasses on the dune
Play no more their reedy tune,
With his head between his paws
He lies on the sandy shores,
So quiet, so quiet, he scarcely snores.

James Reeves

Have you ever thought of the sea as a hungry dog? Point out all the dog qualities the poet uses. Do you like the poem?

Fog

The fog comes
on little cat feet.

It sits looking
over harbor and city
on silent haunches
and then moves on.
Carl Sandburg

Brainstorm some things you could compare to animals, such as helicopter/hummingbird, wind/racehorse, or schoolchildren/puppies. Write a few lines using one of the comparisons you have chosen.

For a wacky poetic experience write several lines comparing an item in column A with an item in column B. Go across or diagonally. For example, you could compare a kalaidoscope to a garbage truck. Begin your comparison like this: A kalaidoscope is a garbage truck. . . . Then add several lines that give the kalaidoscope "garbage truck" characteristics. Think of all the ways you could make this comparison legitimate. Stretch your imagination.

A	B
kaleidoscope	garbage truck
prairie	cucumber

satin	acorn
sunset	golf ball
corkscrew	headlight
mountain	railroad track
hammer	jukebox
symphony	bulldozer
diamond	three-piece suit
trigger	marshmallow
peacock	can opener
love	prune pit
freckle	face lift
baby	skunk
velvet	dill pickle
extension cord	billboard

Circus audiences enjoy seeing circus acrobats pile atop each other. Their staggering human forms get appreciative oohs and ahhs from the crowd. Poetry, too, has special forms. Poets experiment, arranging words to see how they look on the page.

The Unemployment Bureau

The fly on the floor
of the Unemployment Office
                          in Carlisle Street, walks
in quick little spurts as though on wheels, going
          nowhere, circling, tribbling about
          in a circle   :   when, lash, I
          dash my foot out at him, he
flies a few inches away and lands
                          crouched
                          sluggish
       then circles back toward my foot
where it stands in line with other unemployed feet

Poor fly,
March is too early in springtime for you to buzz our heads,
black speck on brown tile floor, you
are probably also
trying to get in line.
                                        Paul Blackburn

The poet "drops" the third line off to the right. This line lands suddenly—much as a fly might alight. Which words does he "drop"? Why do you think he chose these words? Is there anything else unusual in this poem's form?

Medicine

>   Grandma sleeps with
>   my sick
>   grand
>   pa so she
>   can get him
>   during the night
>   medicine
>   to stop
>   the pain
>
>   In
>   the morning
>   clumsily
>   I
>   wake
>   them
>   Her eyes
>   look at me
>   from under-
>   neath
>   his withered
>   arm
>   The
>   medicine
>   is all
>   in
>   her long
>   un-
>   braided
>   hair.

Alice Walker

These lines seem to flow. How do you think Grandma's unbraided hair looks when she is awakened? Do you think the poet is trying to suggest the flow of her hair with the flow of his lines? What are some other explanations for the poet's choice of form?

Growing a Poem

You've been reading poems and discussing poetic feats. Ready or not, it's time for your poetic debut.

If you have never written a poem you like, the whole idea of becoming a poet may seem impossible. But poems are only words and you have plenty of those in your head. Of course, a good poem is a special group of words arranged just so by the poet. Sometimes when it's time to write a poem, those special words don't seem so obvious. We rack our brains and all we get is "moon" and "June." But poems are all around you. Maybe a poem begins by relaxing and really looking at common things around you.

I am sitting here on a quiet, spring day. I don't feel much like a poet, but I'm going to make a jot list of what I see. You can look over my shoulder while I work.

> empty wrapper from cinnamon gum
> smoke curling from my pipe into warm sunlight
> two wirehair fox terriers asleep at my feet
> a philodendron's arms reaching for light
> three carefully sharpened pencils
> a dirty pipe cleaner
> a pile of poetry books with little scraps of paper sticking
>   out
> a bentwood coat rack with a cat diesel power cap on top
> a brown paper bag full of wadded papers
> top-forty on the F.M.
>   "I've been in love with you
>   I am in love with you"
> a fly on the rim of my cup
> worn matchbook, one match left.

Notice that my jot list is just a simple list of what I see from where I'm sitting. It is concrete and photographic. I have not tried to find special words, just precise ones.

Jot List

Getting
It
Started

Make a jot list of what you can see from where you are sitting. Be as specific as you can. Don't stop too soon. Take at least ten minutes.

Now I begin to work the jot list by *selecting* the best details. No one tells me which details are best. I just feel it. I use my own hunches.

> I wait for the words
> A pile of poetry books
> wait with me—little scraps of paper
> stuck between their pages
> A crumpled gum wrapper (cinnamon)
> a sooty pipe cleaner
> three sharpened pencils
> a worn matchbook
> a rubber band
>
> Smoke curls into warm sunlight as
> a fly tightropes on my coffee cup.

Notice that I decided to put myself into the picture by opening with a line about what I'm doing. Look for other changes I have made in wording.

I also began to give the words some *shape* by working them into lines. Again no one guided me. I try to find a natural way to break the lines.

I *ended* the poem with two lines from my jot list which will leave the reader with a picture and a feeling.

First Revision

Getting
It
Down

Follow my steps with your own jot list: *Select*. *Open* with a line about yourself. *Shape* the words into lines. *End* with a feeling picture. Use your own hunches about what works best. Don't hurry. Reread your words aloud and listen to your voice.

My second revision is beginning to *feel* like a poem:

A Writer's Afternoon

I wait for words.
A pile of poetry books
waits with me.

Crumpled gum wrappers (cinnamon),
sooty pipe cleaners,
three sharpened pencils,

a worn matchbook,
and two paper clips (one straightened)
wait with me.

The afternoon curls into warm sunlight,
and
a fly tightropes on the rim of my cup.

                    D.K.

I have found a title and a new image—"afternoon curls." Find other changes in my revision. Do you like them? How would you have revised my poem?

Second Revision

Look at your first revision. Is there a title in there somewhere—maybe "Five Minutes after Lunch" or "Waiting for the Bell" or "Mom, They're Making Me Write Poems Again"? I'm sure you can do better than these. Don't worry about the title; it will come to you.

Look at your lines. Adjust them. Take out a word. Put

Getting
It
Right

in a few words. Tinker with your poem. Work on the last lines. Try for a strong word picture or an honest feeling. Work slowly, rereading and admiring your words.

~~~~~~

Share your poem with a friend. Try it out on the class. Show it to your big sister. Maybe you have found a poem by just listing the everyday things around your desk at school.

Try this approach to poetry writing in other locations around your neighborhood—up in your treehouse, down at the railroad tracks, out in the barn, or off at the laundrymat.

Tightrope walkers depend on the reality of a thin line. Poets, too, must keep a firm grasp on reality. A brief moment described with just the right words is frozen forever.

December

A little boy stood on the corner
And shoveled bits of dirty, soggy snow
Into the sewer—
With a jagged piece of tin.

He was helping spring some.
Sanderson Vanderbilt

Me and My Dad

Me and my Dad
sitting in a tavern eating
liverwurst sandwiches
We laugh and have
a good time
Me and my Dad
James O'Connor, Grade 5

Which of these poems do you like better? Explain. Both poems capture a moment like a photograph captures a scene. Be on the lookout for such moments.

Sometimes we enjoy those circus acts that seems impossible. We like those show-stoppers that tear us away from our cotton candy and popcorn. We're attracted to the complex. The same is true in poetry. You will find poems with many interpretations. These intriguing poems use words and word pictures which leave meaning up to the reader.

The Red Wheelbarrow

so much depends
upon

a red wheel
barrow

glazed with rain
water

beside the white
chickens.
William Carlos Williams

This poem has puzzled both literary critics and scholars. They wonder about the meaning of the colors red and white. They make much of the common objects selected by the poet. While they argue and analyze, readers continue to enjoy this poem. What do you think of it?

If extremes hook your attention, you probably make a point of strolling by the circus sideshow. There you can be entertained by fat people and skinny people, midgets and giants. Not to be outdone, poetry has its short and long, too. One of the shortest poems is called "Fleas":

Adam
Had 'em
Anoymous

This two-line poem is entitled "Drowsy":

Sleep is the gift of many spiders
The webs tie down the sleepers easy.
Carl Sandburg

More is not necessarily better. These two poems pack meaning into a few words. Find a longer poem you like. Try to compress it into just two lines.

Japanese poets have perfected a poetic form which has only seventeen syllables and just three lines. Haiku is a short poem that captures a moment in nature. While it appears simple, the rules governing haiku make it a complex poetic form.

Utsukushiki
  Tako agari keri
    Kojiki-goya.

How beautifully
That kite soars up to the sky
From the beggar's hut.
                                Issa

Amagaeru
  Bashō ni norite
    Soyogi keri.

The little rain frog
Rides on a banana tree
As it softly sways.
                                Kikaku

Haiku

A bitter morning
Sparrows sitting together
Without any necks.
        Andrew Levine, Grade 5

Each line is restricted to a certain number of syllables. Count the syllables in each line. Haiku captures a moment in nature in just three lines. No word is wasted. A crisp image is created.

Cinquain

Can you think of a time when you followed directions to put something together? Maybe it was the time you saved your allowance to buy a model airplane. You gave the salesclerk your money, lovingly tucked the package under your arm, and headed home. Once home you tore into the box, spreading its contents on the floor. A hundred tiny pieces greeted your unbelieving eyes. You wondered if those pieces would ever look like the picture on the box. You followed the directions word for word.

You may remember the first time you baked cookies. Carefully, you mixed and measured. You followed your mother's recipe step by step. When you popped those delicious blobs into the oven, you wondered if you'd have chocolate chew or chocolate goo.

Directions are often helpful. They guide your efforts, helping you create a product you can be proud of. Munching on a cookie you have made or flying your plane overhead gives you a good feeling.

Some poetry depends on special directions, too. Poetic forms often depend on exact word choice, careful syllable counts, specific numbers of lines, and other rules. The tight directions are challenging. Poets must follow a formula to create a mood or express a feeling. They think long and hard before dashing off a word.

The *cinquain* is a formula poem for you to enjoy tinkering with. The French word *cinq* means five. The cinquain is a special five-line poem. Before you write a cinquain, read the following three examples of a simple cinquain:

> Snacks
> junk food
> chips, dips, peanuts
> munch myself, lunch myself
> stuffed
> *Rhonda*

Snakes
Slithering forms
Sliding through grass
Parting my brave smile
Scary.

Leroy

Rain

Damp grass
Cold, misty trees.
Lonely thoughts of you.
Empty.

Dawn

**Getting
It
Started**

In the activities that follow you will experiment with three variations of the cinquain pattern. First brainstorm for subjects. The subjects should be ones you know something about—frogs, school, skating, mini-bikes, cafeteria, food.

Simple Cinquain

**Getting
It
Down**

Follow these directions carefully. Remember, not just any word will do. Search for a word that says what you feel.

Line 1   Write one word. This word is usually the topic of the poem. Notice, in the preceding examples, that Dawn has turned her first word into a title.

Line 2   Now write two words about the subject.

Line 3   Think of three more words.

Line 4   Add four words.

Line 5   Write only one word. Some poets repeat the word used in line 1.

Experiment by writing a few more poems using this pattern.

The regulated cinquain pattern is a little tighter:

> Brother
> brothers, bores
> borrowing, bragging, begging
> but I need him.
> friend
>
> *Carlos*

> Kites
> Light, airy
> Dancing, soaring, plunging
> Tangling dreams in string
> Kites
>
> *Tina*

~~~~~~

Regulated Cinquain

Follow these directions to write a regulated cinquain. Refer to the examples by Carlos and Tina as a guide.

Getting It Down

Line 1   Write the name of a thing. This can be the topic of your poem.

Line 2   Write two words that describe the thing in line 1.

Line 3   Describe an action related to the thing. Limit yourself to three words.

Line 4   Express a feeling about the thing. This time write four words.

Line 5   Repeat the same word as in line 1 or think of a word that refers to the same thing. Notice that Tina used the same word in lines 1 and 5, while Carlos substituted *friend* for *brother*.

Write a few more poems in this pattern.

~~~~~~

The following poems are examples of another pattern, the formal cinquain. These poems look simple. However, they're more challenging than they appear to be.

moon up
over the trees
shadows dance in cold light
something moving down the darkness
silence
Tom

old dog,
lying quiet
dreams of chasing rabbits
and barking down old gopher holes—
lost youth
Germaine

The formal cinquain is so tight it squeaks. Each line must contain a specific number of syllables. Even if they have the right number of syllables, not just any words will do. Every word should add to the poetic picture you want to create.

Formal Cinquain

Getting
It
Down

Write a formal cinquain, using the following pattern of syllables:

Line 1   Two syllables
Line 2   Four syllables
Line 3   Six syllables
Line 4   Eight syllables
Line 5   Two syllables

Poets and circus performers can leave us spellbound. But neither poets nor circus performers began with flawless feats. Instead they began much as you have.

In Chapter 7 you warmed up for your new role as poet. You shook words down and tumbled phrases out. You limbered your imagination by playing with language-bending words here, stretching lines there. You practiced building strong poems without rhyme. You recognized the impact of using carefully selected words. You experimented with sound. You took liberties with language and grappled with the restrictions of poetry. You discovered that in good poetry feeling is first.

Now you're ready to experiment with a more demanding poetic form—concrete poetry.

Concrete Poetry

Form and meaning intertwine in concrete poetry. They wrap around each other tightly. Read this poem aloud. Experience it. Let your eyes be "pulled down to the page below."

Pictures on the Flying Air

A
poem
can play
with the wind
and dart and dance
and fly about in the mind
like a kite in the cloudy white
sky at so dizzy a height it
seems out of reach but
is waiting to be
very gently
pulled
down
to
the
page
below
by a
string
of
musical
words.

Scott Alexander

In what shape is this poem? Why do you think the poet chose this form? Do you like his choice? Explain.

In concrete poetry form and meaning are so close that it is difficult to separate one from the other. Form *is* meaning. Concrete poetry interweaves form and meaning to create concrete forms, or picture poems.

The Roller Coaster

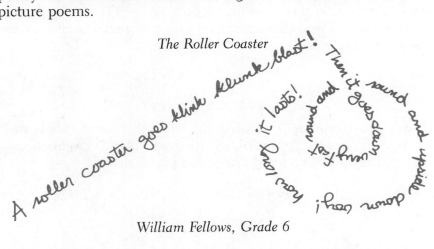

William Fellows, Grade 6

What does this poem say? What does it do? Notice how the poet has arranged his lines. What feeling does this form give you? Do you like this feeling? Would a different form be as effective? Explain.

Concrete poetry is a serious poetic form that taunts the imagination. It demands to be taken playfully. Concrete poetry refuses to be ignored. It reaches out and grabs you. Like quicksand it pulls you in.

Concrete poetry is controversial. Some feel it is an art form. Others insist it is poetry. Actually it is both. Its creators paint intricate picture patterns and write *real* poetry. Concrete poetry is here. It is now.

Poets who choose concrete poetry as their medium of expression are flamboyant. Their poems are dramatic. But it is important not to lose sight of the poetic side, because in concrete poetry, too, feeling is first. To describe it is to destroy it almost. Concrete poetry must be experienced.

On the next few pages are seven options for creating your own concrete poems. Read through all options and poems first. Decide which options challenge the poet in you. At the end of this section select some options to experiment with by yourself and in a small group. Be a daredevil. Take a risk. Manipulate words into new forms. You may just perform a poetic feat of your own.

Options

1. Capture motion.   Like "The Roller Coaster" (page 150) some concrete poems move. How does this poet suggest the speed of racing cars?

The Racers Know

Anonymous

2. Mold an object.   How do the words in this poem relate to its title? Think of some words you would choose for this poem:

A Dog's Life

```
h.
it
sta)                                    'h   el
com                                     tay . :ak
l fetc.                                 .tch speak
 r heei                                 lay down l
  me sit .                              play dead hee.
   ·h come .                          :r jump fetch stay ь.
    .'k play dead sit come ы, uown beg stay roll over sit ь
       i down fetch stay beg speak jump play dead fetch hee'
       s roll over jump play dead beg speak fetch heel si
     . l sit beg lay down speak roll over stay d
       n stay come jump sit heel fetch lay de
       .it roll over speak lay down stay beg·
       ,ed play dead come jump speak roll ovi
     .ed fetch jump heel play dead speak fe
    cch sit stay ·neak jump roll over stay
   ,peak fetch        ·d h nlav dead co
heels cor                    beg lay
stay st:                     roll o
downs                        me lay
'etch roii ь.                ip down sp
 umped pla)                  ·el· play dea
  tch roll ov                ·ay sit ·hee
```

Anonymous

3. <u>Have your poem do what it says.</u>   How does the following poem work? What is your reaction to "Mirror"?

Mirror

When you look	Kool uoy nehW
into a mirror	rorrim a otni
it is not	ton si ti
yourself you see,	,ees uoy flesroy
but a kind	dnik a tub
of apish error	rorre hsipa fo
posed in tearful	lufraet ni desop
symmetry.	.yrtemmys

John Updike

What do these words say? What do they do?

Sailing to the Middle of the Bay

```
Sailing to the middle of the bay,
Pushed
Along
By a sudden
Gust of wind,
A seagull
Flew over the water
Above us,
Ex-
Tend-
Ing
Its wings to the
Full span,
Circling again
```

and again above our boat,

```
Constantly
D
 i
   v
     i
       n
         g
For fish in the
Cold,
Deep water,
S        ng
  u    i
    r  c
      fa
Each time with a prize,
Then
S        g
  o    n
    a i
      r
Back up to the heavens.
```

Student of Arnold Solkov

4. <u>Let your poem speak for itself.</u>   "The Dirty Word" is an example of a sound poem. Read it aloud. Is it difficult or easy to swallow?

The Dirty Word

```
swallow it raw
    awr
      rwa
        arw
          rwa
WAR
```

Eve Merriam

5. <u>Be spacey.</u>   Poets often use the space around words and

letters. Read this poem like windshield wipers. How is this poem different from "Mirror"? How is it similar?

The Hippopotamus

What fun	to be
A Hippo	-potamus
And weigh	a ton
From top	to bottamus

Michael Flanders

6. <u>Make a poster poem.</u>   Look through the Concrete Poetry section. Find some poems that look cramped on a page. Enlarge them. Try using bold colors. Experiment. Look at the effect. Not just any effect will do. Remember, your efforts should enhance the poem. Pick your favorite. Share it with your class.

7. <u>Revise a concrete poem.</u>   Rethink it. Your imagination is your only limitation.

Experimenting with Concrete Poems

Getting It Down

Try a few of the preceding options. Select two or three you find appealing. Don't be afraid to add your own twist. Experiment. Leave a zigzag pattern of concrete poems in your wake.

Checking It Out

When you've written several concrete poems, join a small group. Take your poems and Writer's Notebook. Share your efforts. Talk with the group. Were you successful in communicating a feeling?

Getting It Down

As a group, decide on some options. Write some group poems. Select several to share with the class.

Writer's Workbench 2

Punctuating, Capitalizing, and Spacing

The rules for punctuating, capitalizing, and spacing lines of poetry are slippery. Poets use these rules to help the reader, to add to the feeling of a poem, and to give the poem a special look on the page.

As you know, prose sentences begin with capital letters and end with final punctuation marks. Some poems follow the same rule:

Primer Lesson

Look out how you use proud words.
When you let proud words go, it is
      not easy to call them back.
They wear long boots, hard boots; they
walk off proud; they can't hear you
calling—
Look out how you use proud words.
                              Carl Sandburg

Sandburg's poem reads like a prose piece. The poet uses regular sentences and standard punctuation. He makes his sentences *look* and *sound* like a poem by breaking the sentences into lines.

Find something you have written in your Writer's Notebook, perhaps a short descriptive piece from an earlier activity in this book. Try lining that piece of writing into a poem. Experiment with spacing.

Some poets divide their poems into short lines or phrases. They capitalize each new line and end each stanza with a period.

Dreams

Hold fast to dreams   Hold fast to dreams
For if dreams die   For when dreams go
Life is a broken-winged bird   Life is a barren field
That cannot fly.   Frozen with snow.

                              Langston Hughes

Try using this form with something from your Writer's Notebook.

Many poets invent their own rules for poems. Perhaps the most famous of all unconventional poets is E. E. Cummings. Look at the poet's free and inventive spirit in this favorite poem. Notice particularly how the poet uses spacing to guide the reading of his poem.

Chanson Innocente

in just-
spring   when the world is mud-
luscious the little
lame balloonman

whistles   far   and wee
and eddieandbill come
running from marbles and
piracies and it's
spring

when the world is puddle-wonderful

the queer
old balloonman whistles
far   and   wee
and bettyandisbel come dancing

from hop-scotch and jump-rope and

it's
spring
and
  the

        goat-footed
balloonMan   whistles
far
and
wee

E.E. Cummings

Try using some of Cummings's tricks. Experiment with creative capitalization and spacing.

Don't let all of these options confuse you. You may use any of them, or you may feel more comfortable inventing your own rules as you work with your poems. Here are two bits of advice. Find a poet whose style you like. Model your poems after that style until you find one of your own. Let punctuation, capitalization, and spacing *add* to your poem. Experiment. Read your poem aloud. Try to capture the exact feeling you have in mind.

Just for fun, try organizing the following lines in several different patterns. Use different punctuation, capitalization, and spacing. Share your arrangement with the class and talk about why you like it.

> Down the high ridgespine down from hickory
> and dogwood down into hemlock and shadow
> into water-sound green and where the mountains
> are growing fern whispers light filtering
> leaves down to drink water cold and
> life from a river

After you have tried your own arrangement, look at the poet's finished product. How does his arrangement compare with yours?

Penitentiary Branch Trail
(for Matt, and DRK)

down the high ridgespine
down from hickory and dogwood
down into hemlock and shadow

into water-sound green
and where the mountains are growing
fern whispers light filtering leaves

down to drink water cold
and life from a river
Tom Liner, June 1979

Be on the lookout for interesting uses of punctuation, capitalization, and spacing as you read new poems. Copy poems you like into your Writer's Notebook. Become a collector of good poetry.

CHECKPOINT

Select one of the poems you wrote for either Chapter 7 or 8 to hand in to your teacher. Since your poem will be evaluated according to Checkpoint 4 on the following page, you may wish to revise and polish it. Use all the skills you have been practicing to make this your best poetic effort.

CHECKPOINT 4

1	2	3	4	5

Word Play   ×4=

Loosen up. Let your imagination find new words. Have fun with language!

You use some language play. Practice using strange words in unexpected places.

Your fresh, surprising language s-t-r-e-t-c-h-e-s my imagination.

Word Choice   ×4=

You're using vague words. Start with word-shaking. Choose the most precise words on your list.

I circled concrete words in your poem. Use more of these effective words.

I see strong word pictures. You make every word count.

Experimentation   ×2=

Take more risks. Break out of sing-song rhyme and/or teeter totter lines.

Yes, you're beginning to try things. Go ahead. Plunge in.

Yes, you are working like a poet!

Form   ×4=

Your lines don't seem to fit. Read your poem aloud. Try several different forms. Tap your intuitions. See me.

Some of your lines add to the meaning of your poem. Others leave me a bit confused.

I like the way you arrange your lines. Form and meaning blend smoothly.

Punctuation, Capitalization, Spacing   ×2=

Find a poem you like. Notice how the poet uses punctuation, capitalization, and spacing. Model your poem after this style.

I see you've found a pattern to follow. Works well. Try following your own hunches.

Your punctuation, capitalization, and spacing guide my reading. Interesting, inventive.

Feelings   ×4=

Make another jot list. Begin with your own experiences. Tap the real feelings inside you.

Honest feelings come through in most places.

Magic wrapped in a tightly tied package!

Searching

Chapter 9

Digging in the Decades

If you have read any Nancy Drew or Hardy Boys books, you are no doubt interested in the exciting life of a detective. Investigating crimes, finding clues, and solving mysteries sounds like an adventure. The next two chapters of this book are going to take you through a series of detective-like activities. You won't be solving crimes, but you will be looking for clues to learn more about a subject. You will be acting as a researcher.

Researchers are like detectives. They try to solve difficult problems by finding information, organizing their findings, and drawing conclusions. Some researchers wear white coats and look through microscopes in laboratories. Other researchers gather information by interviewing people and asking questions. Other researchers spend their time in libraries looking through books and magazines. You will not need to wear a white coat to conduct your research in these next two chapters. You will learn to use library and people resources to solve your mystery.

Think for a minute. What are some things we have learned through research? What are some mysteries researchers are still working to solve? Who are some famous researchers?

Researching—An Active Process

Let's face it. Writing a research report could be a dreary experience for both you and your teacher. It could be painful for you if you do not care about your research. It could be boring for your teacher who will have to read and comment on what you write.

The research experience can be rewarding and the reports interesting, however, if *you* can get actively involved in the process. *You* are the center of the research activity. Your excitement about the topic, your careful looking, your active thinking, and your interesting writing can transform all this school work into an adventure. Not all of the information you find on your topic will be helpful or interesting. You will be the manager of the information. You will decide what to use and how to tell others about it. The following diagram of the research process will help illustrate this point:

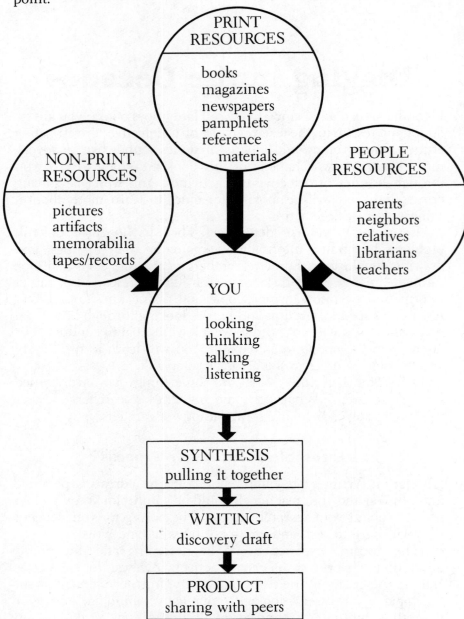

Researcher's Notebook

You are going to need a place to keep track of your research effort. This first and perhaps most important research tool is a good notebook. Get yourself a loose-leaf or spiral-bound notebook and organize it into the following sections:

1. **Jottings.**   This section will be much like your Writer's Notebook. Use this section to:
   > explore topic ideas
   > free write sections of your report
   > talk to yourself
   > sort out your research questions
   > record flashes of brilliance.
2. **Sources.**   In this section you will list books, articles, records, kits, pictures, and people you think might be helpful. In research language, this will be your working bibliography.
3. **Notes and Quotes.**   In this section you will record all the helpful information you find. These notes and quotes will become the heart of your final report. Be careful to record quotations accurately. Also copy the title, author(s), and page numbers for all sources.

With your Researcher's Notebook in hand you are ready to begin researching. If you are nervous about this research business, relax. You are going to walk through it one step at a time.

The Research Plan

Have you heard about the frazzled cowboy who jumped on his horse and rode off in all directions? Sometimes researching can be

confusing. So many things need to be done. There are deadlines and the pressure to find something good to write about. Researchers can avoid the cowboy's fate by developing a plan for the investigation. Good researchers get organized before they begin their investigations. The plan is their road map. It keeps them on the right track and lets them see their progress. Even beginning researchers need a careful plan. The next two chapters will help you follow this plan:

1. Explore topic options. Talk to your teacher, friends, parents, or the librarian. Free write in your Researcher's Notebook. Consider a variety of research possibilities.
2. Select and narrow a topic. Choose one topic you want to know more about.
3. Investigate sources. This is the big hunt. Look through the library and talk to friends.
4. Take notes and collect information. Skim your sources, and pull out a few interesting facts.
5. Organize your findings. Pull them together. Look for an order for your information.
6. Write a discovery draft and formulate conclusions.
7. Prepare a final report.

At the end of these two chapters you will have learned about researching and have written a report you can be proud of.

Finding a Topic

Getting It Started

Some people are good at remembering little facts. Your research is going to take you back through the decades of the 1920s, 30s, 40s, 50s, and 60s. Take out your Researcher's Notebook and see how many of these little facts you remember from those decades:

Trivia Quiz

1. Who were the "Flower Children"?
2. What was a hula hoop?
3. What was the "Charleston"?

4. Who were the Platters?
5. Who was Churchill?
6. When were poodle skirts worn?
7. What was Ed Sullivan famous for?
8. Who first set foot on the moon?
9. What was a sit-in?
10. Who said, "We have nothing to fear, but fear itself"?
11. Who was Clarabell the clown?
12. Who said, "Ask not what your country can do for you, but rather what you can do for your country"?
13. What famous World War II general became president?
14. What does "It's cool, man" mean?
15. What is an Edsel?

How did you do? Try this quiz on a parent or an older adult. These bits of trivia are well-known facts from the past sixty years of American life.

All of us seem fascinated by life in the past. Have you ever looked at old pictures or old magazines? Have you ever listened to old records or seen old newspaper clippings? What was life like in the 1920s or the 1950s? Have you heard your parents or grandparents talk about the "good old days"? In what year were you born? What songs were popular in that year? Who was president? What clothes were popular?

You and your classmates are going to research a decade. Here are some possibilities:

The twenties	flappers, prohibition, the Model T Ford, Babe Ruth, vaudeville, gangsters, 23 skidoo! raccoon coats
The thirties	the depression, bread lines, Jesse Owens, the conservation corps, listening to the radio
The forties	World War II, Hitler, big bands, Jackie Robinson
The fifties	beatniks, rock and roll, Elvis, leather jackets, television
The sixties	a walk on the moon, Vietnam, demonstrations, the Beatles

~~~~~~

Digging in the Decades

Getting
It
Started

Think about these decades. Let your mind wander. What decades interest you? Write a short free writing about the decades in the jottings section of your Researcher's Notebook.

As you think about the decades, be thinking also about specific topics which interest you. Here are some suggestions:

1. dress styles—popular trends, outrageous new styles
2. language—slang expressions, "in" words, slogans, famous sayings
3. sports—star players, great teams, Olympics, new records
4. entertainment—popular songs and singers, movies and movie stars, dances and dancing
5. personalities—important people, newsmakers, creative people, outrageous people
6. news events—important happenings, natural phenomena: earthquakes, storms
7. artifacts—hula hoops, roller skates, frisbees
8. transportation—the automobile, spectacular aviation events
9. scientific discoveries—television, inventions
10. fads—goldfish swallowing, phone booth packing, bicycle riding

~~~~~~

Exploring Options

Getting
It
Started

In the **Jottings** section of your Researcher's Notebook list the decades you are considering. Under each decade, jot down a few reasons why that time period interests you. Also list several topics in each decade which interests you. Jot down a few reasons why you want to know more about that topic.

~~~~~~

Choosing a Topic

In the **Jottings** section of your Researcher's Notebook do a short free writing in which you talk to yourself about the decisions you must make. Write your thoughts about the decade that interests you most. Maybe your mind works like this. . . .

"I think I'll go with the 20's. I don't know much about them, but it sounds like people had fun . . . hmm the "roaring twenties" maybe I'll research the music . . . wonder if my grandmother has any old records? Or maybe clothes. I'm sure I could find pictures of the clothes people wore. Maybe I could even find some old clothes to wear to show the class. I like that. I think I'll do twenties fashions. . . ."

If you are still uncertain about a decade or a topic, try these resources to help you make a decision:

1. Talk to other students to see what they are going to research.
2. Talk to your teacher. Tell him or her what you are thinking about.
3. Ask parents and adult friends for suggestions.
4. See the librarian or media center specialist for ideas.
5. Talk to yourself in another free writing.

Using Key Words

Researching the past is like hunting for treasure. It takes patience and persistence. Now that you have a topic you are ready to get rolling.

Most of the information in your media center is indexed, or catalogued, around key words. Finding the best key words is important to your search. To find the best key words do the following:

Write down your decade and your topic in the **Jottings** section of your Researcher's Notebook:

Twenties   *Fashions*

To find key words look at your topic words and ask yourself these questions:

1. Are there any other words that have the same meaning? Write down any synonyms you can think of for your decade and topic:

    Twenties   *Fashions*
    1920–1929   Clothing styles
                       Dress styles

2. Are there any other ways to spell your topic?
3. Are there any larger topics that might include yours?
4. Does your topic overlap another topic.

Your answers to these questions may give you some good key words to use for your research. Check your topic and key words with your teacher or librarian.

Media Center Resources

Once you have looked thoroughly at your topic and generated your key words, you are ready to begin to search for information. The first part of your search will center around your school library or media center. The information for your research can be found in five primary places:

1. Card catalogue.   This is the most important resource in the library because it can direct and simplify your research. Good researchers usually begin with the card catalogue. As you find your key words in the card catalogue, write down the title, author, and call number of any materials which look promising.
2. Encyclopedia.   This is the place to get an overview of your topic. The encyclopedia provides good background reading to help you get a better feel for your topic. (1) Find the index for the set of encyclopedias you want to use. (2) Look up your key words in the index. (3) Write the titles, volumes, and page numbers of the articles you want to use.

3. <u>Readers' Guide to Periodical Literature.</u>   This index lists articles in well-known magazines by subject and author. Your library may have only a few of the 180 different magazines this guide references, but the *Readers' Guide* is a very important research tool. Write the name, date, and page numbers of any magazines you want to use.

4. <u>Vertical file.</u>   This is the librarian's or media specialist's own private file. Newspaper clippings, pictures, and pamphlets are often collected and organized by the library staff. Ask a media center staff member about the location of the vertical file.

5. <u>Other reference material.</u>   *National Geographic Index, Subject Guide to Children's Magazines*, and numerous other books which discuss and picture American life are in the reference section of your library.

If your class is a large one, and you all descend on the media center at once, you may put a strain on the resources. Thirty students cannot use the card catalogue at once. Don't waste time waiting for the card catalogue. Go to the *Readers' Guide* or an encyclopedia or another reference book. Make your time in the media center count. See how many different potential resources you can list in your Researcher's Notebook.

Writer's Workbench 1

The Card Catalogue

Armed with your key words, you are ready to make an assault on the card catalogue. The card catalogue is the heart of the library. Somewhere in those drawers most of the resources of the library are listed. The card catalogue lists books, records, maps and globes, filmstrips, tapes, charts, pictures, filmloops, transparencies, kits, and films. Learning how to use the card catalogue effectively can greatly simplify your research task.

    The card catalogue is very much like any catalogue. Each resource is listed on a separate card and the cards are in alphabetical order. The cards are filed in drawers. The drawers are also alphabetical and are labeled. These drawers may be removed from the file for easier searching.

    Most books are listed in the card catalogue on *three* different cards. One card is an *author card*. Another is a *title card*, and the third is a *subject card*.

There are several ways to find the information you need for your report. If you are using your key words and do not know the name of any authors or titles of books, look for *subject cards*.

If your subject were fashions in the 1920s, you could begin by looking in the card catalogue under the key words FASHION HISTORY. If you found only one or two books, you could then look under other key words such as UNITED STATES–HISTORY–20TH CENTURY. If you need to, ask your librarian what key words to use. When you find your subject in the card catalogue, look for books that sound as though they will tell you something about your topic. You might find a subject card such as the one in the following illustration:

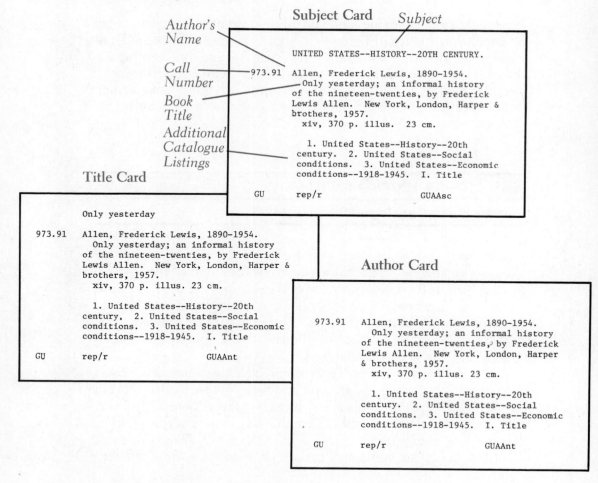

When you find a subject card for a book that looks promising, copy the call number, author's name, and title of the book in the **Sources** section of your Researcher's Notebook. Then look for other helpful books.

On the subject card shown in the illustration, the author's last name is Allen. If you looked under the A's in the card catalogue, you would find an author card for the same book. If you looked up the title *Only Yesterday* under the O's, you would find a title card. The information on all three cards would be the same.

Following is a brief summary of the card catalogue procedure:

1. Take your key words to the card catalogue.
2. Look for subject cards that include your key words. If you have no luck, use your ingenuity or ask your librarian. Take your time.
3. Once you find a helpful subject heading, list the call number, title, and author of any books which may contain important information.
4. Stay with the search. Be thorough. Be patient. Ask for help.

Once you have learned how to use the card catalogue, you are ready to begin to search. Turn to the **Sources** section of your Researcher's Notebook and begin to search for sources related to your subject. Use *all* of your key words.

In many libraries good general sources may be found under the subject heading U.S. HISTORY. This subject is usually divided into decades. Compile a good list of sources before you begin looking for them in the library. For the topic of fashions in the 1920s, you might find the following books:

Key words	Call no.	Author/Title
Fashion History	391.09 Har	Harris, Christie *Figleafing Through History*
History-Modern	909.82	Colton, Joel G. *Twentieth Century*
U.S. History 20th Century	327 G01	Goldston, Robert C. *The Road Between the Wars*

U.S. History 1919–1933	973.91	Allen, Frederick Lewis *Only Yesterday: An Informal History of the Nineteen Twenties*
	973.91 BOA.	Boardman, Fon W. *America and the Jazz Age*
	973.9 Ma	May, Earnest *War, Boom, Bust*

After you have compiled your list of sources, look for them in your library. Take notes from your sources in the **Notes and Quotes** section of your Researcher's Notebook.

As you conduct your research, look for visual materials to include in your report. A photograph such as the one on page 177 could be included in a report on fashions in the 1920s.

Writer's Workbench 2

Using the Encyclopedia

The encyclopedia is a wonderful research tool. Sometimes you can find information in it that fits into your paper perfectly. Since it is difficult to take notes from it, you may be tempted to just copy a section word for word. However, part of becoming a good researcher is learning to take ideas from the encyclopedia and put them into your *own* words. Good research reports are not copied directly from encyclopedias. In this Workbench you will practice reading a section from an encyclopedia and putting the information into your own words. Using the key word CLOTHING, you would find the following information in the encyclopedia:

> **The 1900's.** From 1890 to 1920, improved manufacturing methods brought rapid growth to United States companies that made ready-to-wear clothing. Both men and women began to wear mostly clothing that was *mass-produced* in factories (see MASS PRODUCTION). As a result of mass production, women's

fashions could change more rapidly than ever before. But men's clothing styles changed little until the 1960's.

For a few years around 1910, women wore *hobble skirts.* These skirts were so tight at the bottom that a woman could hardly walk. Clothing became simpler and less formal during World War I (1914–1918). In the 1920's, women adopted the "boyish" look. Dresses were straight and unfitted, and they ended at, or a little above, the knee. In the 1930's, some women began wearing slacks. Skirts became longer during the 1930's and then shorter during the early 1940's. During World War II (1939–1945), women wore many tailored styles with padded shoulders. Slacks—worn by women working in war industries —also became popular.

Women's fashions changed greatly after World War II. Crinolines and long, full skirts returned. Nylon garments, including stockings and *lingerie* (underwear), became available in large quantities for the first time. During the 1950's, straight, tight-fitting *sheath dresses* and shorter hemlines gained popularity. *A-line dresses* and loose-fitting *shifts* came into style during the early 1960's. The very short *miniskirt* quickly spread to other countries following its appearance in England in the mid-1960's.

From 1900 to 1950, both single-breasted and double-breasted men's suits were popular. Shoulders were *natural* (unpadded) about 1910 but gradually became more padded. During the 1950's, many men switched to single-breasted *Ivy League* suits, which had narrow lapels and natural shoulders. They also began wearing colored shirts with business suits.

Both men and women developed great fondness for sportswear and wash-and-wear fabrics during the 1950's and 1960's. Leisure and sports clothes for women included knee-length Bermuda shorts, tapered slacks, and ski and stretch pants. Men wore Bermuda shorts, slacks, and colorful sport shirts. Improvements in sewing machines and in dress patterns brought an increased interest in sewing.

In the 1960's, many young men started to wear colorful fashions, many of which included fancy jewelry. They also grew beards and mustaches. During the early 1970's, men of all ages joined in the change to colorful clothes. They began wearing shirts in checks, stripes, and many colors with business suits. They also wore wide ties in fancy prints, stripes, or bright swirling colors. Men of all ages began growing beards and mustaches. They also began wearing their hair longer than in the 1960's. Women's fashions included skirts of every

length—from the miniskirt to the *maxiskirt,* which
fell to the ankle. Many people seemed to have an
"anything goes" feeling toward clothing styles.

Suppose your topic is fashions in the 1920s. You might begin by
jotting down these notes:

women began to wear factory-made clothes

women liked the boyish look

dresses were straight, unfitted, and ended above the knees

men wore both single- and double-breasted suits with
padded shoulders

Do you see any other important information about fashions in the
1920s?

On a separate sheet of paper take notes from the following
encyclopedia article excerpt on jazz in the 1920s. Do not copy
whole sentences or paragraphs. Select important facts and put them
into your own words.

The Golden Age

During the 1920's, jazz flourished throughout the
United States. This was often called the *golden age*
of jazz. Mamie Smith recorded "Crazy Blues" in
1920, and became the first nationally successful
blues singer. Bessie Smith became the most famous
of the great blues singers.

During the 1920's, ragtime developed into a more
sophisticated and less rigid style known as "stride
piano." This style used the left hand more, alternat-
ing single notes and chords and moving up and down
the scale. One of the early stride pianists was James
P. Johnson, who made his professional debut in
1904. Johnson influenced Thomas "Fats" Waller,
the composer of "Honeysuckle Rose" and other
jazz favorites. Another well-known pianist and composer of the 1920's was "Jelly Roll" Morton, a
colorful figure who claimed he invented jazz.

Louis Armstrong was one of the first great stars of
jazz. He became an outstanding cornet player while
a teen-ager in New Orleans. In 1922, he moved to
Chicago to join the Creole Jazz Band led by his
teacher Joe "King" Oliver. Two years later, Armstrong joined the Fletcher Henderson band.

From 1925 to 1928, Armstrong made records
under the name of the "Hot Five" and "Hot
Seven." These records rank among the greatest in
jazz and feature pianist Earl "Fatha" Hines; trom-

bonist "Kid" Ory; and clarinetist Johnny Dodds and his brother, drummer "Baby" Dodds. Armstrong also became the first well-known male jazz singer, and the first to use *scat singing,* singing meaningless syllables in place of words.

How did you do? What important facts did you select? Did you put them into your own words? Compare your notes with those of your classmates.

Now use the techniques you have just practiced to take notes on your topic. Write your encyclopedia notes in the **Notes and Quotes** section of your Researcher's Notebook.

Readers' Guide to Periodical Literature

The *Readers' Guide* is an index of current periodicals or magazines. Magazine articles often contain information not available in books, and frequently they include pictures. The *Readers' Guide* is indexed like the card catalogue with author, subject, and title entries.

The most frustrating thing about using the *Readers' Guide* (after you learn the abbreviations) is that your media center will have only a few of the magazines listed. Magazines are expensive and most libraries have limited budgets. Somewhere near the *Readers' Guide* you should find a list of titles and dates of magazines your library has filed. Check that list and be sure you know the procedure for using magazines. If you find pictures in the magazines, your librarian may let you check out the magazine long enough to share the pictures with classmates.

Write in the **Sources** section of your Researcher's Notebook at least *three* possible magazine articles on your topic. If the magazines are available, take notes from the articles in the **Notes and Quotes** section of your Researcher's Notebook.

People Resources

Library resources are important, but they are often impersonal and dry. First-hand, eyewitness accounts from people who know things about your decade and your subject can enliven your report. You need to plan to spend an hour or so interviewing an eyewitness.

Take your Researcher's Notebook and brainstorm for the names of some people you might interview. Look around the school first: teachers, the principal, the school secretary, the school custodian, cafeteria staff, bus drivers. Who lives in your neighborhood? Your priest, minister, or rabbi? Someone at your mother or father's place of work? There may be a community center in your neighborhood or a Council on Aging center. Someone there might talk to you. A local merchant might have time to talk to you. Brainstorm a list of possible interviewees in the **Sources** section of your Researcher's Notebook.

Reread Chapter 6, pages 88–94, for interview tips. Take careful notes in the **Notes and Quotes** section of your Researcher's Notebook. Record the *date* of the interview and the *name* of your eyewitness. Ask him or her to remember specific things about your topic. Ask your eyewitness if you can see or borrow pictures, clippings, or clothes from that decade. Collect as much information as you can from your people resources.

CHECKPOINT

You have been living with your topic for several days. You have used library and people resources. You have a working bibliography and notes you have gathered. Before you begin the task of pulling all of this together, take an honest look at your Researcher's Notebook. Think about your work so far and answer the following questions:

1. Do I have a clearly stated and workable topic? If not, what are the problems?
2. Have I looked for information in most of the available sources?
    Card catalogue
    Encyclopedia
    Readers' Guide to Periodical Literature
    Verticle file
    Other reference material
    Personal interview
    Which resources are the most helpful?
3. Do I need more information?
4. Have I looked for visual materials such as pictures from old newspapers and magazines and items family members have saved?
5. Are all my jottings, sources, and notes and quotes carefully recorded in my Researcher's Notebook?

Your Researcher's Notebook material will be evaluated according to the checklist at the end of this chapter. Use the checklist as a guide for strengthening your research.

Writer's Workbench 3

Adding to Your Word Bank

The following ten words were used in this chapter. Some are special words used by researchers. See if you can guess the meaning of these words before you look at their definitions. Look back in the chapter and read the sentence where the word first occurs.

1. bibliography (page 179)   a list of sources used by a researcher
2. formulate (page 166)   to develop a statement about something
3. decade (page 167)   a period of ten years
4. trivia (page 167)   unimportant matters
5. indexed (page 169)   listed in order
6. potential (page 171)   possible, capable of development
7. compile (page 173)   to collect into a whole
8. brilliance (page 165)   great intelligence
9. frazzled (page 165)   physically or emotionally exhausted
10. resources (page 169)   supplies that can be drawn upon

One of the best ways to remember a new word is to see how it is related to other words you already know. Following are some comparisons, or analogies. Number a sheet of paper from 1 to 10. Beside each number write the vocabulary word from the preceding list that best fits in each analogy.

1. Rake is to leaves
    as ___ is to resources.
2. A list of ingredients is to a recipe
    as a ___ is to a research report.
3. Ten is to 100
    as ___ is to century.
4. A bank customer is to a savings account
    as a researcher is to ___.
5. Sawdust is to carpenter
    as ___ is to important information.
6. Sun is to darkness
    as ___ is to dullness.
7. Messy is to neat
    as ___ is to alert.
8. Build is to house
    as ___ is to conclusions.
9. Alphabetized is to card catalogue
    as ___ is to resources.
10. Happy is to sad
    as ___ is to impossible.

CHECKLIST FOR RESEARCHER'S NOTEBOOK

1	2	3	4	5

Jottings

Where are they? Many things are missing. *Please see me.*

You are on your way. Try another free writing about your topic. Be sure you know what you are looking for. Can I help?

Great! Lots of good thinking going on. You are right on track.

Sources

Where are they? Are you having trouble finding things. Have you talked with the librarian? Don't wait too long.

Good beginning. Remember to write down *all* the bibliographic data. Be sure you have listed *all* potential resources.

Good list. Easy to read. I can tell you have been using your time well.

Notes and Quotes

Where are they? You won't be able to write your report without some information.

Be sure you record key words and phrases. Be sure you have page numbers for your sources. You may need more information before you write your paper.

Looks like you're almost ready to write. Your notes are neat and well organized.

Chapter 10

Sharing Discoveries

While you are continuing to dig in your decade looking for interesting information, you also need to begin thinking about pulling together what you have already found. In earlier chapters of this book you learned to use a jot list. You brainstormed that jot list and then used it to free write a first draft. You may want to follow the same general process as you begin writing your research report.

Use the following steps to write a *discovery draft* of your research. A discovery draft is like free writing. You write the draft to discover what you know and to let the words and information you have found begin to take shape. This first discovery draft is an experiment. It may go very well, or you may find you need to do more thinking and planning for your topic.

1. Reread your notes in the **Notes and Quotes** section of your Researcher's Notebook. Mark any bits of information which you think are particularly interesting or important. Think about your audience. Select information that will interest, amuse, and inform them. Look for a good beginning for your report. Maybe an interesting quote or a surprising fact will work. Maybe something from your interview or an anecdote would capture the attention of your audience. Don't worry if you cannot find a good beginning at this point. Just be looking and thinking.

2. Make yourself a jot list from your notes and quotes. Organize the jot list into roughly the order in which you want to use the items in your report. Be thinking about organizing your information.

Getting It Started

Getting It Down

3. Now write the discovery draft. Write quickly without worrying about anything except getting words on the page. If you get stuck on one part of your paper, skip to other parts. Keep writing until you talk through your topic. Don't just copy quotations. Write about your topic in your own words. Just tell your audience what you have learned.

Checking It Out

4. Relax. Reread your draft with a critical eye. Mark the parts which say what you want to say. Mark the parts which don't work. Listen to the sound of your voice. Does it sound like you?
5. Make a list of what your paper needs:
   more facts
   better beginning
   interesting ending
   more information

SPOTLIGHT

Now look at a research paper written by a student, Mindy:

Black Holes: Friend or Foe?

For a long time man's interest in the sky has been limitless. Primitive man must have looked at the stars and wondered. From the Wright brothers' first flight at Kitty Hawk, to man's first step in space, to the unmanned probe circling Saturn now, man puzzles about the unknowns of space. And now yet another "space fad" is on. They are called black holes.

"Not long ago we were confident that we knew what objects could be found in the sky: stars, nebulae, galaxies, planets, and satellites; everything seemed clearcut. Now the whole situation has changed. We have strong evidence of objects so weird it is hard to form any picture of them. And of these the most fantastic of all are black holes." That's what Patrick Moore and Ian Nicolson write on the cover of their book, *Black Holes in Space*. It's very hard to find any bits of information on black holes so if you read carefully you may learn something.

First of all, just what exactly is a black hole? That's a reasonable question and deserves a reasonable answer, so here it is. A gigantic star, hundreds of times larger than our sun, explodes (called a supernova explosion) because of the tremendous gravity pressing on it. Radiation would be scattered trillions of miles in space. The place where it was, will be an unbelievable glob of material. Now that explains how it's formed, but what about the mass, size, and weight? Well that's coming up next. Scientists say that the mass is as much as five billion suns! A teaspoon weighs several tons because of the density. It's so dense even a drop would weigh as much as a battleship. The star keeps condensing until it's the size of a small marble (or smaller!). That tiny object weighs more than our sun and all the planets put together. Enough of all that, so let's go on.

I suppose your next question will probably be, Are black holes affecting the universe? The answer, yes. I'll explain how for you right now. Scientists think that black holes are gnawing at the center of most galaxies including our own Milky Way. Black holes are affecting our universe by sucking it up. In trillions of years our universe may pop into another time and place. If that is going to happen, I wouldn't lose sleep over it because it would be long after man has ceased to exist altogether.

By now you know what a black hole is and how it affects the universe. How about learning some of the discoveries or facts that are recently supporting the black hole theory. Two American scientists found some unexplainable radiation and when they researched it, they found it came from a black hole. These black holes gobble up entire stars, curve space, and warp time. Matter sucked into black holes is crushed out of existence and may disappear from the universe altogether.

It could be that 90% of the mass in the universe has already been swallowed up by black holes and it may only be a matter of time (talking in terms of trillions of years) before the entire universe disappears.

Some scientists think that our universe was created fifteen billion years ago during the "Big Bang" when a gigantic black hole or something else unknown to science containing all matter exploded.

This paper may have you thinking that black holes are terrible and useless. Well that may be true some of the time but they could be used. Scientists think that black holes could be used for super subways through space. Now it's up to you to decide: Black holes, friend or foe?

1. How does Mindy make her report interesting? Point to expressions, words, and sentences you like in her report.
2. Can you hear the sound of the writer's voice in the report? Point to places where you can hear Mindy speaking to her audience.

Writer's Workbench 1

Sexist Language

As a writer you have wrestled with your thoughts. You've worked to get these thoughts into words on paper. You've discovered that thoughts can shape words. But have you stopped to think how words affect your thoughts?

As you read each sentence that follows, concentrate on what you see in your mind's eye. Who are the people that you see?

1. Four hundred *salesmen* attended the Detroit convention.
2. Several *workmen* at the construction site suffered heat exhaustion as the temperatures climbed into the 100° range.
3. Fifty-nine percent of air conditioner *repairmen* across the country agree that the Xanader product is well constructed.
4. Some people think that *stewardesses* have an easy job.
5. *Flagmen* warned motorists of the danger ahead.
6. The *nurses* worked feverishly to save the patient's life.

Did you picture men for the persons in sentences 1, 2, 3, and 5? Did you picture women in sentences 4 and 6? Chances are that many of the salespeople attending the Detroit convention described in sentence 1 were women. If there were women among the workers in sentence 2, they, too, probably suffered from the heat.

Good writers try to be as accurate as possible. They select precise words that reflect life as it really is. When writers are unaware of the potential of words as thought-shapers, they sometimes fall into traps.

Look at Mindy's opening paragraph on page 184. When Mindy wrote that paragraph she was unconsciously using some words which exclude women. As you read that paragraph, list the words which could be changed to include women as well as men. The words on your list are not wrong, but they do exclude women. These words are sexist and sexist words are no longer used by careful writers.

Rewrite Mindy's opening paragraph without sexist words. Share your rewritten paragraph with your classmates. Some of your new word choices may sound strange or even awkward at first. Language habits change slowly. It will take some time before all writers and readers feel comfortable with non-sexist language.

Remember to avoid sexist language in your research report. Proofread your paper with a sharp eye for any words which exclude women or men.

Writer's Workbench 2

Beginnings

Read the opening paragraph of your discovery draft aloud. Do you like the way it sounds? Will it capture your reader's attention? Do you need some ideas for a better beginning?

The List

Look first at Mindy's beginning:

> For a long time man's interest in the sky has been limitless. Primitive man must have looked at the stars and wondered. From the Wright brothers' first flight at Kitty Hawk, to man's first step in space, to the unmanned probe circling Saturn now, man puzzles about the unknowns of space. And now yet another "space fad" is on. They are called black holes.

Mindy hooks the reader on black holes by listing people who have wondered about and explored space. She gives a short history of important space events and then introduces her topic. Perhaps you could use this listing approach to begin your report. What things might go into your list?

Mindy's approach may not work for your paper. Let's explore other beginnings:

Description

One effective way to begin a report is to open with a descriptive paragraph. You learned very early in this book to write with strong verbs and concrete adjectives. You could begin your report with a word picture. Mindy might have begun her report something like this:

> A gigantic star, hundreds of times larger than our sun, explodes (called a supernova explosion) because of the tremendous gravity pressing on it. Radiation is scattered trillions of miles in space. In the place where it was, is an unbelievable glob of material—a black hole.

Is there anything you could describe to begin your report?

Surprising Facts

Sometimes you can interest your reader by beginning your report with a surprising or even startling fact you have discovered in your research.

Do you see any surprising facts Mindy might have used to open her report? Write an opening for Mindy's report using a surprising fact. Your teacher may ask you to share your opening by reading it aloud.

Quotations

Sometimes you find a quotation in a book or magazine which makes a good beginning. Mindy's quotation from Moore and Nicolson might be a good beginning:

> "Not long ago we were confident that we knew what objects could be found in the sky: stars, nebulae, galaxies, planets, and satellites; everything seemed clearcut. Now the whole situation has changed. We have strong evidence of objects so weird it is hard to form any picture of them. And of these the most fantastic of all are black holes." That's what Patrick Moore and Ian Nicolson write on the cover of their book, *Black Holes in Space*.

What do you think? Do you like the quotation beginning better than Mindy's list?

Look through your interview notes. Maybe there is a good beginning quotation in those notes.

Anecdote

Sometimes you can begin a report by telling a story or a short dramatic incident. If you were writing about the Great Depression, you might begin your report by telling a story about people who lost all they had. If you were researching the airplane, you might begin by telling a story about the day the Wright Brothers flew. If you were researching baseball heroes, you might begin by telling about the day Jackie Robinson became the first black man to play the game.

Do you think Mindy could have used an anecdote to begin her paper? If so, discuss how she might have written it.

Questions

Writers sometimes interest readers by asking questions. As the readers read the questions they think and talk back to the writer. A conversation begins. Good reports should be a conversation between the writer and reader.

How has Mindy used questions in her report? Would her beginning have been better if she had put all of those questions in the opening paragraph like this?

What are black holes? How large are they? Are they affecting our universe? Should we be afraid of them? Is there anything good about black holes? These are just some of the questions scientists are trying to answer.

Are there any questions you might use to begin your report?

You now have six different possible ways to begin your research report. Try writing several different beginnings. Share these with a partner. Select the opening paragraph which fits your piece best.

Writer's Workbench 3

Using Quotations from Printed Materials

You may remember that you learned about using the words of other speakers in Chapter 6. In that chapter you interviewed an older person and included some of the person's exact words in your writing. You have used the interview again to gather information for your research paper. You may want to refer to Chapter 6, page 97, to refresh your memory about punctuating direct quotations from interviews.

Using quotations from books, magazines, newspapers, and other printed materials is a slightly different situation. In general, anytime you copy words directly from printed material you should place quotation marks around those words. In her research paper

Mindy used this quotation by Patrick Moore and Ian Nicolson:

> "Not long ago we were confident that we knew what objects could be found in the sky: stars, nebulae, galaxies, planets, and satellites; everything seemed clearcut. Now the whole situation has changed. We have strong evidence of objects so weird it is hard to form any picture of them. And of these the most fantastic of all are black holes." That's what Patrick Moore and Ian Nicolson write on the cover of their book, *Black Holes in Space*.

Notice three things about this quotation:

1. Quotation marks *surround* the exact words copied from the book. Since the words are borrowed directly from the authors and are not Mindy's, she uses quotation marks to give the authors credit.

2. She tells *who* said those words immediately *after* she uses them:

> "That's what Patrick Moore and Ian Nicolson write. . . ."

Anytime you use the exact words of someone else in your research paper, you must give the name or names of the people who said them. You may do that, as Mindy has done, directly following the quotation or you may *introduce* the quotation, as in this example:

> As Patrick Moore and Ian Nicolson put it, "Not long ago we were confident. . . ."

3. Mindy gives the title of the book and indicates where the quotation can be found. Look at the quotation. Could you find those words again if you wanted to? Where would you look?

Anytime you copy the exact words of someone else you must give the *title* of the source and the location, usually a *page number*. It takes time and care to follow this rule, but good researchers are precise about their sources. They want to give other writers credit for their words and they want readers to be able to find any quotations they use.

If your Researcher's Notebook has a carefully organized **Notes and Quotes** section, these guidelines for using quoted material should give you little trouble. If you are using quotations in your research paper, check to be sure you have observed all three guidelines.

Writer's Workbench 4

Preparing the Bibliography

The bibliography for your research report is simply a list of all the sources you used to write your final report. It is not a list of all the sources you found—only the ones you actually used.

Look back in your Researcher's Notebook **Notes and Quotes** section and make a list of the sources you used for your report. Because there are several approved forms for a bibliography, you may want to check with your teacher. When possible, arrange your sources alphabetically by authors' last names. Following are some sample bibliographic entries for books, magazines, encyclopedias, and interviews. Use these as models.

Book

> Allen, Frederick Lewis, Only Yesterday: An Informal History of the Nineteen Twenties. New York: Harper and Brothers, 1957.
> (Notice that the book title is underlined.)

Magazine

> Kazin, Alfred, "Hemingway As His Own Fable," Atlantic, June 1964, pp. 54-57.
> (The magazine title is underlined. The title of the article is in quotation marks.)

Encyclopedia

> "Sitting Bull," Encyclopedia Americana, 1962, vol. XXXV, p. 48.
> (The title of the article is in quotation marks. The encyclopedia title is underlined.)

Interview

> Heinlein, Robert. Interviewed by John White. Colorado Springs, Colorado, April 7, 1959.

These specialized forms for your sources may seem overly precise. Researchers and readers of research are particular about details. Use these models carefully. If you have questions or a special problem your teacher will help you. Double-check your final bibliography carefully. ● For more information about preparing a bibliography, see the Handbook, page H-62.

Revising Your Draft

Your research report is beginning to take shape. It may still be rough in a few spots, but you have a draft you can live with. It is time to prepare the final copy of your report. As you revise and polish your report, you will be working as an editor.

An editor reads the draft with a critical eye, looking for rough spots and making suggestions to improve it. Find a partner and begin to work as each other's editors. Use the following checklist as you read your partner's draft. Make as many helpful suggestions as you can.

Editor's Checklist

1. Opening paragraph.   Does it hook the reader? Has the writer used one of the six suggested beginnings described on pages 187–190. Does the opening need work? Make some suggestions.
2. Quotations.   Has the writer used the exact words of anyone else? Are the words identified correctly as illustrated in Writer's Workbench 3 on page 190? Are authors' names and page numbers given?
3. Organization.   Is the report clear and easy to follow? Are the writer's main points clearly stated? Does the writer need more information to explain or support any main point? Should the writer emphasize other points? Should the writer rearrange any sections? What changes would you suggest?
4. Language.   Has the writer avoided slang expressions? Has the writer made precise and careful word choices? Are there any words or phrases you think the writer should change? Has the writer used any words you did not understand? Make helpful suggestions for word choices and rewording.
5. Audience.   Does the report talk directly to the reader? Has the writer tried to interest the audience?
6. Sources.   Has the writer provided a complete list of

Checking
It
Out

sources for the report? Are they correctly listed in alphabetical order?

Discuss your editorial suggestions with your partner. Be helpful and encouraging.

~~~~~~

CHECKPOINT

~~~~~~

Getting It Right

Rework your own report carefully. Read it aloud to your partner. Work on rough spots. Ask your teacher for help if you need to.

Just before you make the final copy of your report, read it one more time. This time proofread the report with your most careful eyes. Check the following:

Spelling.   Good research reports should be free of spelling errors. Check the dictionary for any spellings you are still uncertain about. Don't be lazy now after all your hard work.

Punctuation.   Read each sentence. Be sure of your punctuation. Check your quotations carefully. Double-check if you are uncertain.

Your finished research report will be evaluated according to Checkpoint 5 on pages 196–197.

~~~~~~

Sharing Your Research

Now that you have finished working hard researching and writing to get your own report just right, you might like to hear from your classmates. This activity is designed to give each class member a chance to share one or two items from his or her research.

Your teacher will divide you into groups by decades. Your job as a group is to plan a 10-15 minute presentation in which you share some interesting and surprising information from your decade. Your group will try to share the flavor of your decade.

Plan your presentation any way you wish but *do not* have your group members just read their papers. That would be more like a medical convention than an exciting group presentation. You may use any props and artifacts you wish. Pictures, records, newspaper clippings, and memorabilia will give lift to your group presentation. Maybe it would be possible to present your information in costume. Maybe your entire group could dress up in clothes from your decade.

Here are the steps to follow in planning your presentation:

1. Make a list of group members and their research topics.
2. Ask each group member to write down several things he or she might like to share with the class.
3. Read over the information that might be shared, commenting as a group on ideas for ordering and presenting the information.
4. Plan together a 10-15 minute group presentation. *All* members of your group should share something. Think about these options:
   a. TV Show.   Prepare a TV show flashback to your decade. Appoint someone to be the moderator or host. Then plan short scenes from your decade. Give the show a title.
   b. Panel Discussion.   If you choose this option, you will need to think about how to keep your presentation interesting. Maybe you have a Johnny Carson or Merv Griffin in your group who can keep things moving. Be sure that each member of your group makes a contribution. Use pictures and objects. Plan your presentation carefully.
   c. News Broadcast.   Your group might decide to present your decade in a television or radio news format. Organize your presentation as though you were presenting the evening news. You may want an anchor person—John Chancellor or Barbara Walters. Each member of your group could be a reporter who presents some interesting information to the audience.
   d. Newspaper.   Maybe the research your group members have done could be presented best as a newspaper. Check to be sure your teacher can duplicate your newspaper because you will need a copy for each class member. Give your newspaper a name such as *The Sixties Sentinel* or *The Thirties Inquirer*. Decide upon a headline. Each member of

your group should write a newsstory for the paper. Pictures and drawings might also be included. Your group will need to be very cooperative to publish a good newspaper.

e. <u>Culture Fair.</u>   If most of your group members worked on topics such as music, fashions, movies, and fads, you may be able to *show* what American life was like in your decade. Sometimes showing is more effective than telling. Think about how you could give the class a feeling for your decade. Maybe you could present a fashion show with music playing. A narrator could tell about your decade while group members show pictures, costumes, and memorabilia.

Discuss these options carefully in your group. Decide which one will work best, and then get busy planning your presentation. Remember that *all* group members must share something with the entire class.

CHECKPOINT 5

1	2	3	4	5

Beginning   ×2=

You didn't capture the reader's attention. See Writer's Workbench 2.	I see you worked at this. Maybe a little more revision time would make this opening even stronger.	Great opening! You hooked me. I wanted to read more.

Quotations   ×3=

You didn't use any. What happened? Did you misunderstand the assignment?	Some quotations are introduced or punctuated correctly. See Writer's Workbench 3.	I'm impressed! Your quotations are used effectively and you have mastered the form. Congrats!

Organization   ×3=

Your paper is difficult to follow. I'm not sure of your main points. Maybe an outline would help.	You have an organization, but the paper is sketchy in places. What are your main points?	Clear, easy to follow. Good transitions between paragraphs. Good job!

Language   ×2=
Too many informal expressions. Language does not match your topic.

You still have a few words and phrases which could be improved. See my marks or check with me.

Excellent word choices. Language is appropriate to your report.

Audience   ×1=
I don't think you understand the idea of writing for audience. See me.

You forgot your audience at times. Remember this was written to inform your classmates.

You spoke to me. I heard your voice. I was interested in your paper.

Sources   ×2=
Where are they? See Writer's Workbench 4.

You didn't take enough time with your sources. Some of them are incomplete. Good researchers are careful about sources.

Sources are well organized, clearly listed, and in proper form. Good, careful work.

Spelling and Punctuation   ×3=
Did you have someone proofread your paper? Research reports must be done more carefully!

Proofread more carefully. There are still too many errors.

Excellent! Very careful job.

Overall Impression   ×4=
Not a very good effort. Good research takes time.

A good effort. You have learned from this report. More time spent editing and proofreading would greatly improve your paper.

Your report shows hard work and careful revision. You should be proud of this report.

UNIT FIVE

Writing to Get Things Done

Chapter 11

Exploring the Family

"We're going to have a wonderful life, Lillie. A wonderful life and a wonderful family. A great big family."

"We'll have children all over the house," Mother smiled. "From the basement to the attic."

"From the floorboards to the chandelier."

"When we go for our Sunday walk we'll look like Mr. and Mrs. Pied Piper."

"Mr. Piper, shake hands with Mrs. Piper. Mrs. Piper, meet Mr. Piper."

Mother put the magazine on the seat between her and Dad, and they held hands beneath it.

"How many would you say we should have, just an estimate?" Mother asked.

"Just as an estimate, many."

"Lots and lots."

"We'll sell out for an even dozen," said Dad. "No less. What do you say to that?"

"I say," said Mother, "a dozen would be just right. No less."

Frank Gilbreth, Jr.,
and Ernestine Gilbreth Carey
CHEAPER BY THE DOZEN

If you have a small family, can you imagine belonging to a family of fourteen? Can you picture living with eleven brothers and sisters? Close your eyes and dream of the good life in an enormous family. Think only of the good parts—games you could play, family outings you could have, fun you could share. Now open your eyes.

~~~~~~

Multiplying Family Memories

Drift to warm family experiences. Whether you are an only child or one of many you have a wealth of family memories. Let your mind wander to a time filled with family love. Just imagine the happiness of that treasured moment multiplied in a family of nine or twelve or even fourteen. Think of how a few extra family members might enliven the scene. Free write about the possibilities of being in a large, loving family.

~~~~~~

Survey classmates to discover the sizes of families in your class. Ask someone to write the numbers 2 through 14 across the board. These numbers represent the total number of people living in the home. Have the recorder poll your class and tally the results. Include yourself and any family members living at home in your count.

Notice the trends. What is the most common family size in your class? What is the average family size? What is the smallest? What is the largest? Do you think your class results represent a majority of American families? Recent trends show the size of the family has shrunk over the years. What do you think are the reasons for this trend?

The Goldilocks Connection

Remember the story of Goldilocks and her pals? Reach back to the fairy tale section of your memory. That's right. Goldilocks is the one who paid a surprise visit to the Bear family. It seems she had to explore the large, the medium, and the small of things before discovering which was just right for her.

~~~~~~

Brainstorming

Join in a discovery adventure of your own. What's so wonderful about being in a large family? Are you sure the small family is just right? Based on the class survey, divide the class into three groups according to family size—small, medium, and large. For your purposes, you may decide that families totaling two through four are small. See what works for your class.

In your groups brainstorm unique advantages of being in a family of your size—small, medium, or large. Then share your group's list of advantages with the class. As you listen to each group's list, decide which family size sounds just right for you.

In these next two chapters you will be at the center of an inquiry into family life. Your experience as a family member will be an important resource. Through small- and large-group activities you will share proud moments from your own family and learn more about the families of your classmates. Your Researcher's Notebook from Chapter 10 will become your Response Notebook. In it you will record your reactions and writings concerning the family. Your work in the Response Notebook will prepare you to write a critical book review in Chapter 12.

In discussion with your classmates you will discover some family life styles much like your own. Others may be quite different. The key word is different—not better, not worse than your own—simply different. Recognizing other styles of living reveals the richness of the American family in its many forms. By listening, sharing, and responding, you will develop respect for and pride in the expanding notion of the American family.

Family Living

Look at the following list of groups of people. Each group lives under the same roof and shares life together. Which groups are families? Make your decisions with the help of a partner. Share opinions with your partner. Trust your intuitions.

Getting It Started

> Newlyweds with no children
> An elderly couple whose children have left home
> A married couple with one adopted child and one of their own
> Four children and an aunt

A single mother with one child
A divorced father with two children
A married couple with three foster children
A widower, his son, and an aunt
A married couple
A father with his three sons from a previous marriage and a mother with her three daughters from a previous marriage
A stepfather and a divorced mother with five children
A mother, a father, and one child
A mother, a father, two children, an uncle, two aunts, a grandfather and a grandmother.

File your decisions in your Response Notebook. At the end of this chapter, you and your partner will consider this list again. Before you move on, take a few minutes to tell each other about your families.

SPOTLIGHT

The Traditional Family

Papa came at last. His steps on the stairs were slow and heavy tonight. It had been a long hard day at the shop with very little business done. Papa looked very tired.

But the children were too eager to spring their surprise to notice. They crowded about him, crying, "Happy birthday, Papa! Happy birthday to you!" They could barely wait.

He smiled a weary little smile. "Thank you all for remembering," he said and started to wash up for supper. Mama, meanwhile, busied herself with putting the hot food on the table.

"Supper is ready," she called.

There was a rush. The children took their usual places quickly. They did not want to miss seeing Papa's face when he found the present.

"What's this?" he asked as he sat down.

"A present from your daughters," Mama told him.

"A present for me?" He'd never gotten a present from the

children before. He couldn't quite believe it. Picking up the package he turned it round and round in his hands.

"Aren't you going to open it?" Henny asked. "Yes, of course," Papa tugged at the cord, the wrapper fell away and the cup and saucer stood in splendor on the table. Papa stared at his present and said not a word.

The children were bewildered. What was wrong? What made Papa's face look so sorrowful? Didn't he like their present?

Papa was thinking: So much money spent on a fancy cup and saucer that I could just as well do without. Haven't we enough cups and saucers in the house now? I have to work so hard to make enough for the necessary things and here they spend money on such a luxury. What if the amount they spent wouldn't help much. It's little spendings like this that add up.

But right through his thoughts, there floated a little disappointed whimper from Gertie, and Papa suddenly remembered his children. He looked down at their faces, so puzzled and sad now. They had been so gay a moment ago. They were young. It was bad enough that they had to be denied so many things because he couldn't afford them. Must he deny them even this pleasure of giving up their small allowance for a present for him?

Ella interrupted his thoughts. She spoke quietly. "Perhaps we should have bought something more useful?"

Papa smiled his wide, gentle smile at his daughters. "No, no, it's wonderful! I've been wanting just such a cup and saucer for years. How did you ever come to think of it? I couldn't tell you right off how happy it made me because I was speechless with delight. Mama, pour me a cup of coffee right now. I can't wait to use my beautiful present."

Again the room flowed over with sunshine and happiness. Papa suddenly found himself covered over with five laughing daughters who tried to hug and kiss him all at the same time.

Sydney Taylor
ALL-OF-A-KIND FAMILY

1. Papa worries about money. Does the family's money situation affect their happiness? Explain.
2. Papa's first reaction causes the children to feel bewildered. What do you think this means?
3. Papa hides his first thoughts. Why does he do this?
4. What is your opinion of Papa?
5. Have you ever hidden your true feelings to keep someone you love from hurting. Has a parent ever spared your feelings?

All-of-a-Kind Family shows the struggles and joys of a Jewish family living in the early 1900s. The family's love for each other is obvious. But there are times when family members show their love in quiet ways.

Displays of affection make you feel warm inside. But sometimes signs of devotion are subtle. They can be easily taken for granted or go unnoticed. Think of some subtle sign of love your mother, father, or guardian has shown you. It may be some incident you have overlooked. Maybe you can recall a hazy recollection from your childhood.

Perhaps your scream pierced the night. Soon your father was holding you in his strong arms. Maybe your mother listened to you tell your tale of how your best friend hurt your feelings. You sobbed your story between salty tears but she didn't seem to mind. It could have been a sacrifice a parent made for you. Perhaps you discovered

that your mother didn't buy a new dress because she wanted you to
have that catcher's mitt for your birthday. It could have been a time
a parent protected you from physical harm.

~~~~~~

Tribute

Think back. Turn over your memories in your mind.
Ponder over how a parent or guardian showed some sign of
love. Write a tribute to this person by creating a poem.
Honor him or her with the gift of your carefully recopied
masterpiece.

Getting
It
Down

~~~~~~

Daddy in the Dream

I was chased by a gang.
I screamed,
"I'm scared!"
Daddy came and carried me on his back.
Daddy was taller than a mountain.
He was wearing a straw hat.
His shadow covered two or three mountains.
                    Yamaguchi Masayo, Age 6

1. What frightened the child?
2. How does the child feel about the father? How can you tell?
3. What does the poem's title tell you?
4. Do you think the poet's father would enjoy the poem? Explain.
5. What is your reaction to "Daddy in the Dream"?

A nuclear, or traditional family, is one limited to a father, a mother, and children. For years this family type was the only acceptable option available to families. Until recently almost all families followed this pattern. Seldom was the pattern broken unless death caused a shake-up in family structure or an elderly relative came to live with the family. Attitudes and institutions supported the nuclear family.

The nuclear family is deeply ingrained in American life. Generations have modeled their families after the traditional families in which they were raised. But why has the traditional family enjoyed such immense popularity? One possible explanation is that people hold strong beliefs about family life. They see in the nuclear family a durable support system. They feel that family life flourishes in a traditional arrangement.

What are other possible explanations for the endurance of the nuclear family. Why do so many champion it? Why do staunch supporters of the traditional family feel so strongly?

Family Values

Adults are not the only ones with strong beliefs. Because of your years of experience as a member of a clan, you too have strong beliefs about the family. These strong beliefs, or values, are as much a part of you as your toothbrush or the hair on your head. You probably don't spend a lot of time considering your beliefs. Like the hair on your head, your values are so close to you it is easy to take them for granted.

Your values are your most cherished beliefs. They tell as much about you as your sense of humor, your personality, or your body language. Taking a closer look at your beliefs is like standing up on tiptoes and peeking inside your own head.

One of the fascinating things about values is that they grow and change. As you encounter new ideas and explore new situations, your beliefs develop. They expand and deepen. Seeing how your values bloom is a way of watching your own growth as a person.

Discovering Your Values

Take a few minutes to concentrate on your values about the family. Wander around in your head. Uncover your strongest beliefs. To help you discover your deepest values, ask yourself some tough questions: What is a family? How many people does it take to make a family? What is absolutely essential in a family? What doesn't matter so much?

In your Response Notebook sketch the following picture of paired heads. In the left balloon jot down your five strongest beliefs about the family. These are private thoughts, so tuck this sheet away in your Response Notebook. Later you will complete this activity.

Getting
It
Started

In Search of the Family

You could put on blinders, scrunch down in your seat, and pretend your family is the only type that exists. That would give you one view of the world, but that view would be limited and not very realistic. Many people believe that most families are just like their own, but there are alternate family styles to be explored and considered. There may be other choices for family living of which you are not aware.

For the next two weeks you are going to immerse yourself in family life. Through your reading and class discussions you will encounter slices of family life in the forms of poetry, short stories, and excerpts from novels.

These readings will give you an overview of the American family, but you will want to do more than scratch the surface of family life. You will want to be the resident expert on two families, your own and one you discover in a novel of your choosing. You may want to reach for literature that reflects family life in the decade you researched or read a novel on contemporary family life. Maybe you're interested in a book that explores the joys of family life or one that shows how someone your age copes with problems in a family. Maybe you want to share the struggles of a young person who seems unhappy or unloved or feels unwanted. Or maybe you want to look over the shoulder of someone who works through the mixed-up emotions of family living. Whatever your interest, there is a book for you.

How will you know where to start? Chapters 9 and 10 introduced you to several tools you can use, such as the card catalogue. Your teacher or media specialist will probably treat you to a book talk. A book talk is an introduction to a number of different books on the same topic. Get your money's worth. Ask lots of questions. Listen for something that hooks your attention—a story line, a description of an unusual character, or a snappy writing style. Write down those titles that sound intriguing.

After the talk, thumb through the books which appeal to you. Read the first few pages of several books before making a decision. Scrounge up a few on your own. Check out at least two books to examine in private.

If you lose interest in a book after reading two or three chapters, return it and start on your second choice. Rejecting a book is one sign of a discriminating reader. Just be sure you make a commitment to read at least one book. Set aside some time for reading every day. Guard that time fiercely. When you finish your book, you will share your expertise with others.

Store your reactions to your reading in your Response Notebook. Write in your notebook every day for the next two weeks. Sometimes you'll just want to jot down a word or two to capture a dazzling insight you have about family living. Other times you'll want to stash pictures you collect in response to your reading.

Following are some suggestions for responding as you read. Try at least three or four of these ideas. Create a few of your own.

1. Guess what's going to happen in the next chapter of the book. Sketch out the details. Read on to see what happens.
2. Imagine what the characters in your book look like. Draw pictures of them or look through magazines to find their doubles.
3. Rewrite a favorite scene in your own words.
4. Write a letter to the author reacting to certain scenes. Give the author advice. When you finish your book, summarize your reactions and mail your letter to the author in care of the publisher.
5. Start a personal dictionary. Make lists of intriguing words and phrases. Note how words are used. Figure out meanings when you can. Consult a dictionary if you get stuck. Write meanings in your own words. Recopy the sentence in which your word or phrase is used or make the word you own by creating your own sentence.
6. Boil the plot down to a fine broth. Try to tell what happens in one paragraph.
7. Jot down questions about the book or questions about the family that come to you as you read.
8. Relate scenes from the book to your own family.
    What would happen if an incident in the book occurred in your family?
    Notice how family members in the book react to certain situations. How would your family members react in a similar situation?
    How does the main character handle difficult family situations? How would you handle the same situations?
9. Think of people you know in life who remind you of characters in the book. Talk about how they are alike and how they are different. Look for similarities between a character and you. How are you alike and how are you different?

10. Record startling insights about the family. Does your book cause you to realize something you never considered? Note that. Does your book reaffirm a belief? Write about that.

Exchange your reactions in a small group. Let your group know how your reading is going. Share humorous, sad, or favorite passages from your book.

SPOTLIGHT

Family Follies

Funny happenings can strike any time, any place in a family. Perhaps you can remember times such as these: Your family was feeling low. You wanted to cheer everybody up, so you and your sister dressed up as clowns and serenaded the family. Your off-key duet cracked up everyone. How about the time your father gave the family a lesson on how to pitch a tent. He told everyone how easy it would be. He painstakingly demonstrated each step only to have the whole tent collapse on top of him. No one dared laugh—then. Now the incident is a family joke. Even your father takes the kidding good-naturedly.

These funny happenings can be told to others as anecdotes. An anecdote is a short, entertaining account. Read this family anecdote written by Mindy :

Christmas is always the best time of the year. Families get together and celebrate. One Christmas our family all met at our mountain cabin in Colorado. My brother was sick with a fever of 101° degrees and was determined to make everyone else feel as miserable as he did. Since he was only two, he couldn't swallow aspirin so we had to mash it up in jelly and put it on toast.

My mother placed his toast on the fireplace hearth and soon forgot about it. My Aunt Mary had opened the gift my uncle had given her and was modeling her pale yellow pants made by a famous designer.

We were all settling down to talk about previous Christmases, when my brother started screaming at the top of his lungs, "My poast! My poast!"

No one knew what on earth he was talking about and so they ignored him. As Mary got up to get some more coffee, something fell off the back of her pants. When she turned around there was a big grape jelly stain right on the back of her new pants!

My brother at once set up a clamor for some more "poast" which set the family into an uproar.

Now, as we gather around the Christmas tree and talk about Christmases past, someone always starts asking for some "poast"!

Mindy

1. What kind of family time does Mindy share? How does she prepare readers for what happens?
2. Point out funny parts in Mindy's story. Do you think her brother's screams for "My poast! My poast!" add to the humor of Mindy's story? Explain.
3. What examples of exaggeration or understatement does Mindy use? Do they add to the humor of the anecdote?

Think of a funny anecdote that happened in your family. It doesn't have to be wildly funny. You may want to choose a story that gently pokes fun at a family life. Stories you star in are especially good. Feel free to exaggerate the funny parts.

If a funny family anecdote doesn't pop into mind, share a happy event. Recall a memorable family vacation or a time of closeness. Think of a happening that brought joy. Put your classmates in touch with a special family feeling.

Getting It Started

Family Anecdote

After you think your story through, put it into writing. As you write keep your audience, your classmates, in mind. Give them a little background information, if necessary. Notice how Mindy fills readers in. If your story is funny, repeat any key phrases that will add to the humor. Use exaggeration or understatement if they will make your

Getting It Down

anecdote more effective. Keep your anecdote brief and light. Split-second timing is important, especially in humor.

~~~~~~~~~~~~~~~~~~~~~~~~~~~~~~~~

SPOTLIGHT

The Extended Family

You may have a grandparent living in your home. Or you may know of someone who does. Traditional families sometimes open their homes to close relatives. If elderly relatives become too sick to care for themselves, they may be invited to move in. Relatives may be added when a death in the family leaves young children unattended. Sometimes close relatives simply tire of living alone. When any situation adds relatives to the home, the family becomes an extended family.

Michael climbed all the way up on the bed and put his whole self alongside his great-great-aunt. He touched her arms. "Are your arms a hundred years old?" he asked. It was their favorite question game.

"Um-hm," Aunt Dew murmured and turned a little away from him.

Michael touched her face. "Is your face and your eyes and fingers a hundred years old too?"

"Michael, I'm tired," Aunt Dew said. "Don't talk so."

"How do you get to be a hundred years old?" Michael asked and raised up from the bed on one elbow and waited for his great-great-aunt to answer.

"First you have to have a hundred penny box," his great-great-aunt finally said.

"Where you get it from?" Michael asked.

"Somebody special got to give it to you," Aunt Dew said. "And soon as they give it to you, you got to be careful less it disappear.

"Aunt Dew ___"

"PRECIOUS LORD ___"

"Aunt Dew?"

"TAKE MY HAND ___"

Michael put his head down on Aunt Dew's thin chest beneath the heavy quilt and listened to her sing her long song.

Sharon Bell Mathis

1. What game do Aunt Dew and Michael play?
2. Why do you think Michael is so interested in the hundred penny box?
3. Why do you suppose Michael enjoys talking to his old aunt?
4. If you had a one-hundred-year-old aunt living with you, what kinds of questions would you want to ask her?

~~~~~~

Exploring Feelings

Pretend you are Aunt Dew's hundred penny box. You have accepted a penny for every year Aunt Dew has lived. Better than anyone you know Aunt Dew. Briefly write the story of how Aunt Dew came to live with Michael's family. Explain

**Getting
It
Down**

the adjustments the family has made since Aunt Dew moved in. Explain how she feels living in someone else's home. Divulge Aunt Dew's deepest feelings.

The Quality of Family Life

There are those who pin their hopes on fanciful dreams. Some work toward great goals. Others devote their lives to significant causes. Some value an exciting life and friendship. Equal rights, world peace, and love are important to many. Most people have definite views on what is important in life. But what about the family? Do you value equal rights or friendship in the family? Is an exciting life a vital part of the family?

Reaching Consensus

With your classmates brainstorm a list of those items that make a difference in the quality of family life. What is important? Keep going until you have a large list.

Form small groups to consider your brainstormed list. Look at it carefully. As a group decide on the ten most important items necessary for quality in family life. There is one catch. You must all agree on the ten words or phrases you put down.

Having everyone in a group agree is called reaching consensus. Consensus, or total agreement, takes patience and skill. It also takes practice. In many activities in this book you have worked on identifying ideas everyone in your group could support. Following are some guidelines to help you fine tune your consensus skills:

1. List.   Make an individual list of the ten most important items for the family in your Response Notebook.
2. Share.   Share lists. Everyone should have a chance to speak.
3. Look.   Search for ideas that pop up on all the lists. If *trust* appears on every person's list, it must be important. Write it on the group list.
4. Open up.   Keep an open mind. Remember that the goal is to list the ten most important items for the family. Someone may say something you never thought of. Another person's thoughts may cause you to see something in a different light.
5. Listen.   Pay atttention to other people when they share their

views. Encourage them to explore their reasoning. Try to see other points of view.

6. <u>Stay calm.</u>   Reaching consensus is always a challenge. Avoid shouting matches. Share your opinions calmly. Accept the opinions of others in the same way.
7. <u>Reach consensus.</u>   Stay away from taking a majority vote. This is not an election. Watch for those who give in too easily. Insist on true agreement. In reaching consensus group members should change their minds only when truly convinced.
8. <u>Record.</u>   Record your group list on a large sheet of paper. Show your agreement by having all members sign the group list.

Review your list. Spend some time sharing your ideas about the influences of the family. How important is the family? Is its impact on people great or small? Share your group lists and opinions with the class.

Changing Times

Nostalgic views of the traditional family are widespread. People like to think of life in the nuclear family as always being wholesome. They have dreamy visions of a life brimming with love, cooperation, and security.

Some believe that problems are new to the traditional family. Your research in Chapters 9 and 10 probably revealed the sentimentality of such a notion. Think of all the challenges faced by the traditional family over the decades. How did these outside forces affect the family: Teen-agers' newly found independence with the Model T in the twenties? The depression of the thirties? World War II in the forties? Rock and roll in the fifties? The Viet Nam War in the sixties? How did these outside forces change the family?

The truth is that life in the traditional family has never been carefree. In earliest times life was hard. People struggled just to survive. They fought diseases that had no known cures. There were outside forces to combat. Just think of living without modern conveniences. Life inside the home was not always perfect either. Nostalgic images sometimes leave out the day-to-day problems faced by all families. In the most loving homes, families had squabbles. So it is not surprising to discover the modern traditional family in difficult times, too.

SPOTLIGHT

My special elective class, "Law for Children and Young People," is about to start. And I definitely have lots of questions. It's a good thing the school started it just in time for everything I have to ask. The first one's going to be "What are the grounds for justifiable homicide?" Can I kill off one or more of the following: an older sister who gets her own room and ends up with all the beauty genes in the family? A mother who lives in a fantasy world always dreaming about winning the lottery or some big prize so we can all live happily ever after? A mother who's always writing letters and going to tryouts for quiz shows? A father who constantly complains about how hard it is to sell insurance and to support a family in this day and age? . . .

It's absolutely disgusting being fourteen. You've got no rights whatsoever. Your parents get to make all the decisions: Who gets the single bedroom. How much allowance is enough. What time you must come in. Who is a proper friend. What your report card is supposed to look like.

Paula Danziger

1. Do you think Lauren, the narrator, is really contemplating homicide? What could make her say such a thing?
2. Do you think Lauren's reaction to life in a traditional family is typical? Why or why not?
3. What are Lauren's complaints about family life? Have you ever had similar feelings?

No one would deny that modern life is complex. It is easy to understand why people get sentimental over what seem like simpler times. Modern life often seems confusing. The frantic pace of contemporary life can be jolting. The effects of modern life are reflected in the family.

Modern family life seems less stable than it once was. Or perhaps the family is simply experiencing growing pains. Family roles are more flexible today than they once were. Fathers sometimes choose to stay at home. Mothers select careers that take them far from home. Some children seem to grow up on their own.

Family mobility is on the increase. Numerous family moves leave many feeling "rootless." Family networks seem more loosely structured. It is not unusual to meet children who have not seen grandparents in years. Others have never met aunts, uncles, or cousins.

While such changes may seem minor, they have left the traditional family in a topsy-turvy state. Changes brought about by modern living have sent shock waves through the traditional family. Complex living has turned the nuclear family inside out.

> Over one million marriages end in divorce every year. One out of every six children lives in a one-parent family. Divorce has become so common in the lives of so many children, that when one little boy wrote a fairy story for his fourth-grade teacher, he ended it by writing, "And so they lived happily together for quite some time."
>
> *Eda LeShan*

What is the usual ending to fairy tales? Why did the little boy end his story this way? Are you shocked by these figures? Are you bewildered? Did you know there are many books for children on coping with divorce? Check with your librarian.

SPOTLIGHT

The Single-Parent Family

Until recent years the traditional family overshadowed all other types. When the word *family* was mentioned, people automatically pictured a father and mother surrounded by children. But the single-parent family is becoming more common.

> Between jobs my mother and I usually lived at the Ritz Hotel which is the kind of hotel where you have to step over derelicts in order to make it through the lobby. Anyway, my mother's full name is Helen Boyd. And my name is Christopher. My friends would call me Chris, but I didn't have any friends. No real friends. I also have no father. Now, once upon a time I did have a father, and my father and Helen really loved each other very much for the first seven years they were married, and then after that they hated each other so much that my father pulled that old trick of saying he was

going out to buy the evening paper but went to Mexico. As far as I know he lived for about three months in Guadalajara and then Helen received the news that he died from an overdose of amoebas. That's one of the first things I learned about Life; it's not always like you read about in your local newspaper. It's more like what you read in the *National Enquirer*. So the first important thing I've confessed to you is that since I was five years old I was raised without a father. I have only a few memories of him like he loved animals and took me to the zoo and he liked dogs and he told me to eat the beets on my plate because they were good for me. I also remember he was bigger than me and I was really impressed by that. One day long after he had left, I saw a chesterfield overcoat in one of our closets and I asked Helen whose it was and she said it had belonged to my father. Now I realize a chesterfield overcoat is not much of a legacy, but I adopted the coat and I always took the coat with me no matter where we moved. It was a terrific-looking coat, a deep gray with a black velvet collar.

End of ancient history!

Paul Zindel

1. When did Chris's father leave? How does he feel about being raised without a father?
2. What is the *National Enquirer?* What does Chris mean when he says life is "more like what you read in the *National Enquirer?*"
3. Do you agree with Chris's opinion about life? Explain.
4. Why do you think Chris put on his father's old chesterfield coat?

Family Reunion

Getting It Down

Chris and his mother take a trip to New Jersey. On a crisp afternoon Chris bundles up and walks to the zoo alone. He strikes up a conversation with a man in a chesterfield overcoat. They spend the day together. Chris soon realizes that this likable man is his father. How does he react? What does he say? Write the scene. Remember to put quotation marks around the words Chris and his father speak.

Share your scene in a small group. Choose one scene from the group to role play for the class.

SPOTLIGHT

Some fear that alternate family life styles signal the downfall of the American family. Shifts in family trends seem threatening to many. People wonder if alternate family types can provide the happiness and well-being children deserve.

What do you think? You have already learned that claims of a carefree life in traditional families are exaggerated. Do you think there are myths associated with the single-parent family? If so, what are they? You have probably heard the term "broken home." What image of family life is suggested by this term? Do you think this image is a stereotype of single-parent families?

The only part that I really mind about Mom not being married is when people ask questions. Otherwise we have a good time, better in some ways than lots of my friends who have mothers and fathers. Like, when I visit Andrew, who was my best friend from my old school, everything has to be done at just a certain time. First we have to do our homework, then we can play, and at just a certain time, we have to have dinner. "Don't you see what time it is?" Andrew's mother keeps saying. In our house we hardly even have clocks. Mom never cares what time it is or when we eat. She says I have to go to bed more or less on time but if I don't, she doesn't really care. Maybe it's because her schedule is so odd. She works at night lots of times, developing pictures in our little back room. Sometimes she works all night and then just leaves me breakfast. I eat it by myself and go off to school by myself, too. Sometimes—which seems funny to some people—she's just getting up when I come home from school. Once she was just having breakfast when Andrew and I came in. "How come your mother is in her pajamas?" he said. "Is she sick?"

I felt funny then, I guess I wanted her to be like Andrew's mother, who is always dressed up and greets us at the door with sandwiches or cookies. So I said she was sick and when Andrew went home, I told Mom she shouldn't just be in pajamas at three in the afternoon. The good thing about Mom is that you can tell her these things. She never gets mad, but she doesn't always do them either. But after that, she tried sleeping in her blue jeans and shirt so that, even if she was just getting up, my friends wouldn't know. I thought that was okay, even though not that many mothers wear blue jeans either. But Mom is just sort of like that. She wears her hair in a pony tail, too, and she never gets dressed up like Evelyn's mother and never puts on makeup. Evelyn and I sometimes watch her mother get dressed up for dates and it takes her hours. She sits in front of this big mirror that makes her face look gigantic, like a pumpkin. Then she puts on all sorts of stuff and lets us try some, too—moon drops and blushers and eye makeup and perfume. Mom never uses that stuff. If she goes out, she just washes her hair and maybe puts on some-thing different but not that different from what she was wear-ing already. She's just that way. Even Andrew says mothers are just a certain way, whatever that way is, and it's silly to think they will ever change. But on the whole, I like Mom the way she is and don't especially mind not having a father.

Norma Klein

1. How does Brett, the narrator, feel about having a mother who wears blue jeans and a pony tail?
2. What parts of her mother's life style cause Brett some discomfort? How do she and her mother work this out?
3. In what ways is Brett's life style different from her classmates' life style?
4. Do you think Brett lives in a healthy, happy home? Explain.

Comedy series based on the family were popular in the fifties and sixties. Following are some shows from that time period. The type of family portrayed in each show is indicated. In the fifties and sixties almost all comedy series focused on white, middle-class Americans. "Amos 'n' Andy," a comedy focusing on blacks, was one of the few exceptions.

| The Adventures of Ozzie and Harriet | traditional |
| The Andy Griffith Show | extended |

Bachelor Father	single-parent
The Danny Thomas Show	traditional
Father Knows Best	traditional
The Honeymooners	other (married, no children)
I Love Lucy	traditional
Leave It to Beaver	traditional
Life with Father	traditional
The Real McCoys	extended
My Three Sons	single-parent

What does the TV scene look like today? How many popular television comedies center on the family? Brainstorm a list on the board. You will need this list later. Are *minority* families represented? A minority is a group of people representing less than half of the total population. Chicanos are a minority group. Can you think of others? Which minority groups are represented in family comedy series?

Writer's Workbench

Family Word Bank

In this chapter the following terms were used in discussing the family. Cover the far right column. Try to remember the meaning of the term as it was used in the chapter. If you get stuck, find the sentence containing the word. Notice how it is used.

1.	anecdote (page 212)	short, entertaining, or amusing story
2.	bewildered (page 205)	puzzled, confused
3.	challenge (page 217)	demanding test or difficult problem
4.	extended family (page 214)	nuclear family that also includes close relatives in the home
5.	life style (page 203)	way of life
6.	nostalgic (page 217)	feeling wistful or sentimental about something from the past
7.	realistic (page 210)	accurate or true-to-life

8. response (page 203)   reaction
9. single-parent family   family headed by a single par-
   (page 219)   ent
10. traditional family (page 208)   nuclear family; family limited
                                                   to a father, a mother, and
                                                   children
11. trends (page 202)   patterns or general movements
                                                   that follow current styles
12. values (page 208)   strongly-held beliefs

Follow these steps to show your understanding of your new word-bank deposits:

1. Break into small groups. Choose a TV family comedy series you would like to work with. Decide on a first, second, and third choice. Be sure everyone in your group is familiar with the series.
2. Declare your decision. Each group will work with a different family comedy.
3. As a group, complete the following word-bank quiz. Appoint a recorder. Complete the quiz based on the show your group has selected.
4. Have a spokesperson read your completed quiz to the class. As a group, share your creative response to question 10.

Word-Bank Quiz

1. What is the family type?   Is the television family an *extended*, *single-parent*, *traditional*, or other family type? Explain your choice.
2. Comment on the family's *values*.   Can you make an accurate guess about the family's *values*? What seem to be their most cherished *values*? Does the family's life style give you any clues?
3. Describe the family's *life style*.   What does the family do for fun? How often are they together? For what occasions? What do family members do for a living? How do they feel about their jobs?
4. Describe a *challenge* faced by the family.   Has the family tackled a serious *challenge*? How well did family members handle the *challenge*? Does the series revolve around a single

challenge? Does the series center on the father's attempt to keep peace in the family? On a running battle with the neighbors?

5. Share a brief *anecdote.*   Is there a show all of you have seen? Write a brief anecdote of a humorous family situation.

6. Which character is most likely to be *bewildered?*   Is there a character who is always perplexed? Can you remember situations in which a character seemed *bewildered?* How do other TV family members react to the character's bewilderment?

7. Find two family *trends* supported by your TV family.   Is the *single-parent* family a *trend?* Is your TV family a *single-parent family?* Be sure you select real trends. Check with your teacher if you're stumped.

8. Does the series give a *nostalgic* or *realistic* picture of family life? Is the show set back in "the good old days"? Does the series show family members as always being cooperative and loving? Is there an attempt to deal with real family problems? How are they handled?

9. Create a *response* to your favorite show.   How do you feel about the show? How can you share your *response* with the class? Would you like to put on a skit or role play a scene? Could each group member create a humorous poem that captures a different TV family member's personality? Devise your own response.

Whatever the family type—traditional, extended, single-parent, or other—all families have much to be proud of. Alternate family life styles show the durability and spunk of the family.

Family Pride

As resident expert you will want to share your knowledge of two families—your own and the family in the book you read. This activity will give you that chance.

Having an audience eager to hear your family stories can be rewarding. Share your expertise with an alert audience of five or six. Learn more about the families of your friends while being introduced to books you might enjoy reading by following these steps:

1. Think about your group project in Chapter 10. How did it go? When you presented your research on the decades, what went

right? What went wrong? How could your time be managed more effectively this time?

2. To share your families select one option from each of the following lists.

3. Get organized. Write your own step-by-step plan. Use the plan on page 195 as a guide. Include your suggestions for streamlining the process.

4. Practice your 10-15 minute presentation. Be sure everyone has an active role. If equipment is available, have your presentation video-taped.

5. Share your live or taped tribute with the rest of the class.

Book Project Options

1. Book fair.   Design new book jackets for the book you have read. On the front, create any design that seems right. Include author and book title. On the back include a brief blurb of twenty-five words or less aimed at hooking potential readers. Prove that you can judge a book by its cover. Set up a book fair. Hawk your books. Lure new readers. Convince them to read your books.

2. Poetry portfolio.   Have each member find two or three poems that capture the spirit of the book's family. Each member should also write at least one original poem. Review all selections. Choose one or two poems for each book's family. Recopy and illustrate the poems. Add finishing touches of your own creation. Set up a display area.

3. Mind movie.   After all members have shared the stories of their book families, brainstorm for a message about the families your group would like to communicate. Look for materials to help you get your message across—records, poems, news articles, magazine clippings, dialogue from the family characters. Organize materials. Think carefully about the order you will use. Decide who will say what. Write a script for your presentation. Set up a tape recorder. Tape your mind movie of music, poems, and dialogue from characters. Replay. Does the tape flow? Rework as necessary.

Family Project Options

1. Family album.   Have each member rummage through the attic, old suitcases and trunks, and dusty dresser drawers in search of family albums. With your parent's permission bring a few to school to share. Design your own group family album, de-

voting one page to each group member's family. Sketch your own pictures or borrow family photographs. <u>Caution:</u> Handle treasured family photos with care.

2. <u>Family favorites.</u>   Many people have a favorite family member. Ask each member to write a special creation for this family favorite. Pull together excerpts from these tributes or include entire pieces if short. Devise your own method of presentation.

3. <u>Family pets.</u>   Families seem to be fond of assorted pets— striped snakes, spirited kittens, personable hamsters, yelping pups. Share stories about a favorite family pet. Compose written anecdotes that star these special family members. Revise, proofread, and publish, making copies available for class members.

~~~~~~

Winding Up

Getting
It
Down

Now that you have completed your exploration of the family do two things. First, jot down your five strongest beliefs about the family. Do this without consulting the list you made at the beginning of this chapter. Now take out the paired-heads activity (page 209). Fill in the right-hand balloon with the beliefs you just wrote. Compare the two balloons. Write a private entry in your Response Notebook. Reflect on the beliefs you listed twice. Talk about any new beliefs you listed.

Second, scrounge up your Family Living list (page 203). Find your original partner. Together review your list. Decide if you want to change any of your decisions. Use the Family Living list to review what you have learned in this chapter.

~~~~~~

Chapter 12

Reviewing the Family

Have you ever heard of Rex Reed or Judith Crist or Gene Shalit? These people are famous film critics. Film critics often see thousands of films over a lifetime. They read hundreds of books and interview countless people in filmmaking.

Film critics help movie-goers decide whether to rush out to the theater or stay home with a good book instead. They do this by criticizing films.

In criticizing films, critics share informed opinions with movie-goers. They comment on the good parts and the not-so-good parts of movies. Film critics do this in film reviews.

A film review gives a brief description of one film. Sometimes the film is compared to other films on a similar subject. The other films may be ones created by the same producer, directed by the same director, or acted in by the same actors. In film reviews critics often comment on how well or how poorly actors perform. They sometimes include their opinions about the work of producers and directors, too. Many movie-goers find film reviews helpful.

SPOTLIGHT

Read this review of an old film entitled *National Velvet*. The film starred Elizabeth Taylor.

National Velvet. The high point in Elizabeth Taylor's acting career came when she was twelve: under Clarence Brown's direction, she gave her best performance to date as Velvet Brown, the heroine of Enid Bagnold's account of a little girl's

sublime folly. Quite possibly the role coincided with the child's own animal-centered universe: she had her own folly, wanting to play the part so badly that she worked out to gain the necessary height (three inches in four months), a process not unlike Velvet's training of The Pie, the horse she wins in a lottery, to ready him for the Grand National Steeplechase. In lots of ways National Velvet isn't a very good movie, but it has a rare and memorable quality: it touches areas in our experience that movies rarely touch—the passions and obsessions of childhood. It's one of the most likeable movies of all time. The cast includes Anne Revere (whose performance as the mother won the Academy Award as Best Supporting Actress of 1945), Mickey Rooney, Jackie "Butch" Jenkins, Donald Crisp, Angela Lansbury, Arthur Treacher. Color.

Pauline Kael

1. Critic Kael tells us that Elizabeth Taylor had a strong desire to

be in *National Velvet*. She calls Elizabeth Taylor's desire *folly*. What do you think the word *folly* means? Why do you think Pauline Kael includes this information in her review?

2. How was Elizabeth Taylor's strong desire to be in this film like the actions of Velvet, the character she played.

3. Have you ever desperately wanted to do something? What did you do to make your wish a reality? Were you successful? Explain.

Think of a time you decided to see a movie or watch a television program based on the advice of a friend. Think back. What did your friend tell you about the show? How helpful was the recommendation? Were you disappointed or delighted? Would you listen to your friend again? Share your experience with the class.

Critic Kael says, "In lots of ways *National Velvet* isn't a very good movie." Taken alone this statement does not seem favorable. But read on. Notice how the critic counterbalances this negative criticism. Discuss the positive comments Pauline Kael makes. Is she recommending this film? Or is she suggesting you skip this one? Based on her comments, do you think you would enjoy *National Velvet*? Notice how short the review is. Ms. Kael tells us a lot about *National Velvet* in a few words. Notice how the critic hooks her readers' attention.

~~~~~~~~~~~~~~~~~~~~~~~~~~~~~~~~~~~~~

The Movie Review

Getting It Down

Have you seen any good movies lately? Think of a film you have seen recently. The film may be one you liked or disliked. It may be a film you enjoyed on television or one you watched at a movie theater. Without summarizing the whole plot, write a brief description telling what the film is about.

Now make a jot list of all the items you might include in a movie review. Go over your list. Remember that a film review helps people make smart decisions about films. Circle those points you think would be helpful to someone your age. Using your hunches, try writing a movie review. Include your opinions in your review. Limit your review to one page.

~~~~~~~~~~~~~~~~~~~~~~~~~~~~~~~~~~~~~

Share your reviews in a small group. As a group, select the best review. Write out specific reasons for your choice. Have one group member read the best review to the class and share reasons for your group's decision.

Book Reviews

Movie reviews can be helpful, especially since movie tickets are expensive. But what about books? Sometimes your time is as valuable as money. How do busy people make good book selections?

A book talk is one solution to the "I can't find a book!" problem. If you are part of a class "diggin' in the decades," exploring the family, or investigating some other topic, a book talk can probably be arranged. However, a book talk is not always possible. It's hard for an individual to ask that much of a librarian's time.

For many, the search for a good book is maddening. Not everyone has such fine-tuned library skills as you have. Some spend time wandering aimlessly from shelf to shelf looking for anything of interest. They pick up books and put them back on shelves. They thumb through books, unable to locate one that feels right. Even someone with your expertise sometimes slips up. The book that held such promise in the library slowly fizzles out after a few pages. Then you're stuck at home, often with no ride to the library and no patience left. Worse yet is giving up on a slow starter. Later you discover that the book is your friends' favorite. Oh well . . . .

Drift back to your original book search in Chapter 11. Discuss what caused you to pick up your book in the first place. Did a weird title snare your attention? Did the promise of nonstop family adventure attract you? Did an irresistible book jacket lure you to the stacks? Once you found a book, how did your reading go?

~~~~~~

The Book Hunt Blues

Almost everyone has experienced the inconvenience of the book search gone sour. Recall one of those unpleasant memories. Freewrite for a few minutes on your exasperating book hunt.

Getting
It
Down

~~~~~~

SPOTLIGHT

Read the following book review written by a student:

The Shattered Stone by Robert Newman, illustrations by John Gretzer; Atheneum: New York, 1975, $6.95.

Although this story seemed to drag at the beginning, it was worth reading on, because the adventure picked up in the middle, and really got exciting. The two main characters, Neva and Ivo, were brave and smart. Neva caught on to tricks more quickly, as when she smelled the wine that the king of Brunn gave them and knew that he was trying to poison them; and Ivo displayed incredible skill when he fought with the Hitis in the desert. I did feel, however, that the characters were not developed enough for me to get involved with. There were no physical descriptions that I could use to picture them, and their attitudes and personalities were not defined. I thought that the children would miss their parents when they discovered that they did not know where they were, but Neva and Ivo showed no feelings here.

There were a few things in the story that were not explained: when Jartan was referred to as Tharlack, I expected an explanation about his past, and I didn't understand who Kenna was. But I think that anyone who loves fantasy and adventure combined, as I do, will have lots of fun with this book. Just as I had thought that the story was coming to an end, and Neva and Ivo would have the secret of the stone revealed to them, I was happily surprised that part of the stone was found to be missing, and another thrilling adventure awaited them.

Kim Mendelson, Age 11

1. Kim explains that her book "got exciting." What events from the book does she choose to share? Are her selections good ones? Explain.
2. What incidents in the book disturb Kim?
3. How does she feel about the main character?
4. According to Kim, what kind of book is *The Shattered Stone?* Does this sound like your kind of book? Explain.
5. Compare Kim's book review to Pauline Kael's movie review. Point out how they are alike. Which review is aimed at an adult audience? Which is intended for people your age? What differences in language choice tip you off?

In Chapter 11 you shared your expertise within the classroom. In Chapter 12 you will have a chance to be a hit as a book reviewer. Your opinions will help other students avoid the frustrating book search.

You will write a review of the book about the family you read in Chapter 11. You will revise and proofread your review with a small group of classmates. You will select a method of publication. Your goal will be an inexpensive, handy publication that students in your school can easily use. The book review you write will help other students choose good books.

To write your review you will follow these steps:

Doing Background Work

1. Read the book.
2. Reread the book with a critical eye.
3. Make notes.

Writing the Review

1. Review your notes.
2. Complete the "Reviewer's Checklist."
3. Write a discovery draft.

Editing

1. Evaluate book reviews.
2. Revise.
3. Proofread.

Publishing

1. Choose a method of publication.
2. Publish.

Good book reviewers, like good film critics, know their business. Before you begin writing your review, jog your memory for books you have read. In your Response Notebook make a list of every book you remember reading. Share your list with a friend. Hearing other titles may jog your memory further.

Look over your list. Place a check mark beside those that have anything to do with the family. Place an asterisk (*) beside books you could use for comparison with the book you review. As a warm-up, do a free writing on books about the family which you have read.

Doing Background Work

Good reviewers do their homework. Background work is as important as the writing itself. Reviewers get audiences by proving that their opinions can be trusted. They take their responsibility to readers seriously. Steps 1–3 will get you started in your new role as reviewer.

1. <u>Read the book.</u>   As a researcher, you often skimmed material. You were interested only in information related to your topic. Reviewing is different. Your first job as reviewer is to read the entire book from cover to cover. You owe it to your author to read every word. The part you skip could well be the best—or the worst. Imagine how upset you would be if your teacher evaluated your writing after having read only the opening paragraph.

2. <u>Reread the book with a critical eye.</u>   After all, first impressions are sometimes unreliable. Your first reading was to find out more about the family. You read for enjoyment, too. Your reactions were honest, first-impression responses. These honest first reactions are valuable. They can give you information about how other readers your age may react. But they are only a beginning. You no longer are just any reader. You are a reviewer. Give your novel a second, more thoughtful reading.

3. <u>Make notes.</u>   Good criticism is fair. It is well-balanced and supported by evidence. Make notes that will help you make a fair evaluation. Good book reviewers seldom depend on their memory. As they read, they jot down impressions—both good and bad. These impressions shape their reviews. Good notes make the difference between a thorough review and a slipshod one.

Knowing what to note and what to leave out can be a bit confusing at first. Following is a plan to help you collect your impressions in a workable form:

Collecting Notes for a Book Review

People continue to read in this electronic age. Why? Perhaps it is because there are so many good books. But what makes a good book? Before you look at the list of characteristics that follows, brainstorm one of your own.

When you have completed your list of characteristics, set aside eight pages in your Response Notebook. Devote one page each to main characters, minor characters, plot, action, believability, author's style, author's attitudes, and author's main idea. These eight sections will help you organize your notes. Use the following ideas to develop each section:

1. Main characters.   Main characters are the ones around which the action centers. Sometimes there is only one main character. Sometimes there are several. The best main characters are like close friends. Often readers report knowing how these characters look, how they act, and just how they feel. Good main characters seem like people you know, friends with both strengths and weaknesses. They seem human. Readers identify with main characters if the author has done a good job.

Write down intriguing personality quirks or striking characteristics the main characters possess. Note your reactions to these. Consider these questions: Has the author described the main characters so that you can visualize them? Can you understand how these characters act and what they feel? Do the main characters act like real people you know? If not, what do they do that is different? Does the author have them behave this way on purpose? Do the main characters have both strengths and weaknesses? What do you like best about them? What do you dislike?

2. Minor characters.   Motion pictures have leading roles played by major stars. Motion pictures also have minor roles played by a supporting cast. Books have stars and a supporting cast, too. Main

characters are the stars. Minor characters are the supporting cast.

You usually know less about the lives of minor characters. Minor characters are not as well developed as main characters. This simply means authors do not give you as much information about them. Like the supporting cast in a movie, minor characters are important.

Notice what happens between main and minor characters. Do the minor characters help you get to know main characters better? Do the comments of minor characters reveal a different or more complete side of the main characters? Do comparisons or contrasts between main and minor characters give you added information?

Good minor characters enrich a story. You should be able to recognize minor characters as real people. If you can't, what went wrong? Did the author give only a sketchy description? Did the actions of minor characters seem unreal? Note points you may want to use in your book review.

3. Plot.   Plot is the series of events that make up a book. These events move the story along. They are sometimes arranged in order; the beginning, the middle, and the end unfold in sequence. This is not always true. Writers, as you know, often experiment. They may plunge in at the middle. They may replay a story over and over, each time having different characters give their versions. Writers may purposely begin at the end, then flash back to the beginning. Techniques like these are part of the writer's craft.

No matter what the style, good events tackle real problems that might happen in a real family. Are the events clear? Do you understand what happens? Can you recognize that the author is using some kind of pattern to string events together? Do the events make a strong story? Jot down your impressions.

4. Action.   A good story often keeps you on the edge of your seat. Some skyrocket at the start but fizzle out at the end. Others are sleepers at first, then snare your attention in the middle. Others never seem to get off the ground. How is the action in your book? Does it keep you turning those pages? How quickly did you read your book? Were you so engrossed in the action that you couldn't put the book down? Did you think it would never end? Think about the action.

5. Believability.   Fantasy and science fiction whisk you off to other worlds. Temporarily you leave the real world behind and enter a land of wonder. Yet even in science fiction and fantasy there is an element of truth. In the not-too-distant future some of the happenings could happen.

You probably have been reading fiction. Fiction is not real but it usually seems to tell the truth. If the fiction you have read is good, family situations will be believable. Characters' actions will be realistic. Solutions to problems will be believable. In the best fiction, you look at the story and say, "Yes, that could happen." Do situations seem real? Have you experienced similar challenges yourself? Do you know anyone who has? Are solutions to family problems too easy? Are consequences explored? Write down your impressions.

6. <u>Author's Style.</u>   Throughout this book you have experimented with different beginnings and endings, the use of strong verbs and concrete detail, language play, and more. In short you have been polishing your skills as a writer. Your voice can now be clearly heard in your writing. You have been developing your writing style. Style is how writers write. It is their unique stamp, their trademark. Style is complex. It includes all the techniques of writing and how these techniques are used by writers.

Do you admire your author's writing? Does the author use any of the special skills you have practiced? Does the author experiment with any unusual techniques you would like to try in your own writing? Describe the special twists you admire. Note those that fall flat. Listen for your author's voice.

7. <u>Author's Attitudes.</u>   After finishing a good book, you have a strong impression of how authors feel toward their topic. Begin with your own feelings. When you put your book down, did you feel hopeful about the family? Were you depressed?

Look at your author's attitudes. Did your author show you a different view or shed light on some part of family life? Did the author make fun of any group of people or were all groups treated with respect? How do you think the author feels about the future of the family? Are the author's attitudes optimistic or pessimistic? Write notes on some of these questions.

8. <u>Author's main idea.</u>   Good books usually have a main idea. What point was your author trying to make? Maybe your author was saying to you that all families have reasons to be proud. Perhaps your author was zeroing in on the love between parents and children.

Search. Think. Look. What is your author trying to say? Does your author's thinking give you new understanding? Did you learn anything that would help your own family? Try jotting down the main idea of your book in one or two sentences.

SPOTLIGHT

Read this selection, "La Peseta," from a book entitled *El Barrio* by Piri Thomas.

La Peseta
(The Quarter)

I

A child wants to have a few *centavos* at least,
Some *dinero* to be able to go to the movies,
To be able to buy a hot dog or a *bacalaito*.
You know, things that other people
That have wealth can enjoy.
To have some money in your pocket
That's a job indeed.
You can go into the candy store
Instead of standing outside deciding
Whether to keep on walking
Or snatch a candy bar, very cool and undetached.

II

My father worked very hard on the WPA
Construction gang with picky *pala*, shovel,
Digging very deep holes and filling them too.
When he left for *trabájo* in the morning
He would give my mother money to buy food,
Always leaving something extra on top of the table
To make sure that we'd also have dessert.
On this day, he put one quarter, some dimes, and a nickel,
Maybe forty-five or fifty cents, a whole lot.
I really wanted to go to that movie
With my new girlfriend named Candida.
I looked at the money and said,
"Well, they would not miss it, you know."

So I took the quarter and put it into my socks,
Pushing it all the way down until it was
    underneath—inside my sneaker—*punto!*

III

As my father started to walk out the door
To go to his job of picky *pala,*
He said to my mother,
"I left some change."
And my mother said, "Bring it to me."
My father came back for the money,
And he looked and he quietly said,
"There is a quarter missing."
Oh, if he had only gone, I thought,
Then Mama would not have known a quarter
    was missing.

IV

I immediately began to look all over the floor
And under the beds and over everything.
And my father just stood there,
Looking at me.
I, who always complained
About going down to the grocery store
Or even washing behind my ears,
I, who always was the last to volunteer,
Was all of a sudden so fantastically willing
To look for the missing peseta.

V

My father said to my sister,
"Have you seen the quarter?"
My sister said, "No."
My father said to me,
"Have you seen it?"
And I said, "No, Poppa,

Can't you see I'm trying hard to find it?"
I was really wishing I had never taken
That *maldita peseta*.
I was not born a criminal,
I just wanted a chance to see what it was like
To have a quarter.

VI

My father looked at me,
And I knew that he knew
That the quarter was somewhere on me.

But not to make me feel completely guilty,
He said, "I'll frisk everybody."
Leaving me there sweating to the last—till
Finally, it was my turn.
"Let me see your pants, son."
I took them off.
He emptied my pockets
And while he was doing all this frisking,
I was loudly proclaiming my innocence complete
    with crossing *corazón*.
"Poppa, how could you even think this?
Poppa, have you ever known me to take
    anything
That didn't belong to me?"

VII

While in my mind justifying it,
As part of my inheritance.
Poppa said, "Take off your sneakers."
Then, . . . I took my smelly sneakers off.
Poppa beat them awfully hard against each
    other—I was so glad it wasn't my *cabeza*.
He said, "Your socks."
And I took one sock off.
The sock with the quarter was the last to go.
I slipped it off, holding the coin inside
With my thumb and forefinger,
And praying to all the Gods in Heaven
That the quarter would stay in the sock,
Which it did not.
Plink-ling-ling the quarter came tumbling out.
My face said, "How . . . did that get
    there?"
I tried to smile, but that didn't work.

VIII

My father dove straight for me
As I dove under the bed.
My father could not get under it because it was
    a very low bed.

So he proceeded very calmly
To take the mattress off.
In the background, my mother seemed undecided
    on child-abuse, 'cause she was saying,
"Don't hit him on the head.
Because you can make him loco.
If you got to hit him,
Around the legs is good enough.
Don't hit him in the head.
I want him to be *intelligente* when he grows up."
I cringed in terror—suppose Poppa broke my legs.

IX

My father ripped off the springs
And then removed his pants' belt.
It looked bigger than the whip
That Zorro used to make his mark.
I broke into a run.
I became the greatest quarterback in the world.
My father went for me
And I ducked him, cut, and split,
Ran, stopped on a dime, and
Returned nine cents change.
I wondered if Poppa would believe that *peseta*
    had just rolled off the table
And without me feeling a thing had slipped into
    my sock and wormed its way under my foot.

X

My father came after me like Superman,
Faster than a speeding bullet, more powerful
Than a locomotive, able to leap backyard fences
In a single bound.
He was a natural-born athlete
Who played for the Cuban Stars, the Black Stars,
The Puerto Rican Stars—*Olé, olé.*
I had to beat my father running . . .
And then—I was caught.
I tried to smile as I waited for the blows that
    were to come,

But my father just looked at me and said,
"Son, why didn't you ask for it?
I would have given it to you.
Did you have to steal it?"
I just looked at Poppa and began to cry,
My sorry tears ran down my cheeks.
I just stood there feeling like a chump.
What can a guy say at a time like that?

Piri Thomas

1. What does "La Peseta" mean? Is this a good title for the story? Explain.
2. Locate any italicized words that are unfamiliar. Read the sentences in which they appear. Guess the meanings of unfamiliar words.
3. Free write a response to "La Peseta." In a small group share your word meanings and free writings.

Getting It Down

"La Peseta" is one story in a collection of stories about life in Spanish Harlem. Practice your reviewer's note-taking skills on "La Peseta." Begin by giving "La Peseta" a careful second reading. This time through collect notes using the ideas listed on pages 236–239. Make your notes for each of the eight sections as complete as possible.

Checking It Out

Share your notes in small groups before handing them in.

Harsh attacks by reviewers are usually not effective. Vicious attacks are distracting. They shift readers' attention away from the book. Instead of finding help, they find themselves drifting to visions of a nasty person.

Protect your reputation as a reviewer. Use negative criticism in place of an attack. The following Workbench will give you some help:

Writer's Workbench 1

Negative and Positive Criticism

Negative criticism plays an important role in the review. It alerts readers to parts you don't understand. It also tells them about things you simply don't like.

Negative criticism has a positive side. It warns readers about confusing sections or garbled language or writing techniques that leave you cold. It is unfair to your readers to leave out negative criticism. They cannot make a smart decision without a complete picture.

Use these pointers to use negative criticism effectively:

1. <u>Identify the problem.</u>   Be specific. A comment such as "I didn't like this book'" is helpful only if you tell readers why you didn't like the book. Pinpoint specific areas that concern you. The eight sections on pages 236–239 are good places to begin. "The action was sluggish" lets the reader know what to expect.

2. <u>Avoid loaded language.</u>   A statement such as "Only a fool would write this" is less helpful than "I am puzzled by the author's description." The first statement is vague. The second is concrete. It comments directly on a problem. Harsh comments and name-calling have no place in the review.

3. <u>Speak for yourself.</u>   Your supported opinions are valuable. Give readers your views. Avoid speaking for others. "Nobody would enjoy this book" might be phrased, "I didn't enjoy this book. Characters were sketchy. I couldn't identify with them."

Positive criticism, too, can be tricky. Give the author credit for good writing, but don't get carried away. Follow these guidelines for using positive criticism effectively:

1. <u>Identify the praiseworthy.</u>   Be specific about what you like. Use the eight sections on pages 236–239 for help. "Everything in this book was wonderful" is too vague. Sharpen your statement: "The author hooked me from the opening sentence. I couldn't put the book down because each chapter had another family adventure I wanted to be in on. I thought her careful descriptions and believable plot were wonderful." Notice the support given here.

2. <u>Temper your language.</u>   Good reviewers avoid extravagant

praise. "This is the world's greatest family novel" is an exaggerated statement. Unless you have read every family novel in the world and have polled all readers, avoid such praise. Maybe you could say, "This is the best of ten books on the family I have read." Then readers would have a more accurate way of judging your opinion.

3. Share your reactions.   Readers want to know your reactions. If you like something, say so. Don't be timid. Your positive reactions can help readers decide to read the book. Comments such as, "I found the private mother-daughter talks touching. I couldn't help crying when Diane told her mom she was engaged," are honest reactions. They also indirectly give readers more information about the author's skill as a writer.

SPOTLIGHT

Read the following review written by a student:

Silas and Con by A. C. Stewart; Atheneum: New York, 1977; $5.95.

Reading *Silas and Con* left me with many different feelings, for although I thought the theme of the book particularly original and interesting, I did not care for the way it was written. Throughout the book was a sort of heavy, ponderous feeling that sort of dominated over everything else, especially the setting. The author seemed to make the worst of the situation, and whenever Silas had a bit of good luck, it was marred by something dreadful happening, or something going wrong.

On the other hand, A. C. Stewart did a commendable job on portraying the characters. It was very real in my mind as to what kind of personality each one of them had. *I* was Silas when he returned home and found his house empty. I was Silas running in terror from the horrid tinker woman, the blood in my veins frozen in horror. I could see the world from Con's eyes, or feel the evil of the life-like toy monkey. And it was like they were all there as I read.

I would not recommend *Silas and Con* to anyone who does not care for slow philosophical reading. If you should decide to read this book you will probably either quit during the first chapter, slog through the whole thing without really reading, or concentrate till the end. If you get to the end, you will probably neither like it or hate it. You will most likely have mixed views somewhere in the middle.

Sean Christopher Kelbley, Age 12

Sean includes both negative and positive criticism in his review. Consider these questions as you discuss your responses to Sean's book review:

1. What negative criticisms does Sean include in his review? What points does he include to support his opinions?
2. Has Sean avoided using loaded language?
3. Has Sean spoken for himself?
4. What does Sean praise? Is he specific? Is his praise wildly extravagant?
5. Does Sean share his reactions? What is Sean's recommendation to the reader?

Writing the Review

Good reviews help readers make smart decisions. Keep your review balanced and informative by giving both positive and negative criticism. Support your criticism. Share your opinions. Enjoy being the expert.

The following steps will help you write your review. Keep your notes handy. You will want to refer to them.

1. Review your notes.   Go over your notes. Circle any comments that highlight the best part of your book. You cannot possibly use all of the notes you took. Don't try. Use your circles to direct your search. Decide on one or two positive points to discuss. Do the same for negative points.
2. Complete the reviewer's checklist.   Your teacher will provide you with a copy of the checklist that follows. It should look familiar to you, since it is similar to checkpoints your teacher has used to evaluate some of your writing. Now it's your turn to be the evaluator. If you're a bit nervous about passing judgment on someone's work of art, relax. You have done your homework. Have confidence in your intuitions as both reader and writer. Draw on your expertise about the family. Rely on your intimate knowledge of the book you read.

REVIEWER'S CHECKLIST

Reviewed by:

BOOK TITLE: PUBLISHER:
AUTHOR: PLACE OF PUBLICATION:
ILLUSTRATOR: COPYRIGHT DATE:

1	2	3	4	5

Main Characters(s)

Is a total stranger. Is stereotyped. Acts like Ned Nurd or Super Hero no matter what.

Is like people I have heard about but have never met. Is wishy-washy. I can't figure this character out.

Is a friend of mine. Is human. Has both strengths and weaknesses.

Minor Characters

Are flat. My sister has paper dolls with more personality.

Are fuzzy.

Seem real.

Take away from the story. I wonder why the author even bothered.

Escape me. I've already forgotten them.

Add to the story.

Plot

Is foggy. Events baffle me.

Seems unconnected. Reads like a jigsaw puzzle.

Is clear. I know why things happen.

Action

Yawn. Zzzzz.

Is draggy in parts, but okay overall.

Keeps you turning those pages. I couldn't wait to see what would happen next.

Believability

Are you kidding?!!

Is shaky. Some of the happenings leave question marks in my mind.

Could happen. Situations seem true to my family experiences or to those of my friends.

Author's Style

Could use a few hints from me.

Uses a few techniques I admired as a writer.

Uses techniques I'd like to try.

Author's Attitudes

Depress me. The author has a gloomy view of family life and humanity.	Puzzle me.	Leave me feeling hopeful about the family in particular and people in general.

Author's Main Idea

Is there a main idea?	Offers no new slant on the family.	Gives me new understanding about the family.
Is one I'm still searching for.	Is like a broken record. Sounds like a sermon.	Is one I'll remember.

My Recommendation

Wait for the movie.	Read only if assigned.	Don't miss this one.

The best part about this book is:

The author could improve on:

Do you know where to find all the information you need to fill in the top of the checklist? When you open your book, one of the first pages you will find will contain the title of the book, the author's complete name, and the name of the illustrator if there is one. It will also contain the publisher and the place of publication. This page is called the *title page*. Look at this example:

Title

Author
Illustrator

Publisher/
Place of Publication

Sister

By Eloise Greenfield
Drawings by Moneta Barnett

THOMAS Y. CROWELL COMPANY · NEW YORK

The *copyright page* is on the back of the *title page*. It gives the copyright date. Having a copyright is important to authors and publishers. It tells who owns the rights to the book. A copyright prevents others from using a work without permission.

Copyright date

Notice that the copyright date is marked by this symbol ©. There is another copyright date on this page. This copyright date is for a quotation, an epigraph, author Greenfield uses in *Sister*. Because the quotation is copyrighted, Eloise Greenfield asked the author, Lucille Clifton, for permission to use her words. What else do you find on this copyright page? Remember to check the copyright page for any information not included on the title page.

Getting
It
Down

3. <u>Write a discovery draft.</u>   A discovery draft is like a free writing in which you discover what you know. See where your notes lead. Try writing your book review. Don't stop too soon. Let the words rain down.

Look at your discovery draft carefully. Have a classmate look at it, too. Have you included both positive and negative criticism? Does your criticism seem evenhanded and fair? Is your criticism specific? Have you included support? Have you shared your opinions?

~~~~~~~~~~~~~~~~~~~~~~~~~~~~~~~~~~~~~~~

You will want your final book review to be written in language that is clear and precise. Before you begin editing your discovery draft, practice subject-verb agreement by doing the following Workbench:

Writer's Workbench 2

Subject-Verb Agreement

Subjects and verbs are old hat to you. You've been working throughout this book to use concrete, specific subjects and strong verbs. You have learned that the verb is the heart of the sentence.

Find the verb in this sentence:

Grandfather was late for dinner.

The verb is *was*. You can find the subject of a sentence by asking the question: Who or what is doing this? Find the subject in the preceding sentence by asking the question: Who was late for dinner? The answer is *Grandfather*, the subject of the sentence.

● (If you need to review definitions of *subject* and *verb*, see the Handbook, pages H-64 and H-66.)

Now rewrite the sentence changing the subject *Grandfather* to *The grandfathers*.

If you changed the verb *was* to *were* when you changed the subject *Grandfather* to *The grandfathers*, you understand subject-verb agreement.

Grandfather ⟨was⟩ late for dinner.

Singular subject—Grandfather
Singular verb—was

The grandfathers late for dinner.

Plural subject—The grandfathers
Plural verb—were

Simple enough, right? Interestingly enough, subject-verb agreement errors are a common writing problem even among college writers. Look at two common subject-verb agreement pitfalls:

Pitfall #1:   Words between subject and verb

The leader of those boys wears red suspenders.

The verb *wears* is singular because the subject *leader* is singular. The words *of those boys* are between the subject and the verb. Avoid the pitfall of selecting the wrong subject. To be sure, ask the question: Who wears red suspenders? The answer is *leader*. Ignore the words that appear in between. Look at these examples:

1. A box of apples costs $7.95 this week.
   What costs $7.95?   box (of apples)
2. The children from Hope School are visiting.
   Who are visiting?   children (from Hope School)
3. The leaves of the elm tree already have turned yellow.
   What have turned yellow?   leaves (of the elm tree)

For practice, do the following exercise orally with a classmate. Ask the question: *Who* or *what* is doing this? Your answer will be the true subject. Don't be tricked by words in between. Then ask a second question: Is the subject singular or plural? If the subject is singular, select a singular verb. Match plural subjects with plural verbs.

1. One of the students (camp, camps) every weekend.
2. Both of the girls (want, wants) to go swimming Friday.
3. A crate of oranges from Aunt Flora (arrive, arrives) at my house every Christmas.
4. The pliers in that drawer (belong, belongs) to you.
5. The boys from Scotsdale (is, are) pinball wizards.
6. Three pairs of shoes (is, are) all I need to take with me.
7. If my friend down the street (come, comes), may I invite Margaret over, too?

8. A grandmother in a road race (turn, turns) some heads.
9. That twerp in science class (tease, teases) me constantly.
10. The stairs at the back of the porch (need, needs) to be repaired.

Pitfall #2:   *I* and singular *You*

In the preceding exercise, did you notice that singular verbs often end in "s." Though this is often the case, there are exceptions:

> I like to write.
> She likes to write.

In these sentences, both pronouns, *I* and *She*, are singular subjects. Notice, however, that they take different verb forms. Look at another example:

> You have homework tonight.
> She has homework, too.

Again, even though the pronouns *You* and *She* are both singular subjects, they do not take the same verb forms.

Choose the appropriate verb form in each of the following sentences. First find the true subject. Decide whether the subject is singular or plural. Keep in mind that *I* and *You* are unique. Write the correct sentences on a sheet of paper.

1. Do you (like, likes) classical music?
2. No, I (prefer, prefers) country and western.
3. My friends from New York (is, are) into rock music.
4. The girls in gymnastics (want, wants) to form a singing group.
5. Billie in front of the lockers over there (hope, hopes) to be their lead singer.
6. The boy behind Billie and her friends (has, have) a rock group of his own.
7. The guys in his band (wear, wears) unusual clothes.
8. In fact many of their outfits (is, are) outrageous.
9. My favorite outfit of their wardrobe (feature, features) skinny ties and pegged pants.
10. All of the people I know (is, are) betting that Billie's group will select conservative costumes.

● For more information about subject-verb agreement, see the Handbook, pages H-7–8.

CHECKPOINT

Complete the editing steps that follow very carefully. Your teacher will use Checkpoint 6 on page 257 to evaluate your review.

Editing

Your review will be published for all students in your school to enjoy. There is nothing quite like the excitement of seeing your writing in print. Once your book review goes public, your skills as a writer and reviewer are on display. That's why the editing stage is so important. Pull out all stops. Stalk errors ruthlessly. Be prepared to shift or even eliminate whole sections. Be a serious editor. Good editors are partners in the writing process. They help writers strengthen their writing.

Complete the editing stage in small groups. Use all the resources at your command, including your teacher. ● Check the Handbook for advice with special problems.

Before you dig in, listen to all reviews written by members of your group. Don't give any negative criticism yet. In fact, focus on the positive parts only. After all reviews have been shared, start the editing stage by doing the following steps:

1. <u>Evaluate book reviews.</u>   Get feedback in the following six areas. Reviewers should make notes about suggestions made for their reviews.

    Description.   Be sure the review describes the book briefly without summarizing the whole plot. Good descriptions hook readers. They usually focus on spine-tingling action or the most intriguing event.

    Negative/positive criticism.   Look for both. Use the guidelines in Writer's Workbench 1, pages 245–246, to evaluate the reviewer's use of criticism.

    Support.   Find specific support for the criticism that is given. There should be evidence for every positive or negative statement made.

    Audience.   Help the reviewer tailor the review to the students at your school. Be sure simple, direct language is used. Think about audience appeal. Help reviewers hook their audience.

Voice.   Listen for the reviewer's distinct voice. If you can't hear the reviewer's voice, say so. Help reviewers by reminding them of previous writings in which you could hear their voices.

Length.   If the review contains more than three paragraphs, it is too long. The beauty of a book review is that it is tightly written. Help reviewers cut back, if necessary.

~~~~~~

2. Revise.   Revise your paper. Use the suggestions of your classmates to create a compact, solid review. Remember that the key is to help other students make an informed decision about the book you are reviewing.

3. Proofread.   Proofread your review with a partner. Check each other's reviews for correct spelling, punctuation, and capitalization. Check for correct subject-verb agreement. ● Refer to the Handbook or a dictionary or ask your teacher for help with problems, if you need to.

Getting
It
Right

~~~~~~

Publishing

Decide on a publication method that

is handy.   If your reviews sit on a shelf collecting dust, they are no help to anyone. Choose a form of publication students can easily use.

is inexpensive.   Publication can be expensive. You probably will have to make some sacrifices. Eliminate frills such as glossy photos and expensive bindings.

looks good.   After all your effort, your reviews should look good in print.   There are many options that are attractive *and* inexpensive.

is easy to put together.   Find a method that is quick and easy.

will last.   Use a method that will hold up.

Think about these possibilities with your teacher or librarian:

1. Ditto copies.   You can type directly on ditto masters. They will make only about fifty clear copies.

2. <u>Mimeograph copies.</u>   Typed stencils will provide several hundred crisp copies. You could make a silk screen cover.
3. <u>Xerographic copies.</u>   You can duplicate as many copies as you need from a master copy.
4. <u>Laminated index cards.</u>   You may prefer to type your reviews on index cards. These can be laminated to provide a thin plastic coating. Cards should be placed in alphabetical order in a file box near the card catalogue.
5. <u>Bulletin board.</u>   Request permission to build your own bulletin board in the library. Use cork squares. Find a local business person willing to donate strips of wood for framing. Use 6½″ × 4″ index cards or bond paper for your reviews.
6. <u>Book.</u>   Why not make your own book of reviews. Your librarian probably has a book that describes the process step by step. Bindings can be simple and attractive.

CHECKPOINT 6

1	2	3	4	5

Description   ×2=

You've told me the whole story. You may be a budding novelist. I'd like to help you in your role as reviewer.

O-o-h, too much summarizing. Describe. Limit yourself to 25 words.

Yes! Your description is brief and focused. It hooked me!

Criticism   ×3=

Whoa! is a little lopsided . . . too harsh or too sugary. See comments below.

Criticism vague. Be specific. Pinpoint criticism.

Excellent balance of negative and positive criticism.

Support   ×3=

Review the pointers on notetaking, pages 236–239.

Back to your notes. Use more of the evidence you've already collected.

I can find at least three of the ideas listed on pages 236–239. Good support.

Audience   ×3=

Oops! You forgot your audience entirely. See me for help.

You don't seem to have a clear picture of your audience. Check with me.

Strong sense of audience. Your simple, direct language is audience-directed. Helpful review.

Voice   ×3=

I don't hear a sound.

I hear someone else??!

I hear you!

Length   ×2=

Ouch! Your review looks like a short novel. See me for help.

L-o-n-g-i-s-h. Get out the scissors.

Compact review.

Publishable   ×4=

Back to the revision stage.

Back to the proofing stage.

The publishers of this text may be in touch. I'll take your autograph now.

Chapter 13

Post Office Power

Allyn and Bacon, Inc.
470 Atlantic Avenue
Boston, MA 02210
June 10, 198____

Dear Student,

Do you ever get any mail? Think about the most exciting letter you ever received. Maybe it was from the boy you met at church camp last summer. Maybe it was a letter from your grandmother on your birthday (with a check in it)! If you are like most people, getting mail is an exciting event. What is so special about letters? Why does a warm, friendly letter make us feel good?

Maybe it's because a letter comes with your name on it and it's for you and no one else. Someone somewhere sat down and had a talk with you. For a few special moments someone thought of you.

This chapter is about writing letters. You probably already write letters and maybe you don't feel like you need a book to tell you how! We hope this chapter will give you more practice in writing good letters to real people.

Friends,

Dan and Gale

P.S. We like to get letters too!

Writing and Talking

When you write a letter to another person, you are having a conversation on paper. Can you remember a letter you received from a friend? Could you hear your friend's voice talking to you as you read the letter? Could you *see* that person writing the letter? Writing a letter to a friend is having a talk with him or her. You tell your friend what has happened in your life and ask questions so he or she will want to write back.

Letters are as different as the people who write them. They are very personal in style. For some kinds of letters, there are few rules to follow. In fact, the most interesting letters are the ones the writers do strange or surprising things with. Other letters are written to transact business. When you write a business letter you may be unsure of who the reader is so you take more care to follow rules of form and punctuation.

Whatever kinds of letters you write, they are a special kind of writing because the audience is usually one other person.

When you write a letter to a friend, it is helpful to picture that person in your mind. Use your imagaination. Put that person beside you and just talk. You may find you can say things in a letter which you would not have the courage to say in person or on the telephone. When you write letters to persons you do not know, your imagination is even more important. You have to *create* the other person.

All around you are people you never notice. Think about that for a minute. The elderly woman who waters plants on her porch each morning as you pass in the school bus may not catch your eye. The construction worker in a hard hat may go unnoticed. At the red light a police officer may direct traffic without so much as a glance from you. These people are familiar strangers. Who are they? What do they think about? Is the elderly woman somebody's grandmother? Is the construction worker lonely? Does the police officer like kids? Who are these unknown people?

~~~~~~

Letter to a Stranger

Getting It Down

Think about familiar strangers in your daily life. Think of people you've seen before but barely noticed. Make a list of these people. Select one and write an imaginary letter to that stranger. Your teacher may ask you to share your stranger-letters. Here's an example to get you thinking:

```
Dear Man With Straw Hat Who Picks Up Roadside Papers,

    You were out there again today. Just like yesterday. And
the day before. I guess I've seen you there a hundred times
without ever really noticing you. I guess you were just a tree
or a lamp post or one of your pieces of paper. But today was
different. For the first time I really looked at you. Your
baggy grey pants and your run-down shoes and that tired look
on your face made me sad. But you smiled and waved. I waved
back and you were a person to me for the first time. I'll be
looking for you tomorrow.

                                        Your new friend,

                                        Mel
```

How does Mel seem to make contact with the man in the straw hat? How does Mel create a real person from a roadside stranger? Point to places in the letter where you heard Mel's voice.

━━━━━━━━━━━━━━━━━━━━━━━━━━━━━━━━━━━━━━━

Do you ever talk to yourself? In your Writer's Notebook you may kick around ideas and try out new techniques as a writer, but have you ever really just had a conversation with yourself? Maybe you look at yourself in the bathroom mirror and say, "Good morning, you handsome devil," as you brush your hair. Maybe you give yourself a pep talk as you sit down to study for a big exam, "You know you can do it. This is no fun but it's got to be done. Nose to the books. If you do well on this test, I'm going to treat you. An extra scoop of Fudge Ripple for you, kid."

Sometimes people talk to themselves when other people are present. The bystanders witness the conversation but aren't really a part of it. Have you ever noticed people talk to themselves around New Year's? "This year is going to be different. I'm going to lift weights every day. This scrawny seventy-five pound weakling will be a hunk by May. And I'm cutting back on the candy bars, too. No more junk food for this body . . ." People stand around and nod their heads but the speaker is not really talking to them. The conversation is with the person inside the speaker.

If you talk to yourself out loud too often, people give you

strange looks. But someone once said that it's okay to talk to yourself as long as you don't start answering. Look at this letter Lucy wrote to herself.

```
Dear Lucy,

   Why are you always so sure people are out to get you? Relax
a little bit and believe in yourself more. Of course, some
people build up your confidence. There's Mrs. Adams down the
street. Just last week she said, "Lucy, you're the most
persistent child I've ever met." I'm not sure what that means
but she said it between clenched teeth after you had rung her
doorbell five days in a row to ask her to buy a candle for the
band fund. She bought that candle, too.

   Of course, you do have room to improve. Take the pledge.
You'll wash your hair every other night and don't wear those
holey jeans to the shopping center again. It's bad for your
image. And maybe you could even give your parents a break.
Maybe, just maybe, you could turn the stereo down two notches
before they scream at you. And then there's little brother,
Chuckie. He really is a pest and a jerk but he is a little
person, and I guess even pint-size brats have feelings. So
lighten up. And don't do obvious things to provoke him—like
when you see him heading for the bathroom. You don't have to
race in ahead of him and lock the door and stay for half an
hour. You know that's not nice, Lucy. Come on.

   Really Lucy, you'll never win the student of the year
award, but you could do better.
                       Your best (sometimes only) friend,

                              Lucy
```

~~~~~~

Letter to Yourself

**Getting
It
Down**

Now try this yourself. Talk about your good and bad qualities or debate with yourself. Talk about both sides of a decision you must make or raise some questions.

Take out a sheet of paper. Begin with Dear (your name) and just write to yourself. You will not have to share the letter with anyone if you do not wish to.

~~~~~~

There are people all around us doing good jobs who get little notice. When a race car wins a big race, the driver gets the trophy and kisses the pretty girl. But behind the scenes are the grease-monkeys who made the car run. When actors win Academy Awards, they get gold statues. But hundreds of unnamed people work together to produce the prize-winning movie.

<hr>

Who are the people behind the scenes in your school or neighborhood who work hard but get little praise? Maybe it's the custodian, or the cafeteria worker, or bus driver. Maybe it's the people who clean the streets at night or deliver the mail in the rain. Brainstorm a list of some of these people at school or in your neighborhood. Choose one to whom you can write a letter of praise.

Getting It Started

<hr>

Letter of Praise

Follow these steps to write your letter of praise:

1. Make a jot list of specific things that your person does which you could praise.
2. Select the three or four most outstanding things and place a check mark beside each.
3. Write one statement that tells what is praiseworthy about this person.
4. Begin your letter with your statement from step 3.
5. Complete your letter including three or four tiems from your jot list. Use a separate, short paragraph for each new point.

Getting It Down

Before you begin, read how Boots followed the preceding steps to write a letter to Shorty.

Jot list

Knows my name
✓ Calls me "Boots"

Teases me
✓ Keeps cafeteria shiny
✓ Picks up milk cartons I leave behind
✓ Always tells me he likes what I'm wearing
Makes me feel good
Smiles at me
Feels sorry for my teacher

Single statement
You're a special person at our school.

194 Weston Street
Gravely, MA 01442
May 2, 198___

Dear Shorty,

You're a special person at our school. You keep the cafeteria shiny, and you pick up milk cartons I sometimes forget.

That's not the only reason you're special. Whenever you see me you always say, "Hey Boots," and that makes me feel good.

You take time to notice me. You tell me you like my outfit. You say, "Let me borrow that shirt sometime."

I just wanted to tell you I like to come in the lunchroom when you are there.

Your friend,

Boots

1. What are Shorty's special qualities? What is his most outstanding quality?
2. Can you hear the sound of Boots's voice in the letter? In what ways does it sound as though Boots is talking to Shorty?

Writer's Workbench 1

Personal Letter Form

In this chapter you will learn about two basic letter forms. These forms will work for most of the letters you write. Use the form that follows whenever you wish to write in a warm, personal voice, usually to someone you know.

1. Return Address.   Write your home address in the upper right corner. Put the date you are writing the letter under it.
   > 194 Weston Street
   > Gravely, MA 01442
   > May 2, 198___

2. Greeting.   Begin your letter with a greeting followed by a comma. ● (See the Handbook, page H-20.)
   > Dear Shorty,

3. Body.   The main part of your letter is called the body. Indent your first sentence:
   > You're a special person at our school. You keep the cafeteria shiny, and you pick up milk cartons I sometimes forget.

4. Closing.   End your letter with a closing followed by a comma. ● (See the Handbook, page H-20.) The closing can be personal. It can express your relationship with the person to whom you are writing.
   > Your friend,
   > *Boots*

With a partner, work on revising your letter of praise. As you read each other's letters, keep these questions in mind: Do you hear your partner's voice in the letter? Is the opening sentence a specific explanation of the person's praiseworthy qualities? Can you find two or three reasons why the person should be praised?

Checking It Out

**Getting
It
Right**

Revise your letter, using any helpful suggestions your partner made. As you recopy your letter, be sure to use the correct form for a personal letter.

Read your partner's letter once again. Does it follow the form for personal letters described in Writer's Workbench 1? Look at the body of the letter. Is the first sentence indented? Does every sentence begin with a capital letter and end with the appropriate end punctuation?

Greeting Cards

Browsing through the card shop can be fun. All types of cards are there—get well cards to make the sick feel better, birthday cards to celebrate those special days, fancy holiday cards to match the spirit of the season.

People seem to enjoy wandering around in card shops. You can hear shoppers giggle out loud or watch couples hover over a rack of designer cards. People of all ages enjoy selecting just the right card for their special person.

There are as many different cards as there are people. Card designers target their message to a specific audience. Think about birthday cards. There are birthday greetings for little children. These cards may be illustrated with balloons, clowns, or toy trains. There are cards designed especially for teenagers, too. Slim girls and handsome boys sip sodas or are draped across sports cars. Fathers and mothers are not missed either. Think of the pictures and greetings used for cards to parents from their children. Describe birthday cards parents give to each other. Talk about birthday cards to grandparents from their grandchildren.

Designers know people have different personalities. They design soft, gentle cards for the romantic, and sentimental ones for the soft-hearted. Witty cards are created for people who like humor. Bold cards are on the racks for the outgoing.

Some cards are traditional. They are the Happy Birthday variety. Others are less conventional. These cards are usually long and narrow. Card designers use slick covers and experiment with surprising ways to express greetings. Here is a contemporary birthday card:

Do you like greeting cards? Which ones are your favorites. Think about a close friend, a parent, and a teacher. Which type of card would you select for each?

Design a Card

Getting
It
Started

You probably have a friend somewhere who owes you a letter. Or maybe there's someone you know who you'd like to hear from. Design a PLEASE WRITE ME card to stir that person into sending you a letter. Follow these steps:

1. <u>Think of a person you haven't heard from lately.</u> Consider your friend's age, interests, and personality. Jot down a few key words to describe this person.

2. <u>Brainstorm.</u>   In a group brainstorm a variety of appeals to hook that non-writing friend. Maybe a humorous approach would work: "I'm getting cramped camping out in my mailbox waiting for your letter." How about a serious, straightforward threat? "If you don't write me, I'll never write you again." Or perhaps you could voice a friendly concern: "It's been a long time since I heard from you. Are you still my friend?" See what you and your classmates can come up with.

~~~~~~~~~~~~~~~~~~~~~~~~~~~~~~~~~~~~~~~

**Getting
It
Down**

3. Write a message for your card. ,   Keep it short, simple, and to the point.
4. Design a format for your card.   Create a way to make your message more dramatic.
5. Make a dummy of your card.   Be sure to include every detail you plan to use in your real card. Don't put the drawings in yet, but do draw blocks where the illustrations belong. Include your message. Check your spelling.
6. Use construction paper to make your card.   Illustrate it with pictures from magazines or create drawings of your own. For now simply pencil in your words.

~~~~~~~~~~~~~~~~~~~~~~~~~~~~~~~~~~~~~~~

**Checking
It
Out**

7. Have a friend carefully review your card.   Look for mistakes in words you may have copied hastily. Go over your words with a thin-tipped magic marker.
8. Mail your card to your reluctant writer-friend.   See if it gets results.

~~~~~~~~~~~~~~~~~~~~~~~~~~~~~~~~~~~~~~~

Voices

When you write a letter, you put your reader beside you. Your letter is a conversation between you and your reader. Think about real conversations. In person you often use different voices.

Sometimes you shift voices according to the person to whom you are speaking. You speak one way to your friends and a different way to your teacher. Your talk is more relaxed with your parents than it is with the school principal. You use different voices for different people.

Sometimes you change voices according to your message, even when you speak to the same person. When you're angry with a friend or your brother or sister, he or she knows it. When you're sad, your voice gives you away. It's hard to hide depression, frustration, or joy.

It is especially important to fine-tune your voice for letter writing. Readers cannot see you. Their only clue to your feelings is to listen for the voice in your letter. They listen for the intensity in your words to know how you feel.

In the activities that follow you will practice using three different voices on the same person. Then you and a partner will choose your most effective-sounding voice. Use one of your brothers and sisters as your audience. If you are an only child, choose a close friend.

One day brothers, sisters, or friends are your trusted allies. The next day they seem more like the enemy. It's hard sometimes to decide how you feel about them. Expressing angry emotions by kicking a wall hurts your foot. Pounding them always leads to trouble—especially if they are bigger or stronger than you. But what are your options? This activity will give you a chance to let go. It will also give you a chance to practice your angry voice.

Brothers, sisters, or friends often make you very angry. Think of something they do all the time, something that makes you want to scream. Or think of something they have done that made you angrier than you've ever been. Think of the situation. Close your eyes right now and remember exactly what happened. Maybe it was the time your little brother flushed your favorite necklace down the toilet because you wouldn't play with him. Or maybe it was the night your sister told your new girlfriend you never brush your teeth. Get mad again. Think hard! Oh-h-h, steam is rolling out of your ears!

The Attack

Blow your top on paper. Take five minutes to say what you feel in a letter. Here's your chance to write all the things you should have said to them. Spill out your anger. Write directly to the person who is making you angry.

Look at Marguerite's letter. Notice how she blasts her brother on paper.

Getting
It
Down

```
Dear Freddy,

    This is your last warning, you little jerk. I told you to
stay out of my room. I mean it. I'm tired of you coming in
without knocking. I'm sick of you taking my things. I have to
look all over for my own things when I want them. I always
find them dirty or broken. If you come in my room again, I'm
```

going to break you into little pieces and stomp your head.
I'll peel your ears down like a banana. I'll slam your lower
lip in a dresser draw. Stay out, creep.

Marguerite

1. Read Marguerite's letter aloud. Listen to her voice. Does she sound angry? Can you "see" what will happen if Marguerite's brother touches her belongings again?
2. Reread Marguerite's threats. Notice that Marguerite hangs on to her sense of humor. Do you think her humorous attack is effective? Explain.
3. Notice that Marguerite leaves out a closing. Why does she do this?

Checking It Out

Read your attack letter to a small group. Discuss how you could make your attack more effective.

Getting It Right

Revise your attack letter. Rework it carefully using the following checklist.

1. Use language creatively. Are there ways to load your language? Can you use loaded labels like "little jerk" or "creep" in place of the person's name? Have you used at least one label? Can you think of better ones?

Is your language vivid? Is it crystal clear? Can you hear your own voice? Do your words leap off the page or lie there flat?

2. Try shorter sentences. Are your sentences abrupt? Is your message delivered in tight, clipped words? Get to the point. Arrange your words in short sentences that have impact. Sprinkle some short sentences throughout your paper.

3. Experiment with repetition. Are there certain points you want to make? Repeat key words and phrases to stress your main points. Have you used any repetition? Have you tried repeating your point by restating it in several ways?

Attacking a person on paper is like going a few rounds with a punching bag. You feel better and nobody gets hurt. But people aren't punching bags. They do have feelings. In a family, harsh attacks can backfire. Feelings can get hurt and angry emotions can surface. Talk about the ways brothers, sisters, or friends might react to The Attack.

~~~~~~~~~~~~~~~~~~~~~~~~~~~~~~~~~~~~~~

Firm but Gentle

Write a second letter defusing your anger. Pull in your fangs. Retract your claws. Try to make strong points by attacking the problem, not the person. Be firm but gentle. Suggest behavior you would find more acceptable. Show a spirit of compromise.

Getting
It
Down

~~~~~~~~~~~~~~~~~~~~~~~~~~~~~~~~~~~~~~

With a small group share your revised attack letters. Then role play the ways your brother, sister, or friend might react to each letter. React as you think he or she would. Get someone else in your group to play your role. As a group, talk about differences between the two letters. Which approach would help remedy the irritating situation in the short run? In the long run? Which approach would you prefer to be used on you? Which approach will you try in the future? Why?

Checking
It
Out

~~~~~~~~~~~~~~~~~~~~~~~~~~~~~~~~~~~~~~

In your attack letter you gave your brother, sister, or close friend a piece of your mind. But how would you react if this same person got hurt? Imagine that this person needs comforting. Maybe you can remember a time your brother or sister was suffering. It might have been a time he or she got into trouble or had no one to play with. Be this person's best friend. Close your eyes and see what is happening. You see sad eyes. You feel so sorry!

~~~~~~~~~~~~~~~~~~~~~~~~~~~~~~~~~~~~~~

The Caress

Write your person another letter. Try a gentle voice. Caress your person with soothing words. Soften his or her heart-ache.

Getting
It
Down

Dear Freddy,

    I know you're wishing you had been more careful. I know
that you didn't mean to slam the baseball into Mr. King's car
door. It was an accident, but nobody will listen. Disappoint-
ing Mom makes you feel sad. Things can be lonely around here
when nobody is speaking to you, but I'm still your friend. I
know you didn't do it on purpose, and I can see how sorry you
are. Mom's just a little upset right now. When you tell her
you want to pay for the damage out of your allowance, she'll
be so proud. Don't worry. Everything's going to be all right.
Mom loves you, and she always forgives.
                    Love,
                         Marguerite

1. Why is Freddy depressed? How does Marguerite respond
   to his feelings?
2. Does Marguerite seem to understand her mother's
   position? Explain.
3. Marguerite likes Freddy's plan to pay for the damages.
   What do you think?
4. Read Marguerite's letter aloud. Do you think her Caress
   sounds soothing? Look at her closing.

Writer's Workbench 2

Sentence-Combining

Do your sentences in "The Caress" jerk along or do they seem to flow? Your sentences should wind around the hurt your person is feeling. Longer sentences are more soothing than short, choppy ones. Look at these sentences from Marguerite's letter:

1. It was an accident, but nobody will listen.
2. Things can be lonely around here when nobody is speaking to you, but I'm still your friend.
3. I know you didn't do it on purpose, and I can see how sorry you are.
4. Mom loves you, and she always forgives.

Each sentence contains two shorter thoughts as shown in this example:

> It was an accident, but nobody will listen.
> > It was an accident.
> > Nobody will listen.

What are the two shorter thoughts within sentences 2–4? What word(s) does Marguerite use to combine these two thoughts into one longer sentence?

On a separate sheet of paper combine the two shorter thoughts in each group that follows into one longer sentence. Use the sentence-combining cues to help you. If you need to review the cues (,and) and (,but), refer to Writer's Workbench 2, page 26.

1. Aunt Mary is going to have a baby.
    My cousin hopes it will be a girl.   (, and)

2. My cousin, Sue, is an only child.
    She is not spoiled.   (, but)

3. She knows siblings can be pests.
    She doesn't care   (, but)

4. I think Sue is crazy.
    She won't listen to me.   (, but)

5. Sue is excited about having a brother or sister.
Nothing I can say will change her mind.   (, and)

This is one way to lengthen your sentences into smooth, flowing ones. When you revise your letter, experiment with this pattern. Include at least two sentences combined by the words *and* or *but*.

**Checking
It
Out**

Now try your "Caress" on a small group. Have them give you some honest feedback. Does your "Caress" communicate understanding? Is your letter like a soothing symphony or does it sound more like a machine gun? Does your letter have a gentle rhythm and even pace?

**Getting
It
Right**

Revise your letter, using any helpful comments made by your group. In your revised letter, remember to:

communicate understanding.   Do you let your person know you understand? Just knowing somebody senses your pain or sees your side can be a comfort. Imagine how your person feels. Concentrate on those feelings. Notice the opening sentences of Marguerite's letter. She spends some time just letting Freddy know she understands how he feels.

use soft words.   Listen to your words. Are there other words that would sound more gentle, less harsh? Use some of your skills as a poet to give a gentle rhythm to your words.

use longer sentences.   Listen to your sentences. Are they smooth and flowing? Combine any short, jerky sentences as you did in Writer's Workbench 2.

So far you have tried "The Attack", a "Firm but Gentle" approach, and "The Caress." With siblings and friends sometimes bullying works. Sometimes babying helps. But there are times when you need a more sophisticated voice.

At times *you* need help. If you're hanging a poster in your room, you can't hold it up, tape it to the wall, and check to see if it's straight at the same time. It's nice to have someone's help. Sometimes you want someone to do something he or she may not want to do. Maybe your sister is curled up with a good book and plans to stay that way. Maybe your father says you can go to a movie but only if your brother goes, too. Often you need support. You know if your sister, alias The Whiz, tells your stepmother how tough school is, she won't be as upset about your "D."

~~~~~~

The Appeal

Think of some situation where you need to appeal to someone. Make it real. Think of something you actually want to borrow or some place you really want a brother, sister, or friend to take you. Come up with an idea you want this person to accept. Use your most convincing voice in a letter.

Getting
It
Down

Dear Freddy,

You got the electronic game you've been wanting. I'm glad. You're a good kid. I helped Mom pick the best model for my favorite brother. Frank is coming over after school. I was wondering if I could borrow your game. I know how generous you are. I will take good care of it. I won't let anyone but Frank touch it and I'll guard it with my life. You know how reliable I am. Please let me use your electronic game. If you do, we'll play any game you want tonight. Tonight will be your night, Fred.

Your favorite sister,

Marguerite

Read through Marguerite's first draft of her letter. Look at the appeals she uses. Glance back at the advertising appeals in Chapter 4, pages 56–58, to refresh your memory.

1. Which appeals does Marguerite use? How does she use them?
2. What do you think of Marguerite's sales pitch? What are some other appeals that might work?

3. Does Marguerite use any appeals that are not listed in Chapter 4? Explain.
4. Think of ways Marguerite might improve her Appeal voice.

~~~~~~

**Checking
It
Out**

Test your letter of appeal on a small group of classmates. Get feedback. Are they convinced?

~~~~~~

**Getting
It
Right**

Rethink your "Appeal" based on the feedback you received. Manipulate your "Appeal." Reshape it. To help you rework your "Appeal" so that it is irresistable, use the following suggestions:

1. <u>Analyze.</u>   Think about your person. Is he or she softhearted? Coldly logical. Use this information to decide which appeals will be most effective.
2. <u>Anticipate.</u>   Think of all the arguments your person will raise. Short-circuit these. If you're sure he or she will say you're too young, explain how mature you are. If your person worries about the care of belongings, make a point of mentioning how responsible you are.
3. <u>Select.</u>   Choose appeals that have the greatest chance of working. Use more than one appeal. If one approach fizzles, you'll have a back-up.
4. <u>Shape.</u>   Woo your person. Deliver your sales pitch. To make your appeal more convincing, shape it up. Do you use sentence patterns that are roughly the same? Look at Marguerite's appeal. Notice how many times she begins with a subject, usually *I* or *You*, and immediately follows the subject with a predicate:

> <u>I helped</u> mom pick the best model for my favorite brother.
> <u>I was wondering</u> if I could borrow your game.
> <u>I know</u> how generous you are.
> <u>You know</u> how reliable I am.

Marguerite speaks directly. Her subject-verb pattern gives her appeal a sense of frankness. Her appeal is straightforward, almost businesslike. Will this pattern work for you? Is there a pattern better suited to your appeal! Experiment. One word of caution: Don't overdo it. Include enough sentence variety to keep your appeal from becoming boring. The same sentence pattern repeated over and over could put your person into a deep sleep.

SPOTLIGHT

Read this excerpt from *The Soul Brothers and Sister Lou*. What appeals does Louretta use on her mother? Notice how Louretta anticipates her mother's reactions. Point out places Louretta shifts gears when her appeals don't work. How does Mrs. Jackson give added support to Louretta's appeals? What do you think of Louretta's tactics? Recall and share a time you convinced a parent to see things your way.

"But don't you fret, Rosetta Hawkins. Just try it my way next time. Take it easy, don't try so hard, and you'll do much better. Just like I'm always tellin' you about this old house and these children. Leave 'em be once in a while and enjoy yourself. They'll be better for it, and so will you."

Louretta saw an opportunity. "Don't you think Momma deserves a Saturday night out, Mrs. Jackson?"

"Why, sure, child," Mrs. Jackson said. "That's what I've just been tellin' her. All work and no play makes the soup taste flat."

Louretta didn't think that was exactly the way the proverb went, but she didn't want to quibble about it just then. "Well, will you please ask Momma to come to our dance next Saturday night? And you come too, Mrs. Jackson."

Momma looked up wearily from her Bible. "Louretta, if you don't stop pestering me about that dance, you'll be sorry. I told you, I don't have time for that kind of foolishness. I'm already behind with the Lord's work."

"Maybe this is the Lord's work too, Rosetta," Mrs. Jackson rebuked gently. "Let's hear what these youngsters are up to."

"Well" Louretta began, "you know we have a music group that meets at my brother's building."

Mrs. Jackson nodded. "Yes, and it's been a fine thing for Jethro. That boy was always so *restless*. But lately he seems to have calmed down some, now he has that place to go to."

"We have a piano and a music teacher and everything. We even compose our own songs," Louretta said proudly, then regretted it under her mother's stern gaze. *Pride is the deadliest of the seven deadly sins. Beware of vanity. Ask the Lord to humble you.*

"Well, anyway," she went on quickly, "this teacher said he would teach the boys to play instruments, and we're giving the dance to raise money to buy them. I think it would be good to have some grown-ups at the dance, just to make sure everything goes all right. And I want you both to come"

Louretta paused, then thought of the final remark that would be sure to remove any remaining doubt from Mrs. Jackson's mind. "Jethro wants to learn the trumpet," she said. "I hope he gets one. I think he's very talented."

"Sho he is," Mrs. Jackson said with pride. "Rosetta, you come on and stir yourself and go to that dance with me. These children are trying to do something fine, and we ought to help them."

"How can I leave this house?" Momma demanded indignantly. "It's different with you, your children are grown. But I have five under twelve. And one of them not yet a year old."

"What's wrong with that lazy oldest girl of yours?" Mrs. Jackson retorted. . . . Let her look after the children.

Momma was getting desperate for an excuse. "I don't have a thing to wear," she said.

"Patch something together, then," Mrs. Jackson said. "Nobody's going to be looking at two old hens like us anyhow. 'Course I *might* get out on the floor one time and cut me a rug."

Holding her skirt up with one hand, Mrs. Jackson did a few steps that must have been from an ancient dance, though they were not too far removed from the Monkey.

Louretta had a hard time restraining her giggles. Momma was scandalized. "Jerutha Jackson, I thought you'd have sense enough to act your age by now."

"Oh, fooey," Mrs. Jackson said, with a fine, nimble pirouette. "What's age? I like to get out and be around young people. They make *me* feel young. They'd do you good, too. You've been cooped up in this house too long."

"Well," Momma said uncertainly.

Louretta clapped her hands delightedly.

"I haven't said yes yet," Momma said with an angry glance at Louretta.

But Mrs. Jackson was already making plans. "What we'll do," she said, "is sell some refreshments to help these children get the money they need. I'll make a mess of fried chicken, and potato salad, just like I always do for the church suppers. You won't have to cook a thing, Rosetta. Since you're much too old for dancing, you can just sit behind a table all night and sell food."

Momma stood up with an indignant sparkle in her eyes. She looked thirty-five at the most.

"I can dance you into a corner any day," she told Mrs. Jackson. "What's more, I can prove it. Louretta, where are those new records William brought home the other day? You know the ones I mean—the real jumpy ones, 'Shooby Doo' and 'Looby Lou,' whatever they're called."

"I'll get them!" Louretta cried, and ran to the front room, eager to turn off the machine that brought upsetting strangers into the house and turn on the one that would make it happy again.

Kristin Hunter

Rework Louretta's appeal into a convincing letter. Share your letters in a small group. Select one letter from the group to share with the class.

**Getting
It
Down**

Reviewing Your Voices

Join a small group. Review your "Attack," "Caress," and "Appeal" letters. Which voice seems to be your strongest? Which letter sounds like a real conversation between you and the person to whom you wrote? Decide on one letter. Give it to that person. Share his or her reaction with the class.

**Checking
It
Out**

The Broken Product

People in the business world are anxious to keep their customers. One way they do this is by helping customers who have complaints. Good business people want to show customers that the company believes in its product. So before you decide never to shop at a store again or ever do business with a company a second time, try putting your complaint into written form.

Look around your home for something that doesn't work well or for some product that doesn't work at all. Maybe it's that blender your mother gets disgusted about. It could be the lamp your father tried to fix but couldn't. It might even be the chain that keeps slipping off your bicycle.

Be sure you have a legitimate complaint. A legitimate complaint is one where the company or the product is at fault. If your bike has a bent fender because you threw it down on the cement instead of using the kick stand, the scratches are your fault. If the toaster burned out after your family used it for ten years, it is probably worn out. Consider the average life of the product. Be reasonable. If you select a pair of tennis shoes with a split down the side, be sure you haven't had them more than a month.

When you send a letter of complaint, you want immediate action. Avoid possible delays by gathering all important information before you begin writing your letter of complaint. Gather information by completing the following steps. Ask for help if you need to.

1. <u>Look for a model number.</u>   If your product is clothing, look for a stock number. Write that down. It may help to give a brief description of the product if you can't find these numbers.
2. <u>Try to find the receipt.</u>   If you can't find the receipt, ask your mother or father if they will give you a copy of their cancelled check. If the item was charged, find the charge slip.
3. <u>Copy down the date of purchase.</u>   Be sure to include the year.
4. <u>Check to see if there is a warranty or other type of guarantee.</u> Some companies give a written promise of guarantee. Copy down the guarantee number and the date if you find one. <u>Helpful hint:</u> Whenever possible, make a copy of sales receipt, cancelled check, charge slip, or guarantee. Include these copies in your letter. Never mail the originals. If they get misplaced at the company, you have lost your proof of purchase. Then you're sunk.
5. <u>Find the complete name and address of the company.</u>   Check

the phone book, the guarantee, or the sales slip.
6. <u>See if you can get the name of the customer service manager,</u>
<u>department manager, or president.</u>   Address your letter to the
person in charge, if possible.

~~~~~~

Before you begin writing your letter, complete the following
four steps:

**Getting
It
Started**

1. Word your main complaint in one short sentence. You
    will begin your letter with this statement.
2. Prepare a jot list. Write down specific support for your
    complaint. For example, jot down things your product
    does that it should not do. Note special quirks. Choose
    two or three support statements and place a check mark
    beside them.
3. Write down exactly what you want the company to do.
4. Decide on some appeal. List convincingly reasons why
    the company should go along with the demand you
    made in step 3. Place an asterisk (*) beside your most
    convincing appeals.

Following are the notes Annette made as she completed the
preceding four steps. Use these as a guide for writing your
own notes.

Statement

I would like to register a complaint about your can opener,
model #412.

Jot list

✓ Can opener is a pain.
  Won't work right.
✓ Cutting wheel misses spots.
  Sometimes it works, sometimes it doesn't.
  It makes me angry.
  I have to hunt for the hand crank can opener.
✓ The hand crank model cost 89¢ and works better than
  the $35 electric can opener.

Demand

I want my money back or I want a new can opener.

Reasons

* Can opener only 3 months old.
  Guaranteed for 6 months.
* I have receipt.
  I have guarantee.
  I'll quit shopping with you.
  I'll tell all my friends you're terrible.
  I couldn't get help from sales clerk.
* Sales clerk told me to contact you.

~~~~~~

Using her notes, Annette wrote the following letter:

> 400 Lexington Heights
> Aiken, MINN 14852
> February 28, 198___
> (612) 444-2210

Customer Service Manager
Kitchen Products, Inc.
7784 Industrial Blvd.
Chicago, ILL 75821

Dear Manager:

   I would like to register a complaint about your can opener, model #412. We purchased your can opener February 2 of this year at a local department store.

Using your can opener is inconvenient. In fact it is often more trouble than it is worth. The cutting wheel does not cut the top off. I end up having to use my old-fashioned hand-crank can opener on most cans.

I tried to return your product to the department store where we bought it. I had my receipt and the guarantee. I am enclosing copies. The store clerk said I should write to you.

I think it is only fair that I get my money back or get a new can opener. I would like to hear from you soon.

Very truly yours,

Annette Johnson

Annette Johnson

Enclosures 2

1. Is Annette's complaint legitimate? Explain.
2. Where does Annette's main statement appear?
3. Find three or four statements of support.
4. What does Annette want the company to do? What reason(s) does she give?
5. If you were the customer service manager, how would you react to Annette's letter?

Writer's Workbench 3

Business Letter Form

Annette's letter is a business letter. This letter form is much like the one described in Writer's Workbench 1, page 265. There are a few additional points to remember. One reason for the differences is the difference in subject matter. You will use this letter form when you write about less personal matters. In the letter of complaint your subject is serious. You mean business. By using this form you signal your seriousness to the reader. Follow these guidelines. Look back at Annette's letter to judge the amount of space to leave between items.

1. <u>Return address.</u>   Write your return address and the date of the letter in the upper right corner. You may also wish to include your telephone number.

> 400 Lexington Heights
> Aiken, MINN 14852
> February 28, 198___
> (612) 444-2210

2. <u>Inside address.</u>   Write the company's name and address in the left corner. If you know the person's name and title, use them. If you do not know the name, simply use the title.

> Customer Service Manager
> Kitchen Products, Inc.
> 7784 Industrial Blvd.
> Chicago, ILL 75821

3. <u>Greeting.</u>   Your greeting will look almost like the greeting in a personal letter. The only difference is the mark of punctuation that follows it. Use a colon (:) instead of a comma(,). ● (See the Handbook, page H-22.)

> Dear Manager:

4. <u>Body.</u>   Indent each paragraph. Make your letter as brief as possible, but include all important information.

> I would like to register a complaint about your can opener, model #412 . . .
> Using your can opener is inconvenient. In fact it is often more trouble . . .
> I tried to return your product to the department . . .

5. <u>Closing.</u>   Make your closing businesslike. Signing "Love," or "Friend," would be too informal. You want to be convincing but polite. *Print or type* your name beneath your signature.

> Very truly yours,
>
> *Annette Johnson*
>
> Annette Johnson

6. <u>Enclosures.</u>   One way to keep your letter short is to include only essential facts. Enclosed copies of documents contain extra information. The word "Enclosure" alerts the reader to look inside the envelope. Show the reader how many enclosures should be

inside. Place this information in the bottom left corner.
Enclosures 2

Letter of Complaint

Use the notes you have gathered to write your own letter of complaint. Write your letter in correct business letter form. Keep your letter brief. State your complaint clearly and quickly. Make your demand.

Be polite. The best letters of complaint are direct but polite. "The Attack" can only backfire. Ranting and raving only weakens your letter. Assume that the company is a good one. Expect the company to follow your suggested action. Show the company that you are cool-headed and confident.

Getting It Down

Revise your letter with the help of a partner. Read each other's letters. Is there an opening sentence that states the complaint? Can you find a specific example or two? Does your partner's letter include a request for action? Is good support for the demand included? Is the letter brief and to the point? Does your partner avoid "The Attack" or other emotional outbursts?

Checking It Out

Revise your letter using any helpful suggestions your partner made. So that you will have a record of your correspondence, make a copy of your final letter to keep. Reread your partner's letter. Is it neat? Does it follow correct business letter form as described in Writer's Workbench 3, page 283? Double-check punctuation. Look closely at the spelling. Consult a dictionary if any words look unusual. Does every sentence begin with a capital letter and end with the appropriate punctuation? Read the letter aloud. How does it sound? Is it direct and serious? Has your partner avoided "The Attack"?

Getting It Right

Telling Tales

Chapter 14

The Wisdom of the People

In Chapters 11 and 12 you took a close look at the family through reading, sharing, and writing activities. You explored the unique characteristics that make different family types special. By exploring family traditions, holidays, and stories you will have a chance to uncover the rich qualities within your own family.

Did you realize your grandfather's story about his adventures as a boy is folklore? So is the lullaby your mother sang to you when you were a young child. Folklore is the fish story your father tells about the gigantic fish that got away. Folklore is elephant jokes and riddles you laugh at with your friends. Circle games like "Here We Go 'Round the Mulberry Bush," and the jump rope songs you sang on the school playground are all part of folklore.

Because folklore is so much a part of our everyday lives, it is called "the wisdom of the people." This "wisdom of the people" doesn't stop with stories, songs, and jokes. It can be broken down into three large areas and includes many different things.

Social Folk Custom includes family traditions and celebrations of holidays, births, deaths, and weddings. Folk games and dances, superstition, folk medicine, and folk humor are also included in this group.

Oral Lore includes those stories and songs you learned as a child. But it goes beyond them to include proverbs, riddles, folk speech, and the poetry found in hand clapping, jump rope and nursery rhymes, and autograph books. Oral stories are called folk narratives. They include myths, legends, fables, ghost lore, and fairy tales.

Material culture includes things you may see daily. Folk

arts and crafts such as quilting, basket weaving, pottery making, and toy making were originally taught in families from designs and methods not written down. These crafts were learned and passed on orally from parent to child. Material culture also includes family recipes and foodlore not learned from books.

In this chapter you will collect examples of both social folk custom and oral lore. A good place to look for information about material culture if you are interested in learning more about it, is in the *Foxfire* series of books and magazines. These books represent work by high school students from north Georgia in their language arts classes. There are many articles about quilting, basket weaving, building log cabins, and many other facets of material culture.

Folklore belongs to all of us. We are all experts in some area of folklore. No matter where you live or where your family comes from, you have personal experiences and knowledge.

Many years ago it was easier for families to keep and share this wisdom with each other. Families were close units isolated from the rest of the world. Families reserved special time for sharing and talking. Folklore was an important part of daily life. Today television, radio, magazines, and books touch and change our lives. Time reserved for family sharing is often absorbed by the complexities of modern life.

Family-sharing time has not completely vanished. Often families congregate for reunions, special celebrations, and holidays. During these times stories are swapped and jokes are told. In this way folklore is kept alive.

Social Folk Custom

Mark's family came from Scotland several generations ago but they have kept their family traditions alive. Does your family have a celebration similar to his?

Tradition is the seed of tomorrow. And our Christmas tradition, known as the McRae Dinner, has indeed been a seed of tomorrow for many years. This family gathering has traditionally consisted of my great grandparents, their children, their children's children, and so on.

Food is always the center of attention at this gathering. My ancestors are of Scottish origin, therefore, the entire meal consists of food eaten by the Scottish hundreds of years ago. Each individual family brings something different.

This traditional family gathering is held at my great-grandparents' house. Gifts are exchanged and opened, then each child reads a religious Christmas poem. However, this tradition of reading a poem has since vanished. This is one of the reasons my family puts so much effort into keeping this traditional dinner alive each year. Because tradition is truly the seed of tomorrow.

Mark Hall

1. How has Mark's family tradition remained the same through the years? How has it changed?
2. Why do you think Mark calls tradition the seed of tomorrow?

Calendar Custom

A family tradition like Mark's, which centers around a specific date on the calendar, is called a *calendar custom*. It is something your family has enjoyed doing for many years. It remains basically unchanged, sometimes for many generations.

Talk to your parents, grandparents, or other older relatives. Let them help you discover a tradition your family has observed since you were a young child. The older the tradition, the better. This tradition may center around any regular calendar holiday. Think back to the way your family has celebrated Christmas, New Year's Day, Hanukkah, St. Patrick's Day, Independence Day, Mother's Day, or any other regular special occasion. Remember that although many people celebrate these special days, all families have something that they add. Families with roots in China, Mexico, or Sweden will celebrate the same holiday in slightly different ways.

Getting It Started

Family Celebration

You have kept a Writer's Notebook in earlier chapters. Because you will be working with folklore in this chapter, you're going to keep a Folklore Journal. In it you will record

Getting It Down

the information you will gather for the activities and the writings you will do.

Write an entry in your Folklore Journal describing your family calendar custom. Tell what calendar holiday you are describing and how long your family has celebrated this holiday in this manner. Tell about any special things you do, the foods you usually eat, and any other activities that make this day unique.

〜〜〜〜〜〜〜〜〜〜〜〜〜〜〜〜〜〜〜〜〜〜〜〜〜〜〜〜〜〜〜〜〜〜

**Checking
It
Out**

Read your description aloud. Discuss with your classmates how they celebrate this same holiday. What are some similarities and differences?

〜〜〜〜〜〜〜〜〜〜〜〜〜〜〜〜〜〜〜〜〜〜〜〜〜〜〜〜〜〜〜〜〜〜

What Is Folklore?

Let's stop right here and decide on a precise definition of folklore. The examples we have looked at can help us.

1. Folklore is oral.   Like grandfather's stories about his child-hood, folklore is *oral*. That means it was not originally written down, but passed on by people talking to each other. Think back to the lullabies your mother sang you. Chances are she learned them from your grandmother, not a book.

2. Folklore is traditional.   When something is traditional it has been around for quite a while. A family celebration, like Mark's family's, is traditional when it has remained unchanged for several generations. Stories are traditional when the basic story doesn't change over a period of many years within a particular group of people. Does your grandmother have a recipe that has been handed down from generation to generation and is a family secret? That, too, is traditional.

3. Folklore has different versions.   Have you ever heard a ghost story you thought you knew except for a few differences? Folklore comes in *different versions* because all the storytellers who use a certain tale may change it a little by adding to it or taking something away. The core of the story remains the same, but storytellers may change details to fit their audience.

"Cinderella" is a story with many versions. The basic story begins with a beautiful girl who is mistreated by a mean woman with two daughters. Cinderella is not allowed to go to a big social event but, by the intervention of a magical power, she gets a fancy dress, and goes anyway. She meets a handsome man and falls in love, but must escape to be home at a certain time. The handsome man searches for her, finds her, and marries her.

In the many versions of this tale, the details are changed according to the audience. In the best-known version, the girl is a stepdaughter who is aided by a fairy godmother. In the mountain version known as "Ashpet," the girl is a hired girl helped by a witch woman. The mountain girl goes to a church social. Cinderella, the girl in the popular version, goes to a fancy dress ball. The details are changed to fit the listeners.

4. <u>Folklore is anonymous.</u>   Anonymous means that the creator or author is unknown. Folklore is anonymous because it belongs to everyone. Since everyone who tells the story may change it somehow, no one person can claim it. Who made up the elephant jokes or the tall tales? Since we don't know, they are anonymous.

Folk Beliefs

Are you a superstitious person? Before you answer "no," think very carefully about the things you do to bring yourself good luck. Have you ever looked for a four-leaf clover or picked up a penny you've seen on the sidewalk? Do you cross your fingers to keep something bad from happening? Is there a special piece of clothing you always wear to take a test or to play in a baseball game? These are superstitions. At one time or another, most of us have crossed our fingers and carried a lucky charm.

But superstition is more than a concern with good and bad luck. Many superstitions deal with the supernatural—witches and ghosts, nature's signs, and death. Have you ever heard someone say, "Howling dogs mean death"? There are people who do believe this. Another old superstition warns you to cover your mouth with your hand when you yawn so the ghosts won't come in.

Folklorists call superstitions "folk beliefs," because, to most people, the word superstition has a negative meaning. Many people will not admit to being superstitious. They may say they are sometimes, or they may say they have heard of some superstitions, but they will usually not answer "yes." If you took the time to question their superstitions, you would see some types of folk beliefs in almost everyone regardless of age or the amount of education they've had.

Another type of folk belief is the home remedy. Years ago doctors were not always around when people become sick. The family had to learn to treat as many illnesses as possible with things they had available to them. Most home remedies used ordinary kitchen supplies such as honey, salt, and mustard. Certainly the home remedies didn't always cure the illness, but they must have worked some of the time or they would not have continued to be used. Has your mother or grandmother ever given you honey and lemon juice for a sore throat or put a piece of tobacco on an insect bite to stop the sting? These are examples of home remedies people still use today.

In this chapter you are going to interview people to find out what they know about superstitions and home remedies. You will need to talk to people in three different age groups. This will show you if there is a difference in beliefs based upon the age of your informant.

Folklorists call the people they interview "informants" because these people are giving information to them. Since you will be acting as a folklorist in this chapter, you will want to know the terminology, too. There are two important things you need to remember while you are acting as a folklorist. Listen carefully to everything your informant tells you. You will not want to write down something the informant didn't say. Ask your informant to repeat any remarks you don't understand. You also need to show the informants that you are serious about the collecting and that you want truthful answers. Show informants that you care to know what they have to share.

Getting
It
Started

Find at least one person in each of the following age groups: under 20, between 20 and 45, and over 45. You will need to collect at least 20 examples of folk beliefs. Even if one informant can give you all 20 examples, interview the other two age groups.

Recording Folk Beliefs

You may collect either superstitions or home remedies. Don't mix them. Record your collections in your Folklore Journal. If any of your informants tell a story, record it to share with your class.

Ask each informant his or her birthplace, the main places lived, and the highest grade of school completed. You will use this information after your collection is complete.

Use the following guidelines as you conduct your interviews:

1. Superstitions.   Ask the persons you interview if they know of any superstitions. If they do, ask if they have ever seen this superstition work. Remember that superstitions pertain to more than luck. Many occupations have their own superstitions. You may want to work only with superstitions believed or known by people in a particular profession, such as police officers, firefighters, truckers, or farmers. You may want to focus on superstitions that pertain to children, animals, or the supernatural.

2. Home remedies.   Ask your informants if they know any home remedies and if they believe these home remedies work. Ask if they remember ever using one or having another person use one on them. Some home remedies will be for preventing illness; others will be for curing it.

Divide into groups according to the topic you chose.

1. Share any unusual folk beliefs you discovered. Did anyone else find the same or similar belief?
2. As a group, look at the educational level of your informants. Can you see any difference in their beliefs based upon the number of years they have attended school?

3. As a group, look at the differences according to age. Do you see any differences in folk beliefs based upon age?
4. Prepare a short summary of what your group has decided. Be ready to explain your findings to the class.

~~~~~~

Oral Lore

Folk Speech

Have you ever listened to new students in class and wondered why they didn't sound like you? It's possible they moved to your town from other parts of the United States. We all speak English, but every region has certain language differences. Some of these differences are noticeable immediately, while others are so slight, the difference may be overlooked. If you live in California or Illinois, a boy from Atlanta, Georgia, would sound different because of his Southern accent. A girl from New York City would sound different to someone from Dallas, Texas. But, even more than the sound of their speech, these people might speak differently because of the words they use for specific things.

Does your family fry eggs in a frying pan, fry pan, skillet, pan, or spider? All these words have the same meaning. The word you use will depend upon where you live, and which word your family and friends use.

Remember your interview with an older person in Chapter 6? You are going to interview people again, but this time you will be looking at the names commonly used for everyday items. You will interview two people who are younger than 20, two people from 20-45, and two people who are over 45. Because you want to see if there is a difference among the people who grew up in the various regions of the United States, you will also want to ask their birthplaces and the main places they have lived. You will record all of this information in your Folklore Notebook.

~~~~~~

What-cha-call-it?

Getting It Down

Show your informants the twelve pictures and sentences on pages 297–298. Tell them to give you the word they most often use when naming the object pictured. Very carefully record each word in your Folklore Journal. Do not write down "frying pan," if you are given "fry pan." Be sure to record the exact pronunciation, too. For example, if someone were to say "spicket" instead of "spigot," write the pronunciation you hear.

1. 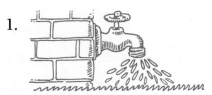   To get water *outside* your house, you turn on the ____.

2.    To get water *inside* your house, you turn on the ____.

3. 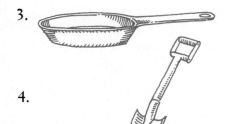   To fry bacon and eggs, you use a ____.

4. 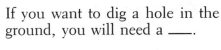   If you want to dig a hole in the ground, you will need a ____.

5. 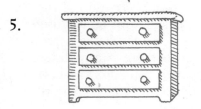   The piece of furniture in which you keep your folded clothes is a ____.

6.    Men wear ____, a two-legged garment reaching from waist to ankles.

7. 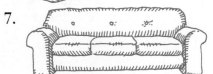   The large piece of furniture which seats several people is a ____.

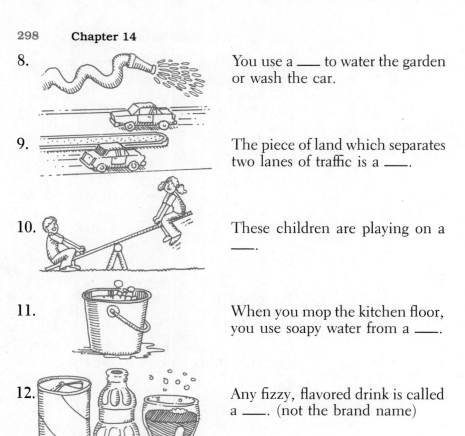

8. You use a ___ to water the garden or wash the car.

9. The piece of land which separates two lanes of traffic is a ___.

10. These children are playing on a ___.

11. When you mop the kitchen floor, you use soapy water from a ___.

12. Any fizzy, flavored drink is called a ___. (not the brand name)

People use a variety of words to name a single object. Did you find any words which surprised you? Which words do you use most of the time? Which words do other members of your family use? Do you consider any of the answers you collected to be old-fashioned? Look carefully at the age groups to see if there is any difference among them. Languages which are spoken daily are in a constant state of change. We are always adding new words to express new ideas and dropping words no longer necessary.

The interviews you conducted may have given you a picture of similarities and differences in people's speech. Look at the answers given by people who have lived in your area for their entire life, and by people who have lived in many different regions of the United States. Do you see any words which seem to belong to natives of a certain area? When a certain pronunciation or a certain word normally appears in a specific area of the country, it belongs to a regional dialect.

Riddles

Do you like to play word games? Riddles are one of the oldest word games known. Riddles are guessing games in which the clues are arranged from the most difficult, most misleading clue to the easiest, most obvious clue.

According to Greek mythology, there was a monster named the Sphinx who sat outside the city gates of Thebes and waited for people to approach. The Sphinx was a monster that had the head of a woman and the body of a lion. When people wanted to enter Thebes, she would ask them a riddle. If they were unable to answer it, she would kill them. A man named Oedipus approached and when she asked him the riddle, he answered it. Can you solve the Sphinx's riddle?

> What has one voice, and walks on four legs in the morning, two legs in the afternoon, and three legs in the evening?

What does the Sphinx mean when she says "morning," "afternoon," and "evening"? Is she really talking about the time periods in a single day? When she says "legs," is she actually speaking of legs every time? These are clues to help you solve the riddle.

Oedipus's answer to the riddle was a human being. A human being crawls on all fours as a baby, walks upright on two legs in adulthood, and may use a cane, an extra leg, for support as an old person.

Many riddles are based on a play on words. This is when a word has more than one meaning and the reader must determine which meaning is correct. A riddle based on a play on words, or a pun, is called a *conundrum*. An example of a conundrum is the riddle, "What has four wheels and flies?" To solve the riddle you must decide what the words mean. In this riddle "flies" doesn't mean to move through the air; it means tiny winged insects. A garbage truck has four wheels and lots of flies!

The creators of a riddle usually know its answer before they write their clues. The answer is the topic. A riddle may be about common objects, qualities, animals, or persons. If you write a riddle about your great Aunt Millie, and no one has ever met her, your riddle will be impossible to solve. That's not fun for either you or the person trying to solve the riddle. But you could decide to write about the president, a local politician, a teacher at your school, or a student whom everyone in your class knows. Choose a topic everyone knows and then carefully select your clues. Then word them to trick your readers.

SPOTLIGHT

These riddles were written by students. See if you can guess the answers.

I share my name with a man who lends money to people illegally. I am gray on top and white on the bottom. There are many different kinds of me. I eat just about anything that moves when I am hungry. I have killed people while they were having fun at the beach. What am I?

Steve

Radiance greater than Hyperion's.
Destructiveness greater than Ares'
Swiftness greater than Hermes'
Like Prometheus bearing fire from
    Zeus' palace
Accompanied by naiads
A crooked spear striking an
    ever-changing target.

Michael

1. Notice how Steve and Michael have organized their clues. Which is the most difficult clue? Which is the easiest?
2. Both riddles refer to people or beings which have something in common with the riddle's answer, but neither riddle is about a person. Sometimes comparing the answer to a different thing will provide a good clue. It will also make you think about the wrong answer. What person is Steve referring to in his first clue? Michael has given a series of clues based upon mythological characters you may have studied. Who are the six mythological beings he uses to explain qualities his subject has?
3. Can you think of any clues Steve or Michael could have omitted or included? Share these ideas with your classmates.

Riddling

Getting It Started

Now create a riddle of your own following these steps:
1. Choose a topic. It may be any object, quality, animal, or person. Don't overlook a topic because you are afraid it is

too easy. Remember the similes and metaphors you worked with in Chapters 7 and 8? You could choose what seems to be an easy topic and make it difficult by using a simile or metaphor in your clues.

2. Brainstorm a jot list of clues. Don't stop too soon! The longer the list, the easier it will be for you to write. Use your five senses. Try to discover a different way to look at the object, quality, animal, or person. If you chose an object, look for words telling how it is used, how it works, or how it was created. If you chose an animal, tell what object it most resembles, how it acts around people, or what it enjoys doing.

3. Now go over your jot list. Which clues are so obvious that anyone could guess your answer right away? If you were describing a lemon, for example, clues that are too obvious might be: yellow, citrus, and egg-shaped. Cross out clues like these. Look at your remaining clues. Do you have three or four good ones? If not, expand your jot list.

4. Arrange your clues from the most confusing, trickiest clue to the easiest clue. Look at Steve's riddle again. His opening clue may fool you if you aren't careful. His second clue is very broad and general because there are many gray and white things. You must add up all his clues to get the answer, a shark.

Michael's riddle also builds to a clue that sums up his answer. The final line is a brief description of lightning.

⚬⚬⚬⚬⚬⚬⚬⚬⚬⚬⚬⚬⚬⚬⚬⚬⚬⚬⚬⚬⚬⚬⚬⚬⚬⚬⚬⚬

5. Now write your clues in sentences, or, if you prefer, create a short poem. Lynn wrote her riddle as a short rhyming poem:

Getting It Down

> What is yellowish-white
> and usually in groups,
> comes out at night
> and makes Zodiac loops?
>
> It is shaped like a jewel
> but yet it is not.
> It sparkles and glows
> because it is hot.
>
> *Lynn*

~~~~~~

**Checking
It
Out**

6. Go over your completed riddle with a partner. If your partner guesses the answer to your riddle too easily, ask which clue gave the answer away and why. Maybe your partner can suggest a change in clue order or wording. If your partner can't solve it at all, talk about your clues. Which clues are too vague? What could be added or taken away to improve your clues?

~~~~~~

**Getting
It
Right**

Fix up your riddle. Then copy it on a sheet of paper. Write the answer upside down on the bottom of the page.

Now share your riddle with your classmates. Either read the riddles to each other or make copies for everyone to keep.

~~~~~~

Legends

The American Indians created many beautiful legends explaining the origin of the animals and plants they found around them. These tales were attempts to explain a world they didn't always understand. The Indians did not have the encyclopedias and books you have available whenever a question arose.

SPOTLIGHT

The following story comes from the Cherokee Indian tribe of Georgia. The story is an explanation of the name given to a spring.

Legend of Thundering Springs

A young Indian chieftain, Bian-wa-wa, lived with members of his tribe in the foothills of Pine Mountain near a crystal-clear spring. On a hunting expedition one day he was wounded and carried to the village of a Cherokee chieftain whose beautiful daughter Theotaska cared for him. They fell in love but the girl's father would not permit her to marry into another tribe.

Bian-wa-wa returned to his tribe alone but later came back
to the Cherokee village and stole Theotaska away to his home,
where a wedding feast was held amid great rejoicing. They
lived together by the spring for several years before a warrior
from a distant tribe came bearing news of an Indian war, and
Bian-wa-wa with his braves again went on the war path.
During the months following most of the young warriors returned, but not Bian-wa-wa.

Theotaska, grieving over the absence of her husband, slowly wasted away and died. She was buried on a knoll near the
spring.

One winter night several years later the few remaining Indians were startled to see a man ride into the village on horseback. The rider was Bian-wa-wa. He had been captured during battle and was just released.

When he learned of his wife's death, his grief was so great that he spurred his horse and plunged down the hillside into the glittering spring below. The Great Spirit, pitying his anguish, let the horse and its rider sink into the bottomless spring and he was never seen again. For many generations the moaning of Bian-wa-wa could be heard beneath the water, like the sound of distant thunder. During the last half of the nineteenth century this moaning stopped and it is believed that Bian-wa-wa has found Theotaska.

1. Why did Theotaska die?
2. Why did Bian-wa-wa not return home for several years?
3. How did Thundering Springs get its name?

This is a story written by Billy to explain how the turtle went through a very big change:

How the Turtle Got Its Shell

When the turtle was young it had no shell, only a dry, gray body. He was also very fast. The turtle used his speed to trick the other animals by stealing food and other things he liked.

One day after tricking many animals, the turtle was walking along when he heard a voice. He turned and there was a man. The man said, "If you trick one more animal I shall punish you," and then he disappeared.

The next day the turtle got up and went out and did his usual trickery, not believing the man. That night the man reappeared saying, "You disobeyed me and now you shall be punished." The man pulled a hollow green rock out of his pocket. It had 5 holes in it. The turtle just stood there in wonderment. Then the man picked up the turtle and squeezed him into the rock and said, "For tricking animals and disobeying me, I put this rock on you. It is heavy and will slow you down forever."

As the turtle got older, it learned to hunt for itself. It also learned to use its burden for protection as he does to this day.

Billy Van Zile

Billy's story has a beginning, a middle, and an end. Look carefully at each part.

1. What did the turtle look like in the beginning of the story? How was it different from the turtles we have around today?
2. Who warned the turtle to change its behavior in the middle of the story? What was the turtle's punishment for disobeying?
3. At the end of the story, the turtle was as it is today. How does Billy describe it?

Pretend that you are a primitive Indian. You have no books, encyclopedias, or science teachers to question. Create a story explaining something in nature.

First brainstorm a list of possible topics. Then choose one topic from your list. You may wish to explain how an animal became the way we now know it, as Billy did. Or you may prefer to explain why there are rainbows, changes of season, or changes in the shape of the moon.

Getting It Started

In your story explain how your animal or natural phenomenon was originally, what caused it to change, and what the change was. Begin by telling where your story takes place. Next, introduce any characters and explain how things were originally. In "Legend of Thundering Springs" Bian-wa-wa and Theotaska were very happily married before Bian-wa-wa went to war.

In the middle of the story tell what events occurred to bring about a change. Bian-wa-wa discovered his wife's death and plunged into the spring.

At the end of your story tell how the events brought about a change in an animal or caused a natural phenomenon. Bian-wa-wa's moaning underwater sounded like thunder, and so the spring was named Thundering Springs. When Bian-wa-wa found Theotaska, the moaning stopped.

Getting It Down

∽∽∽∽∽∽∽∽∽∽∽∽∽∽∽∽∽∽∽∽∽∽∽∽∽∽∽∽

**Checking
It
Out**

Read your completed story aloud to a partner. Your partner will listen to determine whether your story has a beginning that describes what the animal or natural phenomenon was like originally. Your story should have a middle that describes events that brought about a change. It should have an ending that tells how the events caused an animal or natural phenomenon to be as it is today.

∽∽∽∽∽∽∽∽∽∽∽∽∽∽∽∽∽∽∽∽∽∽∽∽∽∽∽∽

Writers Workbench

Adding to Your Word Bank

The following words and terms were used in this chapter. Try to remember the meaning of each term. If you aren't sure, look back in the chapter, find the word, and reread the section explaining its meaning.

folklore (page 289)	calendar custom (page 291)
home remedy (page 294)	anonymous (page 293)
dialect (page 298)	oral (page 292)
conundrum (page 299)	traditional (page 292)
informant (page 294)	folk beliefs (page 293)

Now use the words in the following sentences. Number a sheet of paper from 1-10. Beside each number write the word that best fits in each blank.

1. Something which is spoken rather than written is ___.
2. When the creator or author of something is unknown, it is ___.
3. Many groups of people have ___ celebrations and stories that have been passed on for several generations.
4. A(n)___ is a riddle based upon a play on words, or a pun.
5. A(n)___ is a way people in a certain area of the country speak.
6. The person you, as a folklorist, interview is called a(n)___.

7. —— is called "the wisdom of the people."
8. A(n)—— is any family tradition centering around a specific calendar date.
9. A(n)—— is a way people treat illness at home without a doctor's help.
10. Folklorists call superstitions —— because most people do not like the negative meaning of the word.

Chapter 15

Ghost Writing

In Chapter 14 you became a folklorist and explored a small part of folklore. Did you know that ghost stories are also a part of folklore? Think back to a time when you and your friends tried to frighten each other with scary stories. Maybe you were sitting around a fire at summer camp. It was dark. You could hear dogs barking in the distance, owls hooting, crickets chirping. You just *knew* the ghost in the story would get you any minute. The same story told on a bright, sunny day would not be scary at all.

Now recreate that campfire scene with your classmates. The story of "The Hairy Toe" is sometimes told in other versions. Maybe it was "The Golden Arm" or "The Green Finger" when you heard it. Assign voices, turn down the lights, and do your best to sound frightening.

The Hairy Toe

Voice #1: Once there was a woman went out to pick beans, and she found a Hairy Toe.
She took the Hairy Toe home with her,
and that night, when she went to bed,
the wind began to moan and groan.
Away off in the distance
she seemed to hear a voice crying,
Scary voice: "Who's got my Hair-r-ry To-o-oe?
Who's got my Hair-r-ry To-o-oe?"
Voice #2: The woman scrooched down,
'way under the covers,

and about that time
the wind appeared to hit the house,
Smoosh,
and the old house creaked and cracked
like something was trying to get in.
The voice had come nearer,
almost at the door now,
and it said,

Scary voice: "Where's my Hair-r-ry To-o-oe?
Who's got my Hair-r-ry To-o-oe?"

Voice #3:   The woman scrooched further down
under the covers
and pulled them tight around her head.
The wind growled around the house.
like some big animal
and r-r-um-mbled
over the chimbley.

Voice #4:   All at once she heard the door cr-r-r-a-ack
and something slipped in
and began to creep over the floor.
The floor went
cr-e-eak, cr-e-eak
at every step that thing took towards her bed.

Voice #5:   The woman could almost feel
it bending over her bed.
Then in an awful voice it said:

Scary voice: "Where's my Hair-r-ry To-o-oe?
Who's got my Hair-r-ry To-o-oe?"
(*Said suddenly*) "You've got it!"

Did you notice how the tension built as the voice came closer? The last lines are meant to scare you, not because of the words, but because of the suddenness with which they should be said.

A scary story usually depends upon surprise or mystery to scare you. A scary story is not a bloody, gory tale. The gory tale is only frightening because of grossness. It doesn't have to be planned as carefully as if you were plotting the element of surprise. In a scary story you are left wondering after an unexplained scream or noise. The ending keeps you guessing. A scary story is more difficult to write because you must keep it moving and have a definite plan.

SPOTLIGHT

Many plays are based upon stories writers have heard or read. Troy, a student, wrote a play called "The Silver Hook." He remembered the story from a Boy Scout campout at which everyone tried to outdo friends telling scary stories by firelight.

Assign the parts and read Troy's play aloud. You will need a narrator, an announcer, a boy, a girl, and someone to do sound effects. Turn down the lights and be convincing actors.

Narrator: One night on the way home from a dance, Don is driving through a very old part of the town to take Carol home. Don turns down a dirt road. (*Sound—Car crunching down road*)

Carol: You would never catch me out here at twelve o'clock.

Don: Yea, you're not kidding. (*Pause*) Anyway, why did your parents move out here?

Carol: I don't know.

Don: What time do you have?

Carol: (*Looking at watch*) About ten o'clock.

Don: Well, you don't have to be home until 11:30, so let's listen to some music. (*Sound—popular music*)

Narrator: Don pulls over to the side of the road and turns on the radio. They listen for about fifteen minutes when a radio announcer comes on.

Radio Announcer: (*Offstage*) We have just received news that a prisoner has escaped from the County Prison and he's a killer. He is six feet, nine inches tall, has long black hair, and has a silver hook replacing his left hand. So be on the lookout.

Carol: (*Voice trembling*) Let's go. He could be around here.

Don: O.K.!

Narrator: Don starts the car and leaves fast and when he does there is a loud scream. (*Sound—offstage scream*)

Carol: Oh! What was that?

Don: I don't know!

Narrator: Don takes Carol home and he goes home. The next morning Don goes outside and washes his car, and on the back handle of the door is a silver hook.

THE END

What was the basic story Troy told in his play? Have you heard any variations of this story? Share them with the class.

With a group of classmates you are going to write and present a play based upon a ghost story or mystery. The people in your group will become playwrights, directors, sound effects and props crews, actors, and critics.

The play you will write will be based upon a story you have heard from someone in your group. You may have heard it from another person, or it may be a story you heard at camp, at a slumber party, or late at night in the dark back yard. Remember the distinction between a gory tale and a scary one. You will use surprise and sound effects to make your play scary.

One good place to find scary stories is in the memories of other people. Almost everyone remembers a story that was told on a dark night to scare friends, or the local ghost legend about the "haunted" house down the street or a stretch of lonely highway twisting through the woods.

<hr />

Getting It Started

Talk to a person older than yourself. Ask the person to recall a scary story he or she has heard. Explain the difference between a scary story and a gory one. Explain, too, that the story should be one that was heard, not one that was read or seen at the movies or on television. As your informant tells you the story, take notes so that you will be able to retell it to your group.

1. In your groups share your scary stories. Tell the story your informant told you and any other scary stories you know. Tell the stories in your scariest voices. Ham it up for your group. Everyone should listen carefully.
2. Which stories did you like best? You are choosing a story to rewrite as a play. As a group, choose the two best stories. They should be the scariest ones you heard. They should have characters that speak and actions that the audience will be able to understand.
3. Now think carefully about the stories and the following guidelines. As a group, talk about each area and each story. Use the answers to the questions as your guide for the final choice of a story.

Does the story have a surprise ending or is it just gory?

Does the story need more than two major characters, two minor characters, and a narrator? If so, it may have too many parts to handle in a short play. Your audience may become confused about the actors' identities.

Does the story have more than two settings? Remember the limitations of your classroom or the room where you will present the play. Since your space will probably be limited, you must restrict your settings to make it easy for your audience to follow the action of the play.

Does the story need special effects you won't be able to produce easily in the classroom? This is very important because some scary stories won't work without these special effects. There are some simple things you can do to add that touch of the unknown to your play. You can use sound effects that you have tape-recorded in advance. To make small objects such as hats fly, you can tie a string on the object and loop the string over a light fixture or the film screen. When the object should fly away, a hidden stage hand will pull the string, and magically the object will move through the air.

Once your group has decided which basic story you will use, have someone write the plot on paper so you will have it on hand when you begin writing the play.

Scripting a Play

Look back at Troy's play. What things make a play different from a regular story? The main difference is the way it looks on the page, or its form. Plays tell you how characters should say lines and move on stage. Plays are mostly dialogue, or conversation between the characters. All the lines are identified by characters' names. There is less description in a play than in a story.

Narrator: The Glue in Your Play

In your play, the narrator will be the most important person. The narrator will glue it all together. The narrator will tell you what you cannot see, and explain the many bits of information you will need to follow the play. Troy's narrator describes the scene so that you can imagine that the characters are in a car on a dirt road late at night. Find this description. In Troy's class the students who played Don and Carol sat at two desks placed next to each other to represent a car. The narrator needed to tell the audience that the desks were the car.

A narrator can also explain what is happening offstage. Troy's narrator explains the radio announcer's voice which interrupts the play. Narrators can explain noises heard from offstage, too. Think of your narrator as the person who explains what your audience doesn't see or won't know without explanation.

Characters

Look at the way Troy shows which character is speaking. The name of the character who is speaking is given on the left and is followed by a colon (:). In plays there is no need to place quotation marks around what the characters say.

Sometimes stage directions will precede or follow the characters' words. Stage directions are usually given in parentheses and written in italics or capital letters.

Your characters must sound and act like real people. They shouldn't say or do anything to confuse the audience about who they are. In Troy's play Don and Carol have been to a dance and stop to listen to the radio. They are teenagers and sound and act like teenagers. If your character is an elderly woman, have her say and do what older people do. She would seem peculiar if she read nursery rhymes and Dr. Seuss and rode a Big Wheel. If your characters have lived their entire lives in New York City but speak with a deep Texas drawl, something would seem wrong.

~~~~~~~~~~~~~~~~~~~~~~~~~~~~~~~~~~~~

Describing a Character

Getting It Down

When writing your play you will begin by deciding who your characters are and what they are like. Look at Troy's play again and think about Carol and Don. What do you think they might look like? How old are they? What kind of families and homes do they come from? Use the clues from what they say and do to write a short description of either Carol or Don.

~~~~~~~~~~~~~~~~~~~~~~~~~~~~~~~~~~~~

Share your characterizations with your group when everyone finishes. Which are most descriptive? Which suit the
characters in Troy's play best? Why?

Setting

Much of the information about where the story takes place can be
given by the narrator. Your characters can also give clues. What is
the setting of Troy's play? What do you discover through the
characters' conversations? Troy reveals the time and the lonely,
scary location through Don and Carol's first conversation. The
setting is important to the story. A scary story will seem more
frightening in a location which sounds and looks frightening.
Think back to ghost stories you have heard. Would the same stories
that made you stare into the pitch black night and sneak looks over
your shoulder even make you uneasy at noon on a bright day?

Describing a Setting
The setting is partially described in Troy's play. Use your
imagination and create a description of the setting for Troy's
play. You can model this setting after a place you know as
long as it meets the brief description given in the play.
Remember, the play takes place at night on a lonely road.

When everyone finishes describing the setting, share what
you have written. Which setting is most consistent with
Troy's play? Which one makes you think of a location near
your town or city?

Many times folklore is personalized. This means that the person
who tells the story claims to have been there when it happened, or
knows someone who was. It also means that you add information to

make the story appear to have happened nearby. A story is more scary if it appears to be a local happening than if it occurred on the other side of the world.

~~~~~~

Personalizing Folklore

Getting
It
Down

Read the following ghost story carefully. Rewrite the story adding local landmarks so it will sound as though it took place in your neighborhood or close to it.

The Hitchhiking Ghost

One rainy spring night a university student was driving from Athens to Atlanta when he was surprised to see, hitchhiking along the highway, a lovely young girl dressed in white lace. She quickly explained that she was trying to get home and asked if the driver could help her. Being assured that he certainly could, she got in and gave her address. Because she was drenched she insisted on sitting in the back seat, but she did

accept his proffered coat. The downpour kept the young man's attention on the road, and there was little conversation. Upon arriving at the given address he turned around to find that the girl was gone, but the seat and floor were still wet.

Inquiring at the address he found that the girl had been dead several years, killed while driving home from her senior prom. On the anniversary of her death she is apparently allowed one more try at getting home. The mother of the girl expressed regret that her daughter might have caused him any trouble.

The student was quite dubious about the whole story until he decided to drive to the girl's grave on the following day. There hanging on her gravestone, and still a little damp, was his coat.

Ronald G. Killion and Charles T. Waller
A TREASURY OF GEORGIA FOLKLORE

In your group, compare rewritten stories. What does the addition of local details do to the story? Consider including local details when you write your play.

Checking
It
Out

When you write your play, the words should be clear and easy to understand. Your audience should be able to follow the action of the play without difficulty. One way to make your writing clear is by using pronouns carefully.

Writer's Workbench

Pronouns—Economy Experts

You've been using pronouns successfully since childhood. In toddler days you demanded attention with "I want . . ." and provoked smiles with "Me likes. . . ." Adults seemed to enjoy your creative exploration of language. They didn't seem to worry that you would grow up still saying "Me likes cake" instead of "I like cake."

Those adult intuitions were right. You grew up using language effectively. In learning language you also developed a feeling for pronouns. You seemed to understand the distinction between *she* and *her*, *we* and *us*, and *they* and *them*. You developed a knack for when to say "he" and when to say "him" without formal instruction in pronoun usage.

You can use the intuitions you developed as a child to help you use pronouns effectively in writing. Pronouns are small, but they are workhorses. Without pronouns, nouns bear a heavy load. Pronouns have a special function. They substitute for nouns.

Pronouns are economy experts. They free writers from repeating the names of people and objects unnecessarily. They keep language direct and uncomplicated by eliminating cumbersome repetition.

Pronouns (such as *I, it, we,* and *they*) and their possessive forms (such as *my, its, our* and *their*) are second nature to you now. They are easily taken for granted because they are used so frequently. Read the following passage written without pronouns. Notice the burden put on the nouns.

To Believe Or Not To Believe

Yesterday Karen asked Reggie how Reggie feels about adults encouraging *adults'* kids to believe in Santa Claus. Karen and Reggie discovered that *Karen and Reggie* have opposite views. Karen feels that teaching children to believe in Santa is okay, while Reggie believes the old legend can be harmful.

Reggie said *Reggie* remembered when *Reggie's* brother callously broke the truth to *Reggie.* Reggie said *Reggie* was crushed. Because Reggie thought *Reggie's* parents had been dishonest, Reggie felt betrayed and foolish.

Karen remembered that believing in Santa made the holidays special. Karen recalled *Karen's* dad preparing cookies and cola for Santa. Karen told Reggie that *Karen* tried to be a good girl all year. On Christmas Eve Karen said *Karen* stayed awake as long as possible hoping to see Santa and his eight tiny reindeer. Karen confessed that *Karen* pretended to believe in Santa long after *Karen* knew the truth. Karen explained that Santa made Christmas a magic time of giving for Karen's parent's, too.

Reggie promises *Reggie* will not encourage *Reggie's* children to believe in St. Nick. Karen insists that *Karen* will. How do *readers* feel?

Sluggish, isn't it? The sentences are bogged down in cumbersome repetition. Rescue the passage by eliminating unnecessary repetition. Economize. Rewrite the passage, swapping each underlined word for a pronoun or its possessive form.

Don't let the words *pronoun* and *possessive form* throw you. You are an old pro at pronoun usage. Rely on your writer's intuitions and your reader's ear. Insert words that take the place of nouns.

Read your revised passage to see how it sounds. ● If your pronoun skills are a bit rusty, refer to the Handbook, pages H-5–6.

Special note: Even old pros sometimes confuse these two: *its* and *it's*. *Its* is the possessive pronoun. *It's* is the contraction for *It is*. Don't be fooled. The possessive forms of pronouns do not require apostrophes ('). If you see *it's*, that means *it is*.

Pronoun Antecedents

Pronoun antecedent is a fancy term. Its meaning is really simple though. Remember, pronouns stand for nouns. Those nouns they stand for are called *antecedents*.

Read the following sentence. Look at the relationship between the pronoun and its antecedent.

> *antecedent   pronoun*
> *Cathy* tolerates *her* brother.

In this sentence the pronoun *her* stands for the noun *Cathy*. The noun *Cathy* is the antecedent.

There is a simple trick to finding antecedents. Simply ask: What word does the pronoun stand for? The answer is the antecedent. Try this trick yourself:

> *I* notice Cathy cringe when *her* brother scrapes *his* nails across the chalkboard.

The pronouns in this sentence are italicized. Find each pronoun antecedent by answering the question: What word does the pronoun stand for? Jot your response on a sheet of paper. If your answers look like this, you've got the hang of pronoun antecedents:

Pronoun	*Antecedent*
I	(the speaker)
her	Cathy
his	brother

For practice, identify the pronouns and their antecedents in these sentences. Write them on a sheet of paper. Remember to ask: Who or what does the pronoun stand for? Your answer will be the antecedent.

1. Sonia is having a slumber party at her house.
2. Sonia's mom is usually strict, but she says we can stay up late on Friday.
3. I want to take my own pillow to Sonia's party.
4. My pillow is king-size and it feels fluffier than most pillows.
5. Some of the girls say that they want to have a pillow fight, and I think I know why they want to have it.
6. The girls plan to swipe my pillow when they think I am not looking.
7. The party will be fun even if the girls decide they will hide my pillow.

● For more help with pronoun antecedents, see the Handbook, pages H-5–6.

Confusing Pronoun Antecedents

Readers can't usually ask writers about confusing words or phrases. Where are writers when you really need them? Maybe they're watching a movie, licking an ice cream cone, or shining their shoes, but they certainly aren't around.

This fact puts a special responsibility on writers. Writers have to be as clear in their writing as possible. This is especially true when using pronouns and their antecedents.

Amusing things sometimes happen when writers are sloppy with pronouns:

> When the children showed Ms. Banks the mosquitoes, she swatted them.

Good for laughs but not very helpful. Who did Ms. Banks swat? The children? The mosquitoes? Who knows?

The writer could have made the sentence clearer by rearranging it like this:

> Ms. Banks swatted the mosquitoes *that* the children showed her.

Rearranging the sentence is not always the answer. Doing so sometimes makes the sentence sound strained or unnatural.

Sometimes the writer prefers the original sentence construction. The writer may want to try this second option, eliminating the confusing pronoun:

> When the children showed Ms. Banks the mosquitoes, she swatted the *insects*.

Be sure the pronoun antecedent is clear in sentences you write. If pronoun antecedents are confusing, you may have an unplanned career as a comedian.

On a sheet of paper, rewrite each of the following sentences. First try to rearrange the sentence to make the pronoun antecedent clear. Reread your revised sentence. It should sound natural, not strained.

If the sentence sounds awkward, eliminate the pronoun causing the confusion. Replace the pronoun by renaming the noun for which it stood or by using a synonym for that noun. (A synonym is a word that means the same thing as another word. Example: *Instructor* is a synonym for *teacher*.)

1. When the owner and the burglar collided, *he* leapt out a window.
2. When the woman stooped to milk the cow, *she* tipped over the milk pail.
3. After the ghost entered the old house, *it* ran through the streets in terror.

4. Nora and her aunt chatted and nibbled the cake, crumbs falling to *her* lap.
5. Tony flashed Sam a smile when *he* won.
6. As the bride and mother-in-law calmly sipped coffee, *her* trembling hands betrayed *her.*
7. When the children brought mother the eggs, she beat *them.*
8. After the Red Birds trounced the Blue Birds, *they* slowly crawled to the dugout.
9. As soon as Duke showed Mary the snake, she pummeled *him.*
10. When the mouse scampered up the grandfather clock, *its* sound startled the family.

Make up three sentences in which the pronoun antecedent is confusing. Challenge a partner to clarify the sentences.

Overuse of It

One of the peskiest pronoun problems is the overuse of *it.* A writer leans on the pronoun *it* to carry the entire weight of the passage. Here's an example:

> Sarah put the cat out because *it* was cold. *It* wanted some milk so she gave *it* some. Then *it* wanted to come back into the house, but *it* was too late. The cat disturbed the family's sleep, so *it* had to sleep in the cold.

On a sheet of paper rewrite this passage so the sentences sound clear and natural. Be sure the pronoun antecedents for the *its* you leave in are clear.

Dig up an old writing from your Writer's Notebook. Scrutinize the writing for overuse of *it.* Don't eliminate every *it.* Simply do away with excessive or confusing use of the pronoun *it.*

Play Production Checklist

Your group is almost ready to begin. Everyone in your group should have one of the following special jobs. The entire group will depend upon each person to do the job he or she has been given.

1. Director.   You are in charge of casting and rehearsals. You will look at the presentation and help all the actors give their best possible performance. You will keep order and help see that everyone does the job he or she has been assigned. You will smooth out the rough spots and let your teacher know what is happening in your group.

2. <u>Writers.</u>   It is your responsibility to work with the entire group to write the play. You will check to see that the guidelines for scripting a play (pages 313–317) and writing stage directions (pages 325–326) are followed. It is also your job to give everyone in your group a copy of the play.

3. <u>Sound Effects.</u>   You are responsible for putting the sound effects for your play in order and on tape. You may have to make some of the sounds yourself. You will be in charge of sound effects when the play is presented. Be sure you rehearse using the sound effects tape several times.

4. <u>Props and Costumes.</u>   Props are important to the play because they help make it realistic. You will make up a list of items necessary for your play, and working with your group, find them. Don't overdo your props list. The simpler, the better. Try to choose only one prop for each actor. Use a prop only if it is necessary to the audience's understanding. Many characters will not require anything.

5. <u>Scenery.</u>   You are responsible for setting the stage. You will arrange the furniture. If your group decides to draw a simple background on paper and tape it to the chalkboard, you will get it made.

Most people will not only have one of these five jobs; they will also be actors. Do not do it all alone. Everyone in the group can help to accomplish any job. If the writers are finished, they can help make scenery or props. If the sound effects person has the sounds on tape, he or she can help copy scripts or gather props. Lend a hand wherever it's needed.

Dialogue

Changing your story into a play will require some work with dialogue. Dialogue is simply what your characters say; it is the words they use to tell your story. You will want your dialogue to sound like people talking to each other. Look at Troy's play. How do his characters talk?

One of the best ways to find out how people talk is to listen to people talking. Find a place where two or more people are carrying on a conversation. Some places you might want to try are on your bus or at the bus stop, in the lunchroom, in a room before class begins, at a playground, or at a park. You may want to move around and collect several different conversations.

**Getting
It
Down**

Choose a place where you will be able to write comfortably and hear the conversations clearly. Listen carefully to what is said and write *exactly* what you hear in your Folklore Journal. Don't stop until you have at least one page of conversation recorded. Be sneaky. Don't let people know you're listening. Be a secret agent.

**Checking
It
Out**

1. Read the conversations you wrote down to a partner.
2. What differences do you notice between the way people communicate by speaking and the way they communicate in writing? Do people usually use more complete sentences when writing or speaking?
3. What other things affect the way people communicate face-to-face?

After you and your partner have answered these questions, rejoin your group and compare findings. Be sure that you have evidence to back up what you think.

**Getting
It
Down**

You have chosen a story. You have given everyone in the group a job to do. Now plan and begin writing your play by following these steps:

1. Look at your story. Decide how many characters you will need. Do not plan to have more than two main characters, two minor characters, and a narrator. Each group member should write a short description of one of the characters.
2. Decide on the details of your setting. Write a short description of where the story will take place and any other details necessary to create a setting for the story.

3. Now the writers should write a first draft of the play. Follow the guidelines for scripting a play on pages 313–317. Use your narrator to tell the audience what you cannot show them. Make the conversation sound natural by having the characters say only what they would say if they were real people.

---

4. Read the draft of the play aloud. Do the characters sound real? Does the dialogue flow smoothly? Will the audience be able to follow your story? Rewrite any rough parts. Take the time to get them right.
5. Plan the movement on stage and the emotions you want portrayed. Try out the movements. Remember to have your actors look toward the audience as much as possible so that the spoken words will be clear.
6. Plan your sound effects. The sound effects person will make a tape of the sounds, in order, before the actual rehearsals. To prevent the possibility of doing sound effects out of order, it is usually better to tape them, rather than try to do them "live" during the play. The sound effects should be worked out before the final draft of the play is written so that they can be included in the final script.
7. The costumes, props, and scenery should also be planned at this time. Remember to keep them simple.

Stage Directions

Stage directions are usually enclosed in parentheses. They may be used to set the scene, tell how a line should be read, or give general directions explaining actor movement and sound effects.

In Troy's play, the narrator sets the scene by telling where and when the story takes place. If the setting had been described in the stage directions, his play might have begun like this:

(It is a dark night. The moon is hidden behind clouds. A car moves down a lonely road, slows and stops. Inside the car are two teenagers returning home from a dance at their high school.)

Use either stage directions or the narrator to begin your play.

The second use of stage directions is to explain how a line should be read. The directions tell the actor when to sound happy, when to scream, and when to pause. Look for this type of stage direction in Troy's play.

The third use of stage directions is to tell the actors how to move on stage or to tell the sound effects crew what sound is needed at a certain point. Troy's narrator handles most of this by telling the audience what is happening.

You may not want to use all three types of stage directions. Your narrator can do some of the work. Your group may want to try both methods of setting the scene to see which will work best for you.

CHECKPOINT

Your teacher will use Checkpoint 7 on the following page to evaluate your group's production. Prepare for your production by carefully completing the following steps:

Get ready. . . .

Your writers should be working on the final draft, complete with stage directions. The sound effects crew should be completing the tape needed for rehearsal. The props and scenery crews should know what is needed for the first rehearsal so they will have it on hand.

Get set. . . .

Rehearsals are important. Go through the entire play with all lines, movement, sound effects, and scenery. Act in rehearsal as you would with an audience present. Fix any weak parts. This is your last chance to make your play what you want it to be.

Perhaps you will want to create posters to announce your play and its cast. To form a larger audience, perhaps another class can join yours for a day in the theater.

Go !!!

In the theater, actors never say "Good luck" to each other. Instead, they call, "Break a leg!" Enjoy and give a good show.

CHECKPOINT 7

1	2	3	4	5

Setting   ×3=
This setting doesn't seem to fit the story. Back to the drawing board.

I *think* I know where the play is set, but I'm not sure. You need more scene-setting details.

Good setting! Makes play believable. It's easy to recognize where play takes place.

Characterization   ×3=
Loosen up! Some of you are acting like stick figures. Looks like you need another rehearsal.

Some characters act like real people. Some could use a few pointers. See me.

Characters act like real people. Dialogue, movement, and mannerisms all help us *see* characters.

Sound Effects   ×2=
Did you forget to use sound effects?
                   or
Overdone! Sound effects drown out the play.

A few unnecessary delays. Who's in charge?

No unnecessary delays. Well rehearsed. Great sound effects.

Props   ×2=
Too many props. Keep it simple.
                 or
Where are your props?

Some props get in the way of the actors.

Props are simple and handled smoothly.

Scenery   ×2=
Where is it? Give us a few hints.

Scenery looks good generally. You could have spent more time to get a professional look.

Scenery is appropriate. It adds to the play.

Plot   ×4=
I'm having a hard time following this. Try writing out the play step-by-step. Let's go over it together.

I can usually follow what's happening. Some spots are confusing.

Your story line is easy to follow. The action moves logically.

Practice   ×4=
Oops! Looks like you're playing it by ear. Back to rehearsals.

Most actors seem to know what to say when. Did a few miss practice?

Actors know what to do on stage. A solid performance!

Acknowledgments

Grateful acknowledgment is made to the publishers, authors, or copyright holders for permission to use and adapt the following materials in this book:

Atheneum Publishers: Excerpt from *Very Far Away from Anywhere Else* by Ursula K. Le Guin. Copyright © 1976 by Ursula K. Le Guin. Reprinted by permission of Atheneum Publishers.

Joan Blackburn: "The Unemployment Bureau" from *The Cities* by Paul Blackburn (Grove Press, 1967). Copyright © 1967 by Paul Blackburn.

Cherokee Publishing Company: "The Legend of Thundering Springs" and "The Hitchhiking Ghost" from *A Treasury of Georgia Folklore* by Ronald G. Killion and Charles T. Waller. Used by permission of Cherokee Publishing Company, Atlanta, Ga.

Thomas Y. Crowell, Publishers: Title and Copyright pages from *Sister* by Eloise Greenfield. Courtesy of Thomas Y. Crowell, Publishers.

Delacorte Press: Excerpt from the book *Can You Sue Your Parents for Malpractice?* by Paula Danziger. Copyright © 1979 by Paula Danziger. Reprinted by permission of Delacorte Press; "The Chinese Checkers Players" excerpted from the book *The Pill Versus the Springhill Mine Disaster* by Richard Brautigan. Copyright © 1968 by Richard Brautigan. Reprinted by permission of Delacorte Press/Seymour Lawrence; Excerpt from the book *A Figure of Speech* by Norma Fox Mazer. Copyright © 1973 by Norma Fox Mazer. Reprinted by permission of Delacorte Press.

Dennis Dobson Publishers: "The Hippopotamus" from *Creatures Great and Small* by Michael Flanders and Marcello Minale.

Doubleday & Company, Inc.: "December" by Sanderson Vanderbilt from the book *Creative Youth* by Hughes Mearns. Copyright 1925 by Doubleday & Company, Inc. Reprinted by permission of the publisher; "The Mittens My Grandmother Made" copyright © 1976 by Hanging Loose; originally appeared in *Hanging Loose*, No. 28, August 1976, from the book *The Hocus-Pocus of the Universe* by Laura Gilpin. Reprinted by permission of Doubleday & Company, Inc.

Follett Publishing Company: Excerpt from *All-of-a-Kind Family* by Sydney Taylor. Copyright 1951 by Sydney Taylor. Used by permission of Follett Publishing Company.

Michael Gessner: "In a Moment" by Michael Gessner. Used with permission of Michael Gessner.

Harcourt Brace Jovanovich, Inc.: "Drowsy" from *The Complete Poems of Carl Sandburg*, copyright 1950 by Carl Sandburg; copyright 1978 by Margaret Sandburg, Helga Sandburg Crile, and Janet Sandburg. Reprinted by permission of Harcourt Brace Jovanovich, Inc.; "Fog" from *Chicago Poems* by Carl Sandburg, copyright 1916 by Holt, Rinehart and Winston, Inc., copyright 1944 by Carl Sandburg. Reprinted by permission of Harcourt Brace Jovanovich, Inc.; "Primer Lesson" from *Slabs of the Sunburnt West* by Carl Sandburg, copyright 1922 by Harcourt Brace Jovanovich, Inc.; copyright 1950 by Carl Sandburg. Reprinted by permission of the publisher; "Medicine" from *Once*, copyright © 1968 by Alice Walker. Reprinted by permission of Harcourt Brace Jovanovich, Inc.

Harper & Row, Publishers, Inc.: Page 136 from *Cheaper by the Dozen* by Frank B. Gilbreth, Jr., and Ernestine Gilbreth Carey. Copyright 1948, © 1963 by Frank B. Gilbreth, Jr., and Ernestine Gilbreth Carey. Reprinted by permission of Harper & Row, Publishers, Inc.; Text excerpt from *Confessions of a Teenage Baboon* by Paul Zindel. Copyright © 1977 by Zindel Productions Incorporated. By permission of Harper & Row, Publishers, Inc.; "Mirror" from *The Carpentered Hen and Other Tame Creatures* by John Updike. Copyright © 1957 by John Updike. Originally appeared in *The New Yorker* and reprinted by permission of Harper & Row, Publishers, Inc.

William Heinemann Ltd.: "The Sea" from *The Wandering Moon* by James Reeves. Reprinted by permission of William Heinemann Ltd., Publishers.

Holt, Rinehart and Winston, Publishers: "I Am Waiting" by Michael Goode from *The Voice of the Children* collected by June Jordan and Terri Bush. Copyright © 1968, 1969, 1970 by The Voice of the Children, Inc. Reprinted by permission of Holt, Rinehart and Winston, Publishers.

The Instructor Publications, Inc.: "Pictures on the Flying Air" by Scott Alexander. Reprinted from *Instructor*, March 1966. Copyright © 1966 by F. A. Owens Company. Used by permission of The Instructor Publications, Inc.

Japan Publications Trading Co., Ltd.: Haiku by Issa and Kikaku from *One Hundred Famous Haiku*, translated by Daniel C. Buchanan, Japan Publications, Inc., Tokyo.

David Kherdian: "My Mother and the Hummingbird" from *Looking Over Hills* (The Giligia Press, 1972), by David Kherdian.

Tom Liner: "Penitentiary Branch Trail." Reprinted by permission of Tom Liner.

Little, Brown and Company: "Away From It All" from *Verses from 1929 On* by Ogden Nash. Copyright 1935 by Ogden Nash. First appeared in *The New Yorker*. By permission of Little, Brown and Company; "National Velvet" from *Kiss Kiss Bang Bang* by Pauline Kael. Copyright © 1968 by Pauline Kael. By permission of Little, Brown and Company in association with the Atlantic Monthly Press.

Liveright Publishing Corporation: "in Just-" and "Spring is like a perhaps hand," reprinted from *Tulips & Chimneys* by E. E. Cummings, by permission of Liveright Publishing Corporation. Copyright 1923, 1925 and renewed 1951, 1953 by E. E. Cummings. Copyright © 1973, 1976 by Nancy T. Andrews. Copyright © 1973, 1976 by George James Firmage.

Macmillan Publishing Co., Inc.: "Haiku" by Andrew Levine, "Me and My Dad" by James O'Connor, and "The Roller Coaster" by William Fellows. Reprinted with permission of Macmillan Publishing Co., Inc., from *Young Voices*, compiled by Charles E. Schaefer and Kathleen C. Mellor (Bruce/Macmillan, 1971).

Eve Merriam: "The Dirty Word" and "Ping-Pong," reprinted from *Finding a Poem* by Eve Merriam. Copyright © 1970 by Eve Merriam. Reprinted by permission of the author; "Spring Fever" from *It Doesn't Always Have to Rhyme* by Eve Merriam. Copyright © 1964 by Eve Merriam. Reprinted by permission of the author.

NCTE: "Sailing to the Middle of the Bay" by a student of Arnold Solkov. Used with permission of the National Council of Teachers of English.

New Directions Publishing Corporation: "Constantly Risking Absurdity" from Lawrence Ferlinghetti, *A Coney Island of the Mind*. Copyright © 1958 by Lawrence Ferlinghetti. Reprinted by permission of New Directions; "To the Snake" from *Collected Earlier Poems 1940-1960* of Denise Levertov. Copyright © 1958, 1959 by Denise Levertov Goodman. Reprinted by permission of New Directions; "The Red Wheelbarrow" from *Collected Earlier Poems* by William Carlos Williams. Copyright 1938 by New Directions Publishing Corporation. Reprinted by permission of New Directions.

Random House, Inc.: "Dreams" by Langston Hughes. Copyright 1932 by Alfred A. Knopf, Inc., and renewed 1960 by Langston Hughes. Reprinted from *The Dream Keeper and Other Poems* by Langston Hughes, by permission of Alfred A. Knopf, Inc.; Excerpt from *I Am the Cheese* by Robert Cormier. © 1977 by Robert Cormier. Reprinted by permission of Pantheon Books, a Division of Random House, Inc.; "La Peseta" from *Stories from El Barrio* by Piri Thomas. Copyright © 1978 by Piri Thomas. Reprinted by permission of Alfred A. Knopf, Inc.; Excerpt from *Mom, The Wolfman and Me* by Norma Klein. Copyright © 1972 by Norma Klein. Reprinted by permission of Pantheon Books, a Division of Random House, Inc.; Excerpts from *The Real Me* by Betty Miles. Copyright © 1974 by Betty Miles. Reprinted by permission of Alfred A. Knopf, Inc.; Excerpt from *The Temple of Gold* by William Goldman. Copyright © 1957 by William Goldman. Reprinted by permission of Alfred A. Knopf, Inc.

Marian Reiner: "The Night" from *Whispers and Other Poems* by Myra Cohn Livingston. Copyright © 1958 by Myra Cohn Livingston. Reprinted by permission of Marian Reiner for the author.

Scholastic Inc.: Excerpt reprinted from Four Winds Press, a division of Scholastic Inc. from *What's Going to Happen to Me* by Eda LeShan. Copyright © 1978 by Eda LeShan.

Charles Scribner's Sons: Excerpt from Kristin Hunter, *The Soul Brothers and Sister Lou*. Copyright © 1968 by Kristin Hunter. (New York: Charles Scribner's Sons, 1968). Reprinted with the permission of Charles Scribner's Sons.

Seaver Books: Excerpt from "Indian Song: Survival" by Leslie Marmon Silko. Copyright © 1975 by Leslie Marmon Silko. Reprinted from *Voices of the Rainbow*, edited by Kenneth Rosen, published by Seaver Books, New York, 1980.

Simon & Schuster: "Daddy in the Dream" by Yamaguchi Masayo, from *There Are Two Lives*, Richard Lewis, ed., translated by Haruna Kimura. Copyright © 1970 by Richard Lewis and Haruna Kimura. Reprinted by permission of Simon & Schuster, a Division of Gulf & Western Corporation.

Stone Soup: Book review by Kim Mendelson from Volume 8, number 4; Book review by Sean Christopher Kelbley from Volume 7, Number 1. Reprinted by permission.

Viking Penguin Inc.: An excerpt from "Flight" from *The Long Valley* by John Steinbeck. Copyright 1938 © renewed 1966 by John Steinbeck. Reprinted by permission of Viking Penguin Inc.; An excerpt from *The Hundred Penny Box* by Sharon Bell Mathis. Copyright © 1975 by Sharon Bell Mathis. Reprinted by permission of Viking Penguin Inc.; "Jack Sprat" and "Pease-pudding Hot" from *Mother Goose Nursery Rhymes*. Published in 1975 by The Viking Press, Inc.

The World Book Encyclopedia: Encyclopedia excerpts on pages 174–177. Adapted from *The World Book Encyclopedia*. © 1981 Worldbook-Childcraft International, Inc.

Xerox Education Publications: "The Racers Know" (page 151) and "A Dog's Life" (page 151) from *Concrete Is Not Always Hard*, edited by A. Barbara Pilon, Xerox Education Publications, Middletown, Ct., 1972.

Writer's Handbook

Special Problems in Writing

Most writers operate with a "first-things-first" method. They get their ideas down on paper and then worry about following the conventions of spelling, punctuation, and usage. We certainly suggest you do the same. The sections which follow are here to help you with problems you might encounter when you revise your rough draft. There are several sections, each serving a special purpose.

The following table of contents indicates the areas covered and the pages on which assistance may be found.

USAGE	PAGE
Use of Pronouns	H-5
Subject-Verb Agreement	H-7
Verb Tense	H-9
Active and Passive Voice	H-9
The Imperative	H-10
Placement of Modifiers	H-10
Run-ons and Fragments	H-11

PUNCTUATION AND CAPITALIZATION	
Comma	H-13
Semicolon	H-21
Colon	H-21
Apostrophe	H-23
Dash	H-25
Hyphen	H-25
Parentheses	H-26
Brackets	H-27
Period	H-27
Question Mark	H-28
Exclamation Mark	H-28
Ellipses	H-29
Quotation Marks	H-29
Capitalization	H-31

COMMONLY CONFUSED WORDS	H-36

A LIST OF FREQUENTLY MISSPELLED WORDS   H-40

SPELLING HELPS

    Visualizing   H-43

    Mnemonic Techniques   H-43

    Selected Spelling Rules   H-44

THE RESEARCH PAPER   H-48

A GLOSSARY OF GRAMMATICAL TERMS   H-63

THE BUSINESS LETTER   H-73

A BRIEF GRAMMAR   H-77

    Sentences   H-77

       Elements of the Sentence   H-77

       Basic Sentence Patterns   H-79

       Sentence Expansion—Modification   H-83

    Nouns   H-87

    Pronouns   H-89

    Verbs   H-90

    Prepositions   H-97

Usage

USE OF PRONOUNS

The following examples provide models which should guide you in the proper use of pronouns. Refer to the sample sentences and find one which is similar to the sentence you are concerned about. Then see how the pronouns have been used and make sure that your sentence uses the pronouns similarly.

Subject

____ liked the movie.   ____ and ____ liked the movie.

I	I	I
We	We	we
You	You	you
He	He	he
She	She	she
They	They	they
It	It	it

Direct Object

The kangaroo chased ____.   The kangaroo chased ____ and ____.

me	me	me
us	us	us
you	you	you
him	him	him
her	her	her
them	them	them
it	it	it

Predicate Pronoun

The winner is ____.   The winners are ____.
    was   were

I	we
you	you
she	they
he	

Object of the preposition

The fight was with ___.   The fight was between ___ and ___.

me	me	me
us	us	us
you	you	you
her	her	her
him	him	him
them	them	them
it	it	it

Possession

___ running impressed the judges.

My
Your
His
Her
Their
Its

Indirect Object

The faculty sent ___ the book.

me
us
you
him
her
them
it

The faculty sent ___ and ___ the book.

me	me
us	us
you	you
him	him
her	her
them	them
it	it

SUBJECT-VERB AGREEMENT

A verb must agree in number with its subject. A singular subject takes a singular verb; a plural subject takes a plural verb.

That *man owns* the store.   (singular subject and singular verb)

Those two *women own* the store.   (plural subject and plural verb)

Past tense verbs are the same in singular and plural except for forms of the verb "be."

it *missed*, they *missed*   I *looked*, we *looked*

he *shared*, they *shared*   he *was*, they *were* (changes for
                                             a form of the verb "be")

Compound subjects joined by *and* take a plural verb, whether the subjects are singular, plural, or mixed:

Sue and her father *cook* delicious family meals.

The actors and actresses *need* more rehearsals.

Only three students and one teacher *want* to come along.

The number of the verb is not affected by words or phrases between the verb and its subject:

A *resolution* of these problems *is* vital.

Diplomacy, as well as intelligence, *is* crucial.

The *construction* of more skyscrapers *is* unavoidable.

The following pronoun subjects use a singular verb: anybody, anyone, each, either, everybody, everyone, neither, one, no one, someone, somebody:

Does anybody want to learn? *Each* of the boys *has* money.

No one cares enough. *Someone has* to accept the responsibility.

The following pronoun subjects use a plural verb: both, few, many, several:

Both Larry and Tony *are* excellent divers.

Many are supportive of the administration's stance.

Several of the teachers *were* angry.

The following pronoun subjects use either a singular or plural verb depending on the meaning of the sentence: any, all, most, none, some:

Some of the merchandise *was* stolen.

Some of the dresses *were* stolen.
All of the fruit *is* ripe.
All of the bananas *are* ripe.
None of the construction *is* completed.
None of the buildings *are* completed.

Whether the subject precedes or follows the verb, the verb must agree with its subject in number:

Has anyone seen Jim?
The *assignment was* scribbled on the chalkboard.
On the chalkboard *was* scribbled the *assignment*.
Here *comes* the *sun*.
Here *come* the football *players*.

Singular subjects joined by *or* or *nor* use a singular verb; when a singular and a plural subject are joined by *or* or *nor*, use the verb that agrees with the nearer subject:

Either the *lawyer* or the *witness is* lying.
Either the *lawyer* or the *witnesses are* lying.
Neither the *students* nor the *teacher knows* how to balance the
    equation.

A collective noun used as a subject takes a singular verb when the subject refers to a unit. If the subject refers to the individuals of a group rather than to a unit, use a plural verb:

The *audience is* thrilled with the performance.
The *audience are* clapping their hands wildly.
The *number* of car accidents *increases* each year.
A *number* of teachers *are* retiring in June.

When the subject of a subordinate clause is a relative pronoun (which, that, who), the number of the verb agrees with the antecedent.

He spread a <u>rumor</u> *that was* unforgivable.
He spread <u>rumors</u> *that were* unforgivable.
Sue is a <u>person</u> *who loves* music.
Sue is one of those <u>people</u> *who love* music.

Plural subjects which indicate amount, distance, or other singular units of measure require singular verbs:

A hundred *dollars is* a lot of money.
1,000 *miles seems* like a long drive.
Three *inches* off the bottom *makes* the skirt a lot shorter.

VERB TENSE

Do not mix present, past, and future time within a passage.

Mr. Browning had been my friend for years. When I was a little girl he even took me horseback riding a few times. After I was saddled onto the horse, he looks at me and says, "I wish I had a little girl like you for a daughter."

The underscored verbs are present tense. Past tense should have been maintained by using the following verbs . . . he *looked* at me and *said*,"

When statements either occur in the present or are "timeless" (meaning true in both the present and the past), use the present tense even though the rest of the sentence or paragraph uses the past.

Dr. Williams believed that Albert Einstein, who uncovered the principles of relativity and expanded on other laws of physics, is the first and foremost scientific genius of all time.

Use the present participle to indicate an action or state of being that occurs at the same time as the main verb:

Glancing carefully from side to side, Eleanor *led* Jeramie across the street.

Being the eldest, Sue *felt* responsible for her younger sister.

Use either the past participle or the perfect participle to indicate an action or state of being that occurs before the time of the main verb:

Left alone by her wealthy husband's sudden death, my client naturally distrusted her flock of sudden admirers.   (past participle)

Having completed the exam early, Jim went outside for some fresh air.   (perfect participle)

Concerned by her son's sudden unwillingness to communicate, Mrs. Frank sought the help of a psychologist.   (past participle)

ACTIVE AND PASSIVE VOICE

An *active* voice verb expresses an action performed by the subject. A *passive* voice verb expresses an action performed upon the subject.

Active Voice   Passive Voice

          action   action
His bat struck the ball.   The ball was struck by his bat.

Use the active voice, which is more immediate and lively, whenever possible in narrative and descriptive writing.

When the doer of the action is unknown or when the direct object (the receiver of the action) is of more interest than the doer of that action, use the passive voice.

On the way to the airport, I stopped at my bank's special services window and *was given* travelers' checks for cash.

THE IMPERATIVE

When giving directions, avoid shifting between the imperative and other verb forms.

Correct:

Before you go to bed, *turn* off the sprinkler, *cover* the plants, and *turn* off the lights.

Incorrect:

Before you go to bed, *turn* off the sprinkler, *cover* the plants, and *you need to turn* off the lights.

PLACEMENT OF MODIFIERS

Avoid "dangling" introductory phrases and clauses that do not sensibly and clearly modify a word in the main clause.

Strong:

Overcooked and tough, the meat was inedible.

Dangling Modifier:

Overcooked and tough, I could not eat the meat.   (*Overcooked and tough* mistakenly appears to modify *I*.)

Strong:

Straining under a load of books, he caught his toe on the edge of the step.

Dangling Modifier:

Straining under a load of books, his toe caught on the edge of the step.   (*Straining under a load of books* seems to modify *toe*.)

Strong:

After I graduated from high school, my mother bought me a new car.

Dangling Modifier:

After graduating from high school, my mother bought me a new car. (*After graduating from high school* seems to modify *mother*.)

RUN-ONS AND FRAGMENTS

Be careful not to fuse two or more sentences together without using either a conjunction or the proper punctuation. Here are sentence-combining exercises which show how two simple sentences can be joined in different ways.

1. Joining with *and, but,* or *or*
    The apples were green_x   (, but)
    ⟨The oranges were red.
        The apples were green, but the oranges were red.

2. Joining with a *semicolon*
    The apples were green_x   (;)
    ⟨The oranges were red.
        The apples were green; the oranges were red.

3. Joining with *a semicolon followed by a conjunctive adverb*
    The apples were green_x   (; however,)
    ⟨The oranges were red.
        The apples were green; however, the oranges were red.

A fragment is an incomplete sentence or a group of words that is not complete. Usually it lacks either a complete verb or a subject. Be sure not to let a fragment stand alone, as if it were a sentence. Here are a few examples of sentence fragments:

> The reason being that I was too tired to stick around.
> Although I could have done the job better than the person she hired.

There are two easily identifiable types of sentence fragments: the phrase fragment and the subordinate clause.
    Do not separate either a phrase or a subordinate clause from the sentence.

The Phrase Fragment

Complete sentence

> My parents' new townhouse is on the east side of a small Wisconsin lake in a wooded area full of ravines.

Fragment

My parents' new townhouse is on the east side of a small Wisconsin lake. *In a wooded area full of ravines.* (Prepositional fragment)

Complete sentence

As I drove by her house, I saw Jean struggling to push a clunky old lawnmower across a lawn overtaken by weeds.

Fragment

As I drove by her house, I saw Jean. *Struggling to push a clunky old lawnmower across a lawn overtaken by weeds.* (Participial fragment)

The Subordinate Clause Fragment

Complete sentence

Although I won't be able to attend next Monday's meeting, I will attend Thursday's session.

Subordinate clause fragment

Although I won't be able to attend next Monday's meeting. I will attend Thursday's session.

Complete sentence

When the rains come and the breeze is warm, it feels like spring.

Subordinate clause fragment

When the rains come and the breeze is warm. It feels like spring.

Punctuation and Capitalization

COMMA

The comma (,) is the most frequently used punctuation mark within the sentence. When used effectively, it can make lengthy sentences easy to understand. When used carelessly, it can cause your reader to miss the point of your writing. The following examples show you how commas are used by many writers. Emphasis is placed on the kind of materials that you will be writing in school.

Commas Between Items in a Series

Three or more words, phrases, or clauses used together in a sentence make up a series (*words*, *phrases*, or *clauses* in this very sentence make a series of words). The commas help you use a shorthand form of repeating part of a sentence several times. Look at the following example:

The Great Hall was decorated with paper flowers.

~~The Great Hall was decorated with~~ streamers.   (,)

, and
~~The Great Hall was decorated with~~ two giant gazeboes.   (, and)

> The Great Hall was decorated with paper flowers, streamers, and two giant gazeboes.

The commas allow you to say three things about the decorations in the Great Hall without repeating "The Great Hall was decorated with" three times.

In this next sentence, the phrases in the series are expanded and moved to another position.

Paper flowers ~~decorated the Great Hall.~~
Streamers of twisted crepe paper ~~decorated the Great Hall.~~   (,)
and , Two giant gazeboes surrounded by green plants decorated the Great Hall.   (, and)

> Paper flowers, streamers of twisted crepe paper, and two giant gazeboes surrounded by green plants decorated the Great Hall.

A series ordered with commas can be made of single words:

<u>Nouns</u>

Jim placed in the semi-finals competition.

,   <u>Jose</u> placed in the semi-finals competition.   (,)

, and   <u>Michelle</u> placed in the semi-finals competition.   (, and)

Jim, Jose, and Michelle placed in the semi-finals competition.

Erica likes <u>pickles</u> on her sandwich.

, Erica likes <u>mustard</u> on her sandwich.   (,)

, and Erica likes <u>sprouts</u> on her sandwich.   (, and)

Erica likes pickles, mustard, and sprouts on her sandwich.

<u>Adjectives</u>

The streamers made the gym look like a Fourth-of-July celebration.

The streamers were <u>red</u>.

, The streamers were <u>white</u>.   (,)

, and The streamers were <u>blue</u>.   (, and)

The red, white, and blue streamers made the gym look like a Fourth-of-July celebration.

If you add words that modify <u>red</u>, <u>white</u>, <u>blue</u>, and <u>streamers</u>, use the same two commas.

The red, white, and blue streamers made the gym look like a Fourth-of-July celebration.

The red was <u>brilliant</u>.

The white was <u>chalky</u>.

The blue was <u>royal</u>.

The streamers were <u>crepe</u>.

The <u>brilliant</u> red, <u>chalky</u> white, and <u>royal</u> blue <u>crepe</u> streamers made the <u>gym</u> look like a Fourth-of-July celebration.

A series ordered with commas can be made of simple sentences:

The clouds appeared.

,   The wind came up.   (,)

, and   The rains fell for hours.   (, and)

The clouds appeared,   the wind came up,   and the rains fell for hours.

A series ordered with words such as <u>and,</u> <u>or,</u> or <u>nor</u> does **not** need commas.

Neither   Wind kept New Year's Eve motorists off the roads.   (Neither)

nor   <u>Snow</u> kept New Year's Eve motorists off the roads.   (nor)

nor   <u>Ice</u> kept New Year's Eve motorists off the roads.   (nor)

Neither wind nor snow nor ice kept New Year's Eve motorists off the roads.

Commas Between Pairs or Items

Two clauses are usually combined with commas even if the items are already joined with a conjunction such as <u>and,</u> <u>but,</u> <u>yet,</u> <u>or,</u> <u>nor,</u> or <u>for.</u>

Long independent clauses need commas:

This arrangement would be more convenient for me.

, but   You must consider the others in the group.   (, but)

This arrangement would be more <u>convenient</u> for <u>me</u>, but <u>you</u> must consider the others in the group.

Short independent clauses do **not** need commas:

You go ahead.

and   I'll come later.   (and)

<u>You</u> <u>go</u> <u>ahead</u> and <u>I'll</u> <u>come</u> <u>later.</u>

Dependent clauses in pairs do **not** need commas:

When   The trees begin to bud.   (When)

and   The ice melts.   (and)

It will feel like spring.   (, then)

When the trees begin to bud and the ice melts, then it will feel
like spring.

Paired phrases of any length are not separated from each other by
commas:

Adverb Phrases:

mopping
While   Burt ~~mops~~ up the mess in the kitchen.   (While ____-ing)

answering
and   Burt ~~answers~~ the phone with his free hand.   (and ____-ing)

,   Burt had his first misgivings about having his own apartment.   (,)

While mopping up the mess in the kitchen and answering the
phone with his free hand, Burt had his first misgivings about
having his own apartment.

Verb Phrases:

We looked around everywhere.
but   ~~We~~ couldn't find him   (but)

We looked around everywhere but couldn't find him.

Adjective Phrases:

The ball was quite large.

and
~~The ball was~~ somewhat deflated.   (and)

The ball was quite large and somewhat deflated.

Noun Phrases

The Sulphur Street gang met at noon.

their
and   ~~The Sulphur Street gang's~~ uptown rivals met at noon   (and)

The Sulphur Street gang and their uptown rivals met at noon.

Commas After Introductory Items in a Sentence

It is sometimes effective to set the stage for your readers with an introductory item before you give them the content of your sentence. When you do so, use a comma to set off the introduction from the main part of the sentence. If you don't, you might confuse your readers.

Introductory Words

> Above, the thick clouds began to disperse and let the sun peek
>   through.
> Somewhere, somehow, we've got to get to the bottom of this.

Introductory Phrases

> By the way, Jim was looking for you.
> As a matter of fact, I am pretty tired of listening to you complain
>   about school.

Introductory Clauses

> When you finish playing, the piano needs to be dusted.

Commas Before and After Items That Interrupt Sentences

Appositives

Words, phrases, or clauses in apposition are nouns that follow another noun in the sentence; appositives further explain or identify or restate the noun that they follow. Notice how the appositives interrupt the flow of the sentences they are in and add needed information.

Words

> Lena Wilson played the piano in the concert.
>
> ~~Lena Wilson is~~ a student.   (, —— ,)
>
> Lena Wilson, a student, played the piano in the concert.

Phrases

> Pierre is returning to Paris next week.
>
> ~~Pierre is~~ our foreign exchange student.   (, —— ,)
>
> Pierre, our foreign exchange student, is returning to Paris next
>   week.

Miss Johnston loved to talk about Hamlet's insanity.

~~Miss Johnston was~~ our English teacher.   , (, —,)

Miss Johnston, our English teacher, loved to talk about Hamlet's insanity.

She removed the egg carefully from the nest to examine it more closely.

~~The egg was~~ a small, fragile one.   , (, —,)

She removed the egg, a small, fragile one, carefully from the nest to examine it more closely.

Clauses

Erica won the singles tennis competition without much effort

, She's my sister.   , (, —,)

Erica, she's my sister, won the singles tennis competition without much effort.

Non-restrictive Clauses, Phrases, and Words

A non-restrictive clause is a dependent clause that modifies the noun it follows; it is an adjective. It does not change (restrict) the meaning of the sentence it joins. It simply interrupts it to add information the reader may not know. Non-restrictive phrases and words interrupt in the same manner. All non-restrictive items are set off by commas.

Clause

Arlene Turner is my best friend.

, who   ~~Arlene Turner~~ lives right down the street   , (, who —,)

Arlene Turner, who lives right down the street, is my best friend.

Phrase

Jacquie reached the bottom of the slope in 35 seconds!

    skiing
, ~~Jacquie skis~~ furiously through the storm.   , (, -ing —,)

Jacquie, skiing furiously through the storm, reached the bottom of the slope in 35 seconds!

Words

Fido chased Fluffy away.

Fido is unfriendly.   (, —— ,)

Fluffy is friendly.   (, —— ,)

Fido, unfriendly, chased Fluffy, friendly, away.

Nouns of Direct Address

Sometimes you may interrupt your sentence to address your readers directly. You may simply want to get their attention or you may want to convince them of your seriousness. Set off their names with commas.

We are proud to present, ladies and gentlemen, "The Greatest Show on Earth!"

You can be assured, Carol, of the money by the end of the month.

Parenthetical Expressions

Parenthetical expressions are words or phrases used to explain, emphasize, or qualify a statement. Some common parenthetical expressions are: as a matter of fact, consequently, however, for example, for instance, I believe (think, hope), indeed, moreover, on the other hand, therefore.

He is, I believe, the only person who can do the job well.

Jim did say, however, that he would think it over before making his final decision.

The house next door, as a matter of fact, is for sale right now.

I can't wait around this town for two more weeks; consequently, we'll have to make the decision this week.

Embedded Questions

Short questions within a sentence are set off with commas as well.

Team A is the stronger of the two.

Don't you agree?   (, —— ,)

Team A is, don't you agree, the stronger of the two?

Phrases Used for Emphasis

A sleek limousine pulled into the driveway.

A limousine was hardly the car I expected   (, —— ,)

A sleek limousine, <u>hardly the car I expected,</u> pulled into the driveway.

Speaker Tags in Direct Quotations

"I am not the only student who thinks so!"

" She argued.   (," —— ,")

"I am not," <u>she argued,</u> "the only student who thinks so!"

"Those will have to do until I can afford new radial tires."

" Jim mumbled,   (," —— ,")

"Those will have to do," <u>Jim mumbled,</u> "until I can afford new radial tires."

Commas in Certain Conventional Situations

Items in dates and addresses:
> On Monday, February 5, 1981, the building was destroyed.
> He has lived at 1500 Park Avenue, New York, New York, since August, 1956.

The salutation of a friendly letter and the closing of any letter:

> Dear Nancy,   Dear Father,   Love,   Sincerely,

Degrees and titles that follow names:

> Joseph Lytle, Ph.D., authored the Preface to the book.
> James Johnson, Jr., will talk on endangered species of birds in Newfoundland this Sunday.

SEMICOLON

There are three primary uses for semicolons in more formal papers:

<u>Independent Clauses without Conjunctions</u>

     Walter started walking toward the car.

;   Nothing would make him turn back.   (;)

         Walter started walking toward the car; nothing would make him turn back.

<u>Independent Clauses with Certain Conjunctions</u>   (for example, for instance, however)

     The bell rings at 11:30.

; however   It has been late before today.   (; however,)

        The bell rings at 11:30; however, it has been late before today.

<u>Between Word Groups Containing Commas</u>

     The paper was full of humor.

,   ~~The paper was full of~~ life.   (,)

, and   ~~The paper was full of~~ happiness.   (, and)

; but   Its punctuation ~~was horrible.~~   (; but)

,   Its spelling ~~was horrible.~~   (,)

        were

, and   Its capitalization was horrible.   (, and)

        The paper was full of humor, life, and happiness; but its punctuation, spelling, and capitalization were horrible.

COLON

There are four uses for the colon in writing:

<u>At the Introduction of a list of items</u>

Our guidebook recommended the following items.

:   ~~It recommended~~ a knife.   (:)

,   ~~It recommended~~ a compass.   (,)

, ~~It recommended~~ a small backpack.   (,)

, ~~It recommended~~ some edibles.   (,)

, ~~It recommended~~ a canteen.   (,)

, ~~It recommended~~ matches.   (,)

, ~~It recommended~~ a sweater.   (,)

, and ~~It recommended~~ a camera.   (, and)

> Our guidebook recommended the following items: a knife, a compass, a small backpack, some edibles, a canteen, matches, a sweater, and a camera.

At the Introduction of a Formal Statement or Address

The world will never forget Theodore Roosevelt.

or ~~The world will never forget~~ his famous words.   (or)

: "Walk softly and carry a big stick."   (;)

> The world will never forget Theodore Roosevelt or his famous words: "Walk softly and carry a big stick."

After an Independent Clause that is explained by a second clause

Clothing isn't made the way it used to be.

: Seams tear easily.   (:)

, Zippers break.   (,)

, and Fabric isn't very durable.   (, and)

> Clothing isn't made the way it used to be: seams tear easily, zippers break, and the fabric isn't very durable.

Certain Conventional Situations

Salutation of a formal letter:
   Dear Sirs: Gentlemen: Ladies: To Whom It May Concern:
In noting time:
   1:15 a.m.   12:30 p.m.
Biblical references and other bibliographical references:
   John 19:57   James 9:1   Hebrews 2:7   Proverbs 34:50
   Boston: Allyn and Bacon, Inc.

APOSTROPHE

You may use the apostrophe (') for three different purposes in writing: it can signal possession (Erin's book), plurals (I made two A's.), or an omission of letters (aren't for are not, we've for we have).

Possession

To show possession for one person or thing (any singular noun), place the apostrophe and then an s after the noun or indefinite pronoun ('s).
The opinion was written on the board.

The opinion belonged to the teacher   ('s)   's

The teacher's opinion was written on the board.

The taxi came to a screeching halt.

The taxi belonged to Gus   ('s)   's

Gus's taxi came to a screeching halt.

> Other Examples: brother's gloves, Caroline's hat, the elephant's trunk, Rawl's grocery, Mr. Comb's glasses, bus's brakes, everybody's loss, anybody's guess, someone else's problem

To show possession for several people or things (any plural noun), place only an apostrophe after the noun   (') . . .
The swimming pool is now empty.

The swimming pool belongs to the girls.   (')   '

The girls' swimming pool is now empty.

If the plural form does **not** end in s. Plurals such as deer, children and women are made possessive by adding 's.
deer's,   children's,   women's

When two or more nouns possess something individually, indicate the possession (according to the rules above) for each noun.

The departments are on different floors of the store.

's

~~One department is for~~ men.   ('s)

and   's

~~Another department is for~~ women.   (and ____'s)

The men's and women's departments are on different floors of
the store.

When words indicate joint possession, indicate possession (according to
the preceding rules) for only the last noun.
The records were the hit of the party.

's

The records belonged to Jose and Marguerita.   ('s)

Jose and Marguerita's records were the hit of the party.

Other examples: the cat and dog's dinner time,
mom and dad's vacation

When using a personal pronoun to replace any possessive noun, do **not**
add an apostrophe.
The dress was two sizes too large for me.

her

The dress belonged to Evelyn.   (her)

Her dress was two sizes too large for me.

Other examples: his gloves, its profit, their mistake   (Don't confuse the possessive pronoun, its with
the contraction of it is—it's. They are easy to mix up.)

Plural

To indicate the plural of numbers, symbols, letters of the alphabet, and
words referred to as words, use 's.
How many is three 3's and four 4's?
Count the +'s and the −'s in this equation.
Occasion is spelled with two c's.
Try to cut down on the number of and's and but's in your paragraph.

Omission of Letters

We have only just begun.	('ve)	We've only just begun.
There is no doubt about it.	('s)	There's no doubt about it.
You have not told everything.	(n't)	You haven't told everything.

DASH

The dash is used somewhat as the comma is. It is more appropriate to use a dash than a comma . . .

when the shift in thought is *sudden*
> I hope that next time he has the sense to—but perhaps, we should first hear what he has to say for himself.

or when the interruption in the sentence is especially abrupt
> He could have—and indeed should have—been a bit more considerate.
>> Other examples: His goal—if you can even call it a goal—should have been to get himself out of debt.

or when the series ordered by commas is long and possibly confusing
> You should use sections—the table of contents, chapters with headings, tables and graphs, appendixes, and references—to make your research paper easy to read.

HYPHEN

Use a hyphen between syllables to divide a word at the end of a line.
> regis-/ter
> oppor-/tunity
> indica-/tive

Be sure to leave more than one letter of a divided word at the end of or at the start of a line.
> e-/lope (faulty)   (Put the entire word on the next line.)
> speed-/y (faulty)   (Put the entire word on the line.)

When there is a prefix or a suffix, divide the word just after the prefix or just before the suffix.

    inter-/dependent   (not in-/terdependent)
    merri-/ment   (not mer-/riment)
    sub-/ordinate   (not subor-/dinate)
    elusive-/ly   (not elu-/sively)

Often, a good place to divide a word is between double consonants.

    run-/ning
    Missis-/sippi

Use hyphens when two or more words combine to form a modifier.

    a would-be movie star
    a well-kept beard
    a don't-care-if-you-do attitude

If the first word of the modifier unit is an adverb ending in *ly*, do not use a hyphen.

    a neatly dressed woman
    a poorly worded sentence

Hyphenate compound numbers from twenty-one through ninety-nine, and fractions.

    Thirty-three years old hardly makes you old!
    A one-fourth portion goes to charity; the other three-fourths is
        needed to pay back expenses incurred.

Use a hyphen to avoid confusion or between awkward letter combinations.

    re-collect   (collect again; prevents confusion with recollect mean-
        ing *to remember*)
    semi-interesting   (avoids awkwardness of *semiinteresting*)

PARENTHESES

Parentheses indicate another kind of interruption in a sentence. When the interruption includes material most people already know, but some may not, use parentheses.

    Mayor Daley (Chicago) had more political control than any other
        mayor in the country.

The make-up of carbon dioxide molecules (see Diagram B) consists
of two atoms of oxygen and one of carbon.
The film *Gone with the Wind* (1939) was aired on television recently.
Sen. Percy (R., Ill.) was re-elected by a narrow margin.

All other punctuation near the parentheses must come after and not
before them. When a parenthetical item is added to a clause that ends
with a comma, extend the comma beyond the parenthetical information.
The ghost of Hamlet's father commanded Hamlet's friends to "swear
by the sword" (the sword itself was, ironically, symbolic of the cross),
forbidding them to tell anybody about his appearance.

BRACKETS

Use brackets to enclose explanations within quoted material when the
explanation is not part of the quotation.
Mr. McDonough calmly addressed the audience with these words: "I
am honored by it [the nomination for presidency], and if elected I
will do my utmost to carry out the awesome responsibilities of this
honored position."

Use brackets to enclose explanations within parentheses when the
explanation is not part of the material in parentheses.
The molecular structure of more complex molecules is harder to
understand. (See page 219 [Chart A] for detailed breakdowns of five
complex molecules.)

THE PERIOD

Use a period to follow a statement or a command.
The trees shivered in the cold.
Please keep the noise down.

Use a period after abbreviations.
Dr.   Mr.   Mrs.   Ms.   Nov.   B.C.   Ave.

Abbreviations of various governmental agencies and social, professional,
or business organizations are **not** followed by periods.
NATO   UNICEF   CIA   HEW
IBM   dbs (decibals)   mph (miles per hour)

Avoid abbreviating common words in ordinary writing.

Unclear:
>   Two new mfg. cos. were just built on Co. Blvd. last Oct., just
>   next door to my two bros., Chas. and Jim.

Clear:
>   Two new manufacturing companies were just built on Colorado
>   Boulevard last October, just next door to my brothers, Charles
>   and Jim.

Indirect questions are followed by a period.
>   She asked whether I wanted to come.
>   We wondered how much longer we should wait.

Polite requests in formal business letters are followed by a period.
>   Will you please send me ten extra copies and bill me for them.

THE QUESTION MARK

Use a question mark to follow a question.
>   Do you want to come?
>   How much longer should we wait?

A question mark should be placed inside quotation marks **only** if the
quotation itself is a question.
>   "Do you think you'll come?" he asked me.
>   *BUT*
>   Who said, "All the world's a stage . . ."?

THE EXCLAMATION POINT

Use an exclamation point after statements expressing strong, excited
feeling.
>   Wow! What a dress!
>   "Cut it out!" he yelled at me sharply. (Note the period after *sharply*
>   and the exclamation mark within the quotation marks.)

ELLIPSES

Use three periods to show where words have been omitted within a quotation; use four periods where words have been omitted at the end of a sentence or where two or more sentences have been omitted.

> I pledge allegiance to the flag . . . and to the republic . . . with liberty and justice for all.

> Speak properly and in as few words as you can, but always plainly, for the end of speech is not to make a show but to be understood. . . .

> Be reserved but not sour . . . cheerful, not light. . . .

QUOTATION MARKS

Use quotation marks before and after a person's exact words. If you aren't quoting a person exactly, you needn't use quotation marks at all.

> She told us to think about our attitude.

If the person's words ask a question, state a command, or simply make a statement, use the appropriate end punctuation inside the second quotation mark.

> I asked, "Why don't you go along?"

When a person's words are interrupted with a quotation stem (said mother, replied George), place a comma and quotation mark before and after the stem.

> "How would you feel," asked Mother, "if Aunt Ruth didn't even mention your birthday?"
> "Leave me alone," I shouted, "before I lose my temper!"

If you use a semi-colon which is not a part of the quotation, place it outside the quotation marks.

> Father said, "I don't want to discuss it at all"; unfortunately, Mr. Rogers thought it was an important matter and refused to drop it.
> He grumbled, "They just don't make clothes the way they used to"; from the looks of what he was wearing, I knew what he meant!

If the sentence is a question, but the quotation is not, place the question mark outside the quotation marks.

Didn't you tell Mark, "Forget it"?
You said to me, "Forget it!" didn't you?

Use quotation marks before and after words referred to as words.

Don't use "but" or "and" at the start of a sentence.
I tried to explain to the psychiatrist my hostility against the world and
against the "dopes" that controlled it.

Use quotation marks before and after titles of songs, short stories, short poems, essays, articles, and subdivisions of books (chapters, sub-headings, etc.).

"Georgia On My Mind" is Ray Charles' most popular tune.
E.E. Cummings "In Just Spring" is my favorite poem.
I read a fascinating article entitled "Computer Art" in yesterday's
newspaper.

BUT
No quotation marks are used for the title of a poem of book length.

Walt Whitman's *Leaves of Grass* is an American classic.

Begin a new paragraph each time a speaker changes.

"I can't wait until Christmas," Jamie babbled, "and school's out
for awhile."
"I know what you mean," Sarah sighed wishfully. "I think I'm
going skiing for the week between Christmas and New Years."
"Too bad it's not summer vacation coming up," Ralph inter-
vened. "I have a good job this summer!"

When you quote the same person for more than two paragraphs, use quotation marks at the start of each paragraph and at the end of the final paragraph.

"I'll never forget that vacation, because everything seemed to go
right.
"First, the weather was perfect. The sun was out every day, the
snow was fresh, light, and powdery, just the way I like it. The slopes
weren't even crowded. I remembered how sunburned my nose was at
the end of the first day.
"Then Sue and Deborah came up. On Sunday morning we all
went cross-country skiing, out away from the crowds into some of the
back country. All of us worked up a sweat and laughed a lot. At one

point, we even ran into a herd of elk and took some great photographs."

"Photographs?" Jim interrupted. "Do you have them here?"

Extensive quotations are indented five extra spaces from both the left and right margins (ten spaces if beginning a new paragraph) and single-spaced, even if the rest of the paper is double- or triple-spaced. Leave an extra line above and below the indented quoted material to separate it clearly from the rest of the copy. No quotation marks are necessary.

"However that may be," Taylor related, "neither the President nor Secretary of Defense Robert McNamara gave objective review to Westmoreland's operations." Townsend Hoopes further states:

> The Pentagon simply lost sight of the truth that protection for the people against Viet Cong terrors had to be achieved by means that did not themselves alienate the people by causing heavy casualties and wanton physical destruction.

Use single quotation marks to enclose a quotation within a quotation.

"What do you mean by saying, 'Put the news peg in the upper lefthand corner of the first page'?" I asked Mrs. Weber.

CAPITALIZATION

Capitalize the first word in any sentence or in any quoted sentence or fragment.

Everyone agreed that the rooms needed painting. "Do you think that we'll have time to do them next week?" asked Charles.

BUT

"Do you think," asked Charles, "that we'll have time to do them next week?" [Note: "that" is *not* capitalized since it is a continuation of the direct quotation beginning with "Do you think . . .]

Traditionally, the first word in each line of poetry is capitalized. In modern poetry, while this observance is still common, it is **not** a hard and fast rule.

I think that I shall never see
A poem lovely as a tree . . .

Capitalize proper nouns.

Capitalize the names of persons.

Miles Davis   Picasso   Hamlet   Charles Dickens   Mr. McDonald   Mrs. MacDuff   John O'Brien

Capitalize geographical names, including:

Cities, counties, states, countries, continents

Atlantic City, New Jersey, Boulder County, Canada, Europe

Bodies of water

Atlantic Ocean, Black Sea, Lake Michigan, Mississippi River, Beaver Pond, Chipmunk Creek

Islands, peninsulas, straits, canals, beaches, mountains

Hawaii, Florida Peninsula, Strait of Gibraltar, Panama Canal, Daytona Beach, Grand Tetons, Longs Peak

Streets, specific buildings

Broadway, Main Street, Birch Boulevard, Fifty-ninth Street, Highway 119, Sears Tower, White House, Conrad Hilton Hotel

Parks, forests, dams, canyons, valleys

Yellowstone National Park, Pike National Forest, Hoover Dam, Poudre Canyon, Beaver Valley

Recognized parts of the country or world

the North, the Middle East

Note: The words *north*, *south*, *east*, and *west* are *not* capitalized when they refer to directions, but *are* capitalized when they refer to sections of the country.

Drive *east* from Colorado for 1,000 miles and you will be in the *Middle West*.

Capitalize the names of ships, boats, planes, trains, awards, and monuments:

S.S. Titanic, the Lucille (name of boat), the Blue Angels, Olympic Gold Medal, the Statue of Liberty

Capitalize the brand names of consumer products—do **not** capitalize any common nouns which may follow the brand name:

Seven-Up, Crest, IBM typewriter, Volkswagon Rabbit, Jay's potato chips, Butternut bread, Sunkist oranges

Capitalize the names of specific rooms and other nouns followed by a numeral or letter;

Room 607   School District 12   Chapter 8   Diagram B

Capitalize the names of school classes—however, the words *freshman*, *sophomore*, *junior*, *senior* are not capitalized when they refer to either a student or a year:

Jim Stone is valedictorian of the *Senior Class*.

They were a fine group of *Seniors*.

Sue is a *junior* this year.

Al's grade point average rose dramatically his *sophomore* year.

Capitalize the names of specific business firms, and governmental, scholastic, professional, and social organizations or departments

Business firms

United Airlines, Xerox Corporation, Sperry Rand, Inc., Flatirons Theatre, Fred's Cafe

Governmental, scholastic, and social organizations

Congress; Department of Health, Education and Welfare; United Nations; French Club; American Honor Society; Phi Beta Kappa; Lions Club, Shriners, Pep Club; Photographic Society of America

Institutions

Harvard University, Lawrence College, Glenbard East High School, Ford Foundation, Institute for Peace Studies, Language Arts Department

Capitalize the names of nationalities, races, and religions

American, French, Oriental, Caucasian, Protestant, Moslem, Catholic, Jewish

Capitalize the names of specific deities or prophets and possessive pronouns or nouns referring to those deities

God, Christ, Buddha, Mohammed, John the Baptist, Zeus, Apollo, Simon Peter

God gave the world *His* only *Son*.

Capitalize proper adjectives, but not the common nouns that follow them.

America, American *people*   Canada, Canadian *winters*

Elizabethan *drama*, Gothic *architecture*, Renaissance *literature*

Capitalize the names of events

Capitalize historical events and periods of time

World War I, Civil War, Battle of Bunker Hill, Dark Ages, Iron Age, the Renaissance

Capitalize special events

the Super Bowl, the Olympics, the World Series

Capitalize political or religious holidays

Fourth of July, Memorial Day, Christmas, Easter

Capitalize calendar items including the days of the week and the months of the year

Book Week, National Secretaries' Week, Sunday, April

Do **not** capitalize the names of seasons unless personified.

I can't wait for spring.

BUT

There was Spring, tripping in all dressed in green with flowers in her hair.

Capitalize specific titles of persons

Capitalize the title of a person when used preceding a name

Superintendent John Knolls   Reverend Philips

Dean Williams   General Eisenhower

Capitalize a title either used alone or after a name only if referring to a high government official or in order to show special respect.

Hello, Reverend   What next, Coach?   President Roosevelt

Jim Withers, president of the Senior Class

John Daley, ex-Mayor of Chicago (**Note:** the prefix *ex-* is not capitalized.)

the Senator

BUT

a committee of six senators

the Chief of Police

Vice-President Johnson (Two capitals are required only when referring to the Vice-President of a nation.)

Capitalize the first word and all important words in titles of books, short stories, poems, plays, periodicals, articles, documents, songs, films, and works of art. Articles (*a, an, the*) and conjunctions and prepositions of fewer than five letters are not capitalized unless they are the first word in the title.

Have you ever read the *Chicago Tribune?*

"Snows of Kilimanjaro" is, perhaps, illustrative of Hemingway at his best.

I Never Promised You a Rose Garden is the story of the rehabilitation of a precocious, teen-age schizophrenic named Deborah.

The award-winning film, "One Flew over the Cuckoo's Nest," was aired for the first time on television in 1979.

Capitalize the titles of academic subjects only if they refer to languages or specific course titles.

French, Spanish, English, History II, Algebra I, American Poetry, Advanced Placement English

BUT

home economics, history, algebra, chemistry

Capitalize words showing a family relationship when used with a person's name or in place of that person's name, but **not** when preceded by a possessive.

> my *u*ncle, his *a*unt, Uncle Remus, Aunt Sally,
> my *c*ousin Ralph, my *s*ister Ruth
> I told my *m*other all about it.
> *BUT*
> I told Mother all about it.

Always capitalize the pronoun "I."

> *I* know what *I* know when *I* know it.

UNDERLINING (ITALICS)

Underline (or use italics) for titles of books, periodicals, names of ships, and works of art. Do not underline or italicize *a*, *an*, or *the* preceding a title unless it is part of the title.

> *The Scarlet Letter* by Hawthorne
> Have you read the *Wall Street Journal?*
> My favorite painting is *Portrait of an Artist's Son* by Renoir.
> The *Titanic* is a well-known ship.

Underline (or use italics) for words, numbers, letters, and figures referred to as such.

> The number 6 looks like the number 9 upside down.
> The word *and* is the most common conjunction.

Underline (or use italics) for foreign words or phrases.

> She always used the words *c'est la vie* when something problematic
>   but unavoidable happened.

Commonly Confused Words

The following words are commonly confused. Sometimes the problem is with spelling; sometimes it is with meaning.

accept/except	I accept your settlement offer except for the part on the first page.
advice/advise	I advise you to take my advice and be careful.
affect/effect	The smell affects me so much I feel sick. What effect does it have on you? Could you effect a change in the ventilation?
already/all ready	John has already gone. My friends, are you all ready to go?
alter/altar	We can't alter the past. The altar was covered with flowers.
altogether/ all together	I don't altogether dislike the taste. The flavors are blended all together in the drink.
angel/angle	A triangle has three angles. Much early art portrays angels as babies.
assent/ascent/ ascend	Will your parents assent to your making the ascent? Don't ascend without their permission.
bath/bathe	I decided to bathe in the warm bath water.
bear/bare	The only kind of bear I have seen is a bare bear.
berth/birth	She gave birth to a baby in the berth of a Pullman car.
bore/boar	Bore holes in the tree and attach the fence. That will keep the boar away. However, without any excitement, the country may bore you.
born/borne	Where were you born? They have borne their troubles well.
brake/break	Step on the brake lightly. These glasses I'm holding break easily.
capital/capitol	Springfield is the capital city where they voted on capital punishment. It takes lots of capital to start a business. The Capitol building is in Washington.
cite/site/sight	He cited Shakespeare in his paper. The site of our new home has not been picked yet. A beautiful sight greeted us when we saw the lovely valley.

cloths/clothes — There are six new wash cloths under the pile of clean clothes in the linen closet.

coarse/course — The wool shirt felt coarse against my skin. The plane followed a straight course. Chicken Kiev was the main course. I signed up for the course in Latin.

consul/council/counsel — I called the British consul in Rome to get help. Jeremy was elected to the school council. I tried to get counsel from the best lawyer in town. She agreed to be my counsel.

desert/dessert — The Sahara Desert is huge. Grandpa would never desert the family. We had chocolate mousse for dessert.

diary/dairy — I once wrote in my diary about my experiences milking cows at my uncle's dairy.

dissent/descent/descend — Did your parents dissent when you asked them if you could make the descent? You didn't descend in spite of their dissent, did you?

formerly/formally — She was formerly Miss America. She formally addressed the group.

forth/fourth — Go forth to battle in the fourth company of infantry.

its/it's — The cat licked its paws. It's too late now.

later/latter — I'll see you later. I'll choose the latter of the two.

lose/loose — Don't lose your temper. I have to tie up some loose ends.

moral/morale — You have to have strong moral character to keep your morale high these days.

miner/minor — My father was a coal miner. A sixteen-year-old is considered a minor in some states. I have one minor objection.

muscle/mussel — There are many mussels at our beach. The athlete has very strong muscles.

pair/pare — Please pare a pair of apples.

past/passed — Grandma lives in the past. We drove right past your house. I passed up a great opportunity.

peace/piece — I feel at peace in the mountains when I have a big piece of pie.

personal/personnel — I don't want a personal involvement. I took the job because I liked the personnel working there.

plane/plain — They hired four planes to spray herbicides. She had a plain dress on. The settlers traveled across the plain.

precede/proceed — I will precede you as you proceed down the aisle.

presence/presents	She had a mysterious, self-contained presence. We opened our presents on Jim's birthday.
principal/ principle	Greed was his principal motivation. Who is principal of the school? He has strong principles.
prophecy/ prophesy	Does the prophet prophesy? Or is his prophecy just a lot of words?
quiet/quite	Be quiet. I'm quite sure we'll go.
rain/reign/rein	The king began his reign in a heavy rain; it was pouring so hard his horse would barely respond to the rein.
sheathe/sheath	Sheathe your sword in its sheath.
stationary/ stationery	The seats were stationary and couldn't be moved. I received a letter on perfumed stationery.
straight/strait	We went straight through the Strait of Gibraltar on our ship.
than/then	I am taller than he. If he puts on elevator shoes, then he'll be taller.
their/they're there	It's all their fault. They're waiting at the club. Put the flowers over there. There are three of us.
to/too/two	Give it to me. He is too young for me. I'm coming, too. Here are two of my best recipes.
waist/waste	She has a 24-inch waist. Do you know what we should do with nuclear waste?
weather/whether	We're going whether the weather cooperates or not.
wholly/holy	The group was wholly in agreement. The saint was holy.
whose/who's	Whose hat is this? Who's responsible here?
your/you're	This is your copy. You're too young to drive.

Lie and Lay

Lie means "to recline" or "to be in a horizontal position." The verb *lie* is intransitive; it never takes an object. *Lay* means "to put or place something down in a resting position." The verb *lay* is transitive; it requires an object.

    I think I'll *lie* down.   (intransitive)

    Lay the book on the table.   (transitive; *book* is the direct object)

Below are the principal forms of these verbs:

Present	*Present Participle*	*Past*	*Past Participle*
lie	lying	lay	lain
lay	laying	laid	laid

Lie down. I *am lying* down. Five minutes ago, I *lay* down for a nap. Perhaps they have *lain* down for a while.

Lay the book on the table. He *is laying* the book on the table. He *laid* the book on the table. I *have laid* the book on the table.

Sit and Set

Sit means "to assume an upright position." *Sit* is almost always an intransitive verb; it rarely takes an object. *Set* means "to put or place something down." *Set* is a transitive verb; it usually requires an object.

Sit down on the sofa.   (intransitive)

Set the packages down on the table.   (transitive)

Below are the principal forms of these verbs:

Present	Present Participle	Past	Past Participle
sit	sitting	sat	sat
set	setting	set	set

Sit down over there.

He *is sitting* on the floor. He *sat* on the floor.

We *have sat* here waiting for you for hours.

Set the packages on the table. Jane *is setting* the groceries on the front steps.

They *set* the boxes on the floor. We *have set* the larger boxes on the floor.

Rise and Raise

Rise means "to go up" or "to get up." It is intransitive; it never takes an object.

Raise means "to force something to move upward." *Raise* is transitive; it takes an object.

What time does the sun *rise*?

Can you *raise* the flag?

Below are the principal parts of these verbs:

Present	Present Participle	Past	Past Participle
rise	rising	rose	risen
raise	raising	raised	raised

Rise to your feet. He *is rising* to his feet. The crowd *rose* during the Pledge of Allegiance. The moon *has risen* at sunset for the last five days. *Raise* the flag. The janitor *is raising* the flag. Two students *raised* their hands. I *have raised* my hand three times in the last five minutes.

A List of Frequently Misspelled Words

The following list includes many of the words in English which are thought to be difficult to spell. You can solve many spelling problems by checking this list or a dictionary.

A

abbreviate
absence
abundant
accelerator
accidentally
acclimated
accommodate
accompanied
accompaniment
accomplishment
accumulate
accuracy
achievement
acknowledgment
acquaintance
acquire
adequately
adolescent
advantageous
aerial
aggravate
allegiance
allusion
amateur
among
analysis
analyze
angel
angle
annihilate
anonymous
answer
anxiety
anxious
apologetically
apparatus
apparent
appearance
appreciate
appropriate
arctic
argument
arrangement
ascend
ascent
assent
association
atheistic
athletic
attendance
audience
auxiliary
awkward

B

bachelor
ballet
bankruptcy
barbarian
bath
bathe
bear
beggar
beginning
behavior
beneficial
benefit
benefited
berth
bibliography
birth
biscuit
blasphemy
boar
bore
boulevard
boundaries
breath
breathe
brilliant
buffet
buoy
bureau
business
busy

C

calendar
campaign
candidate
captain
carburetor
caricature
catalogue
catastrophe
category
cellar
cemetery
certain
changeable
characteristic
choose
chose
circumstantial
colossal
column
committee
communist
comparative
compelled
competent
competitor
completely
complexion
compulsory
conference
confidentially
connoisseur
conscience
conscientious
consciousness
consistent
controversial
criticism
criticize
curiosity
curious
curriculum

D

dairy
decadent
deceitful
decision
definite

H-40

descend
descendant
descent
describe
description
desirable
despair
desperate
devise
diary
different
dilapidated
dilemma
diligence
disappear
disappoint
disapprove
disastrous
disciple
discipline
discrimination
dissatisfied
dissent
dissipate
divide
divine
doesn't
dormitory

E

ecstasy
efficiency
eligible
eliminate
embarrass
emperor
emphasize
endeavor
enthusiastically
environment
equivalent
especially
espionage
exaggerate
exceed
excellent

exceptionally
exhaustion
exhibition
exhilaration
existence
extraordinary
extremely
exuberant

F

familiar
fascinate
fascism
February
feminine
foreign
forfeit
forth
forty
fourth
frantically
freight
fulfill
fundamental

G

gaiety
galaxy
gauge
generally
government
governor
grammar
grammatically
grievous
guarantee

H

handsome
harassment
height
hereditary
hindrance
holy
hospital

horizontal
humorous
hygiene
hypocrisy

I

illusion
imaginary
immediately
incidentally
incredible
independent
indispensable
inevitable
influential
ingenious
initiative
innocent
intellectual
intelligence
interesting
interpretation
interrupt
irrelevant
irresponsible

K

kerosene
knew
knowledge

L

laboratory
larynx
legitimate
leisure
liable
library
license
lightning
liquor
literature
livelihood
loneliness
luxurious

M

magnificence
maintenance
manageable
maneuver
marriage
martyr
mathematics
meant
mediocre
melancholy
melodious
merely
miniature
minute
mischievous
misspell
moral
morale
mortgage
mosquito
municipal
murmuring
muscle
mussel
mysterious

N

naive
necessity
neither
neurotic
nickel
ninety
ninth
noticeable
nuclear

O

obedience
occasion
occurred
omission
opinion
opportunity

optimistic
orchestra
original
outrageous

P

pageant
paid
pain
pamphlet
pane
parallel
paralysis
parliament
particularly
pastime
peasant
penicillin
permanent
permissible
perseverance
persistent
perspiration
persuade
phenomenon
physically
physician
picnicking
playwright
pneumonia
politician
possess
practically
precede
preference
preferred
prejudice
presence
prestige
presumption
prevalent
privilege
probably
procedure
proceed

prominent
pronunciation
propaganda
prophecy
prophesy
psychiatrist
psychoanalysis
pursue

Q

quantity
quietly
quite

R

rain
rebellion
receive
recognize
recommend
reference
rehearsal
reign
rein
religious
remembrance
reminiscent
remittance
repetition
representative
respectful
responsibility
restaurant
rhyme
rhythm

S

sandwich
satisfactorily
saxophone
schedule
secretary
seize
separate

sergeant
sheath
sheathe
siege
significant
similar
sophomore
souvenir
speak
specifically
specimen
speech
sponsor
straight
strait
strictly
stubbornness
succeed
success
superintendent
supersede
surprise
surroundings
susceptible
syllable
symbolic
symmetrical
symphonic
synonymous

T

tariff
temperament
temperature
tendency
thorough
together
tolerance
tomorrow
tortoise
tragedy
transcend
tries
truly
twelfth

typical
tyranny

U

unanimous
undoubtedly
universal
unmistakable
unnatural
unnecessarily
unscrupulous
until
usually

V

vaccine
vacuum
valuable
variation
various
vegetable
vehicle
vengeance
versatile
vigilant
village
villain
vinegar

W

weather
Wednesday
weird
whether
whisper
whistle
wholly
withhold

Y

yacht
yawn

Spelling Helps

VISUALIZING

One of the most successful techniques for remembering the spelling of a word is to see the word in your "mind's eye." If you have this ability, you will be able to retrieve a correct spelling easily, and you will be able to spot misspelled words, too. Most visualizers look at the word on a page, then look away and try to "see" the word in their memories.

MNEMONIC TECHNIQUES

Some people remember correct spellings by developing "hints" which are based on some characteristic of the words they are to spell. The following examples are presented so that you can see how the process works. Only a few of these "hints" are presented, since the best way to use this process is for you to develop your own. Use the examples here as suggestions; then, make up your own tricks to help you remember.

absence	I will "c" you at the end. absence
accompanied	An "a" is accompanied by two "c's" in this word. *acc*ompanied
captain	Don't let it r*ain* on the capt*ain*.
describe	There is a *scribe* in de*scribe*.
excellent	There is a prison *cell* in ex*cell*ent.
fundamental	*Fun* is *mental*.
independent	Put a *dent* in indepen*dent*.
knew	The "k" is new.
paid	How is it that *I* always get involved when something is to be *paid*?
parliament	Can there be a *liar* in a par*lia*ment?
pronunciation	A *nun* always has good pro*nun*ciation habits.
speak	Give him an "*a*" and let him sp*ea*k.
succeed	It takes double letters to su*cc*eed.
vegetable	Your vege*table* is waiting at the *table*.
Wednesday	We hope to *wed* on *Wed*nesday.

SELECTED SPELLING RULES

IE or EI

Use I before E except after C for the long "E" sound.

believe	priest	after C
fiend	relieve	ceiling
grievance	retrieve	conceit
niece	shriek	deceive
piece	thief	receive

Learn the exceptions to this rule by memorizing this nonsense sentence (Note the spelling of each word):

Neither financier seized either species of weird leisure.

Use E before I when the sound is not a long "E"

freight	neighbor
height	weight

Adding Prefixes

When you add a prefix to a word, the spelling of the word itself does not change.

un + natural = unnatural	over + run = overrun
mis + spell = misspell	im + mobile = immobile
un + excused = unexcused	re + supply = resupply

Adding Suffixes

When adding the suffixes -NESS and -LY, the spelling of the word does not change.

dry + ness = dryness	mere + ly = merely
kind + ness = kindness	shy + ly = shyly

Exceptions: For words that end in Y not representing the long "I" sound, change the Y to I before adding -NESS or -LY.

happy + ness = happiness	ready + ly = readily

Drop the final E before adding a suffix that begins with a vowel.

> hope + ing = hoping   live + able = livable
> use + able = usable

Retain the final E after C or G if the suffix begins with A or O.

> advantage + ous = advantageous   notice + able = noticeable
> courage + ous = courageous   service + able = serviceable

Retain the final E before adding a suffix that begins with a consonant.

> care + ful = careful   hope + ful = hopeful

Exceptions: argument, awful, ninth, wholly, wisdom

For words ending in Y preceded by a consonant, change the Y to I before adding a suffix. Retain the Y if it is preceded by a vowel.

> funny + est = funniest   boy + ish = boyish
> happy + ness = happiness   enjoy + ing = enjoying
> merry + ment = merriment   stay + ing = staying

Exceptions: Retain the y in words such as *babyish, ladylike, studying.*

Double the final consonant before adding a suffix beginning with a vowel if both of the following two conditions exist: 1) the word has only one syllable *or* the accent is on the second syllable; and 2) if the word ends in a consonant preceded by a vowel.

> control + ed = controlled   propel + er = propeller
> occur + ence = occurrence   quit + ing = quitting
> plan + ing = planning   refer + ed = referred

> *BUT*
> cancel + ed = cancelled (Accent not on last syllable, but final
>   consonant is doubled)
> prefer + able = preferable (Accent shifts to first syllable)

Add K before adding ING, ED or Y to words ending in a hard C.

> picnic + ed = picnicked   mimic + ing = mimicking
> panic + ed = panicked   traffic + ing = trafficking

Plurals

To form the plural of nouns, observe the following rules:

The most common way to form the plural of a noun is to add S.
   book, books   table, tables   desk, desks

The plural of nouns ending in S, SH, CH and X is formed by adding ES.
   box, boxes   church, churches   dress, dresses

To form the plural of nouns ending in Y *preceded by a consonant*, change the Y to I and add ES.
   army, armies   enemy, enemies   fly, flies

To form the plural of nouns ending in Y *preceded by a vowel*, add S.
   donkey, donkeys   key, keys   monkey, monkeys

To form the plural of most nouns ending in F or FE, add S. However, the plural of a few nouns ending in F or FE is formed by changing the F to V and adding either S or ES.

   chief, chiefs   dwarf, dwarfs
   BUT
   calf, calves   elf, elves
   hoof, hooves   knife, knives
   leaf, leaves   loaf, loaves

To form the plural of nouns ending in O *preceded by a vowel* add S. If the final O is preceded by a consonant, the plural is formed by adding S or ES.

   (O preceded by a vowel)
   rodeo, rodeos   radio, radios

   (O preceded by a consonant)
   domino, dominoes or dominos   tomato, tomatoes
   hero, heroes

All words ending in O that pertain to music, form the plural by adding S.

   alto, altos   piano, pianos
   crescendo, crescendos   solo, solos

To form the plural of compound nouns written as one word, add <u>ES</u> if the word ends in <u>S</u>, <u>SH</u>, <u>CH</u> or <u>X</u> and <u>S</u> if it ends in anything else.
    spoonful, spoonfuls   strongbox, strongboxes

The plural of hyphenated compound nouns consisting of a noun plus modifiers is formed by making the noun plural.
    mother-in-law, mothers-in-law   passer-by, passers-by

Some nouns are the same in the singular and plural.
    deer, sheep, species, trout

Many words of foreign origin have two plurals. Others have a plural that is irregular by English standards. When in doubt, check your dictionary.

Singular	*Plural*
alumna (feminine)	alumnae (feminine)
alumnus (masculine or mixed)	alumni (masculine or mixed)
curriculum	curriculums, curricula
appendix	appendixes, appendices
beau	beaus, beaux
focus	focuses, foci
memorandum	memorandums, memoranda
fungus	funguses, fungi
index	indexes, indices
analysis	analyses
basis	bases
crisis	crises
criterion	criteria

The plural of numbers, letters and symbols is formed by adding an *apostrophe* and <u>S</u>.
    two 5's,   three x's,   How many +'s are there in that equation?

The Research Paper

A research paper is a formal composition that includes information from a number of sources. It is essentially a summary of the information the writer has discovered about a particular subject.

Many research papers simply present the information the writer has found. Others attempt to draw a conclusion which persuades the reader to adopt a particular point of view. A paper on the origins of American jazz would probably be informational; one on ways in which the federal tax system could be reformed could proceed from the facts to a conclusion and then to a recommendation for a future course of action.

Strictly personal opinions are usually out of place in a research paper. As a result, the word "I" is seldom used. It is important in a research paper to "let the facts speak for themselves." You should let the authorities you cite carry the weight. It is much more convincing for a research paper to say, *Thomas Jefferson* thought the taxing system should . . ." than to say, "*I* think the taxing system should . . ."

If you wish to draw a persuasive conclusion in a research paper, you should generally present a series of facts in an "If . . ., then . . ." statement such as:

"If Jefferson's view that . . . can be applied today, and if the constitutional principle that . . . is still valid, then the tax system of the United States is not what the Founding Fathers intended."

This writer presents information from one of the Founding Fathers (the argument would probably be stronger if the writer had presented information from others as well); there are also appropriate facts from the U.S. Constitution. Then, in a conclusion, the writer brings those facts together into a summary statement. The careful reader would probably have picked up the differences between present practice and the intent of the Founding Fathers as they were presented throughout the paper. By stating the conclusion in the final paragraph, the author makes sure that no reader misses the point.

Parts of the Research Paper

1. Title Page

The title page includes at least the title of the paper and the author's name, both centered in the middle of the page. Often, the name of the course, the teacher's name, and the date are also included on three separate lines in the lower right-hand corner of the page (see Figure 1).

figure 1

USING EXISTING KNOWLEDGE AND TECHNOLOGY
TO DEAL WITH THE ENERGY DILEMMA

By

Susan Spangler

Introduction to Science
Mrs. Pomranka
April 6, 198—

2. The Abstract (optional)

An abstract is a brief summary of the content of the paper. It should state the central idea and main divisions of the paper as well as summarize any inferences made or comparisons drawn from the author's research. If the paper attempts to solve a problem or recommend a future course of action, the abstract should also state how the author arrived at the problem, how the research was done (reading, interviews, questionnaires, etc.), how the results were compiled, and how the conclusion was formulated.

3. Table of Contents

The Table of Contents lists the main divisions of the paper and their corresponding page numbers (see Figure 2).

4. List of Illustrations (if any)

(see Figure 3).

5. Introduction (optional)

The purpose of an introduction is to inform the reader of the intent or purpose of the paper and the extent of the research involved. If the paper covers a problem or a controversial issue, the problem should be clearly introduced, the necessary background given, a statement included about the method of research, and information given telling how the conclusions are derived.

Figure 2

TABLE OF CONTENTS

	Page
Introduction	5
The Music of Black Africa	6
Importation and Treatment of Black Slaves	8
Early Black Music	10
Emergence of Urban Blues	12
Early Blues Greats	15
New Orleans Ragtime Influences the Blues	17
The Influence of Black Oppression on the Blues	21
Conclusion	24
Appendix A, Rhythmic Notation of Present-day Blues	25
Appendix B, Historical Presentation of Blues Rhythms	29
Bibliography	37

Figure 3

LIST OF ILLUSTRATIONS

	Page
<u>Figure 1</u>, Primary Rhythmic Configurations of Present-day Blues	5
<u>Figure 2</u>, Major Slave Routes	8
<u>Figure 3</u>, Early Work-Song Rhythmic Configurations	11
<u>Figure 4</u>, Historical Events and Songs Growing Out of Them	22

6.   Text

(This is the main body of the paper).

7.   Appendixes (if any).

Supplementary or explanatory material not essential to the text but of importance should be included in the appendixes at the end of the paper.

8.   Bibliography

The bibliography is a listing of all reference material used in preparing the paper. It includes published material such as books and magazines; it also includes such things as interviews, letters, and the like which may have been used but which are not commercially published. A later section provides specific information about the form to be used in the bibliography.

Choosing a Topic

Choosing a topic is the most important part of writing a research paper. If you choose an unsuitable topic or write on one which is too broad, your paper will not be successful.

Here are two suggestions which are very important to consider in choosing a topic. First, be sure to *select a topic which you find interesting*. If you write about something you have no interest in, you will probably not write well.

Then, be sure *the topic is in an area you would like to learn more about*. Having insurance against boredom is important for anyone writing any paper, but it is especially important in the case of a research paper, since you will spend a considerable amount of time with the topic.

Where do ideas for topics come from? For most writers, they come from one or more of at least three places:

1. Often topics come from *assignments given by teachers*. Usually a teacher will provide you with a broad area, however, and you will be expected to narrow the topic to something specific which you feel to be an important dimension of the area and something which is interesting to you.

2. Many times topics come from *your own experience*. For example, if you were concerned about the conservation of energy resources, you certainly could find a specific topic for research in that area. Sometimes, your interests and general topics assigned by a teacher coincide in strange ways. A student interested in engineering might respond to an assignment to write a research paper on Shakespeare's plays by writing about the stage machinery which performers of Shakespeare's time used.

3. Sometimes, especially as you read widely, you will find topics arising from *articles or books which you read*. If you keep your eyes open and search for topics when you are reading, you will find some excellent ideas. Most often, you will find the main thrust of the article provides an idea for a topic. But sometimes you will be struck by a single sentence or idea hidden in an article. If you are alert, always looking for ideas to write about, you will spot those hidden topics.

When you choose a topic, you should keep in mind the availability of materials that you will need for your research. Once you have an idea, go to your school, community, or home library and see if there is sufficient material to use as a basis for a paper. If you can't find at least ten sources which apply to your topic, you should probably look for another area. Use the card catalogue, the *Readers' Guide to Periodical Literature*, and other appropriate indexes to determine whether your library has enough material to provide you with a good base to work from.

Limiting the Topic

Once you find you have enough material, limit your topic. Imagine trying to write a paper on a topic such as "World History." You could literally write for a lifetime and never complete the work. You need to narrow that broad topic.

The key to limiting your topic is to select a subject for writing which you can cover *completely* in the time available to you. You must also consider the length of your paper. An illustration of the process of limiting a topic follows:

   History
      U.S. History
         The Depression Years
           Roosevelt's Anti-Depression Activities
            Government Work Programs
               The Works Progress Administration (W.P.A)
               Highways Built by the W.P.A.

An eventual title for a paper emerging from this process might be "The Impact of the W.P.A. on Transportation in the United States from 1935 to 1950." Included in the paper could be a description of W.P.A. sponsored activities, the costs of W.P.A. highway building programs, and the like. It would be possible in such a paper to develop a conclusion based on the benefits of the activity as it is related to its cost.

Taking Notes

Prepare a preliminary outline to guide you in note-taking.

In order to begin researching a topic in an organized way, you need to write some kind of outline that includes the topics on which you need information. Sometimes you will need to begin reading before such an outline can be written; at other times you will already know enough about your topic to anticipate the main sections of your paper.

Suppose you were going to write a research paper on the origin of modern-day blues music. Your tentative outline might look something like this:

1. The music of black Africa
2. The importation of black Africans to America and the treatment of black slaves.
3. Early black work songs, religious and gospel spirituals, and "plantation blues"
4. The emergence of urban blues in cities with high black populations
5. The music of early blues greats such as Louis Armstrong, Bessie Smith, and Billie Holliday
6. The influence of New Orleans ragtime and big band sounds on the blues
7. Progressive problems of black people and how these problems changed their music

Prepare a "heading card" for each topic of your outline.

A heading card is a single card, usually 3″ by 5″, which you use at the front of all note cards containing information on that particular area. An example of a heading card is shown below.

Heading Card

```
┌─────────────────────────────────────────────┐
│                                             │
│                                             │
│         1.    The Music of Black Africa     │
│                                             │
│                                             │
│                                             │
│                                             │
│                                             │
│                                             │
└─────────────────────────────────────────────┘
```

As you read, you may find that topics need to be added to your outline. As you add them, prepare heading cards for them as well.

Prepare a "bibliography card" for each source you use.

The moment you begin using a source (book, magazine, interview, letter) prepare a bibliography card for it. Use cards that are the same size as your heading cards.

The bibliography card serves two purposes: First, it provides a correct identification for each note you will take, and it saves you the effort of writing the complete source on each note card. Second, it provides a bibliography entry in correct form so that when the final draft of the paper is written, you need only arrange your "bib" cards in alphabetical order and copy them on the page.

If you were writing a research paper on energy conservation, you might use a book by Davis and Schubert entitled, *Alternate Natural Energy Sources in Building Design*. Your "bib" card would look like this:

Bibliography Card

Davis, Albert J. and Robert P. Schubert,
Alternate Natural Energy Sources in Building Design,
New York: Van Nostrand Reinhold Company, 1977.

Specific directions about how to prepare bibliographic entries are included in the "bibliography" section of this Handbook. Be sure to follow the directions very carefully. If your "bib" cards are carefully and accurately done, you will save yourself considerable time and trouble later on.

Prepare a note card for each potentially useful idea you encounter in your sources.

When you encounter something in your reading which you feel may be useful for your paper, either write it on a 3″ by 5″ notecard in your own words (paraphrase it) or copy it directly. If you copy it directly, enclose it in quotation marks. If you paraphrase the material, be sure you do not use the author's exact words.

Once you have written your note, write the author's last name, the publication date, and the page number(s) of the source at the top left of the card. At the top right, write the number of the topic (from your outline) to which the note refers. Here is an example of a notecard from Davis and Schubert's book, *Alternate Natural Energy Sources in Building Design*:

Note Card

Davis and Schubert, 1977, p. 42   #4
  "There are three basic types of light. First there is <u>direct</u> sunlight, which originates from the southeast to southwest (high angle), and east to west (low angle). <u>Ground</u> light, a secondary source, is reflected from the earth's surface and varies in intensity in relationship to ground surface, angle toward the sun, and the slope of the ground. <u>Diffused</u> light or skylight is direct light diffused by the particles of the atmosphere."

You know several things from the form of the notecard: first, you know the source from which the material came; second, you know the page from which it came; third, you know that it is quoted directly (note that the material is enclosed in quotation marks); finally, you know which outline topic the quoted material refers to (**#4** refers to topic number 4 in the outline).

Notice that you do not write the entire bibliographical entry on each card, but only the author's name, date of publication, and page. You also do not write out the entire topic from the outline; rather, you simply identify the card according to the number of the topic from the outline.

When you have finished the notecard, place it immediately behind the header card for the appropriate outline topic. Most people like to place rubber bands around the cards to keep them together.

It is important that you use a fresh notecard for each idea you identify, so that you can have all cards for a single topic together and not have single cards which fit under several headings. Also, when you arrange your cards in the best order to help organize your paper, you will be able to shift ideas around as you shift cards. If you have many ideas on a single card, it becomes much more difficult to organize your paper. Most students get a pack of 100 3″ by 5″ notecards when they begin a research paper. Those following good procedures will frequently use all of the cards as they prepare a 10-12 page paper.

Writing the Paper

Review your outline.

As you have been taking notes, you have probably been modifying your outline. You have probably encountered new topics, and found that certain topics you originally felt important are no longer worth including. As you modified your outline during the notetaking stage, you probably modified the numbers on your notecards to conform to your changing outline. However, once you finish your notetaking, it is important to step back for a short time and look at the outline carefully. Ask yourself the following questions:

1. Do the main topics reflect the major ideas I want to present?
2. Are the topics reasonably independent of one another?
3. Are the topics arranged in the sequence that will be the most effective in presenting the information?
4. Do the topics lend themselves to an appropriate conclusion?

Based on your answers to the questions, modify your outline as necessary. You may find this to be a good time to add sub-categories to help you organize your materials even better. Some people like to develop very detailed outlines at this point; others go directly to the first draft of the paper.

The Thesis Statement.

Some writers like to write a single sentence which sums up where they intend to go with their research before the research effort gets underway. Most beginners like to let the major idea of the paper evolve as they become familiar with the sources they intend to use. Whatever your preference is, the first step in writing the first draft is to write a *single sentence* which sets the stage for what you will write in your paper. You may never use the precise sentence you write as your initial thesis sentence; in fact, you will probably revise it several times before you write your final draft. However, that single sentence is very important to you. It guides you as you organize your material and as you select which material to use.

A good thesis statement does at least two things: it tells the reader what your paper will be about, and it captures his or her interest. In the case of a research paper which intends to persuade, it also hints that the reader will be asked to accept the writer's conclusions. The following thesis statements may serve as examples:

1. The emphasis in the Constitution of the United States on the rights and responsibilities of the common person is due in large measure to Benjamin Franklin.
2. The world has a serious energy problem, but it can be solved through the intelligent use of existing knowledge and technology.
3. Jane Smith has the qualities Hamilton looked for in a governor.

Usually the thesis statement appears in the final draft of the paper at the end of the first paragraph; however, under some circumstances, it may not be explicitly stated until the end of the paper. A useful model for the research paper is the following:

First paragraph.

This sets the stage for the paper by catching the reader's attention; then it quickly moves to the thesis statement. The following is an example of an introductory paragraph:

The world's fossil fuels will be used up in less than one hundred years if consumption continues at present rates (Ernhardt, 1981, p. 18). Numerous high-technology solutions such as generation of electricity through panels in space with micro-waves transmitting the energy to earth have been proposed to solve the problem. Most solutions involve considerable governmental expenditure. What has been ignored by officials is the abundant supply of answers to the energy problem that we already have. The world has a serious energy problem, but it can be solved through the intelligent use of existing knowledge and technology.

The Text.

Once the first paragraph (with its thesis statement) has been written, organize your notecards according to the outline and begin to juggle them until they seem to fit an appropriate order within the topics. Then, using the notecards, begin writing, using the cards as guides. Often you will use only bits and pieces of the material on the cards; sometimes you will have to go back to the original source to get additional information (although if you have been careful in the notetaking process, this will rarely happen).

Sections of the paper should correspond to the topics of the outline, and you may wish to title those sections. Should you wish to do so, center the titles on the page and underline them. They should be included in the Table of Contents once you finish your final draft.

The Conclusion.

Usually research papers will have a conclusion. More often than not, the conclusion is a re-statement of the first paragraph and its thesis statement. The following is an example of a concluding paragraph:

> The intelligent use of the energy sources supplied by the wind, by the seas, and by the sun can eliminate the problem posed by rapidly diminishing fossil-fuel supplies. But rather than waiting for high technology to capture those energy sources, the common, ordinary citizen can make a common-sense application of techniques that go back to the cave dweller and thus delay the onset of a crisis in energy. Ultimate answers to the energy problem may involve complex technology, but immediate answers involve common sense and common people.

Conventions

Headings.

Most research papers use three levels of headings to sub-divide the content and to provide helpful cues to the reader.

A centered main heading
A flush-left side heading
An indented paragraph heading

Here are examples of the three headings:

METHODS OF RESEARCH
Library Research
Procedure
Written Results
Questionnaires
Writing the Questions
Procedure
Written Results

Proper Presentation of Numbers

When referring to numbers in a research paper, use *words* to express the following:

The numbers zero through nine
five others
We questioned *eight* doctors regarding their knowledge of the latest in cancer research.

Any number that begins a sentence
>   *Sixty* percent of those questioned answered, "yes".
>   *One hundred forty* students were given scholarships.

Use figures to express
Numbers 10 or greater
>   They tabulated a total of 48 responses.

Units of measurement or time
>   He was given 500-mg doses for 2 weeks.

Ages
>   Her daughter is 7 years old.

Times and Dates
>   8:25 A.M., January 29, 1988

Percentages
>   A total of 18% responded to the letter.

Ratios
>   The people voted 4:1 in favor of the bond issue.

Exact sums of money
>   Each person who completed the petition was paid $5.

Page numbers, figure or table numbers
>   Table 4 on page 26 shows the 1952 election results.

Numbers grouped for comparison within a single sentence
>   Of the 25 cases, 11 were settled out of court, 3 were settled in court, and 1 is still pending.

Commas in numbers
In figures of 1,000 or more, use commas between groups of three digits.
>   1,000 children 84,396 Libyans

Illustrative Material

Illustrative material such as tables, figures, charts, graphs, and photographs can increase understanding of the text in ways that words cannot. Just as "one picture is worth 1,000 words," one table or chart can show pages of written description at a glance, making it easy for the reader to assimilate and compare vital information.

- Figures, charts and graphs should be clear, properly labeled, and easy to read.
- Use heavy lines for vertical and horizontal axes clearly labelling the units in which they are measured.
- If possible, color-code each separate line placed on graphs.
- Number each figure, chart, or graph throughout the paper.
- If there are many figures within each chapter, number the figures by chapter (figure 3.8—the 8th figure in chapter 3).

Footnotes

There are three common kinds of footnotes, each serving a different purpose:

1. Content footnotes

Content footnotes explain or amplify the information in the paper. An example of a content footnote would be a reference to something in an appendix.[1]

[1]See appendix B for Solar Tables for North America.

> Most often, especially in short papers, you will place information such as this in parentheses at an appropriate point in the paper instead of putting it at the foot of the page. (See Appendix B for Solar Tables for North America.)

2. Reference footnotes

Reference footnotes are used to inform the reader about the source from which material was taken. Footnotes of this sort are used for all ideas taken from other sources, whether or not the sources are quoted directly. Avoid the mistake of footnoting only quoted material.

The most common way of indicating the source of referenced material is to use the following format: (Davis and Schubert, 1977, p. 42) immediately following the quoted material. The sequence of material is: a parenthesis, the name(s) of the author(s), the date of publication, the page(s) on which the material appeared, and a parenthesis. This reference appears in the text of the paper, not at the bottom of a page. Should the reader wish to find the specific article to which the reference refers, he or she should go to the bibliography, where a book entitled, *Alternate Natural Energy Sources in Building Design* appears under the authorship of Davis and Schubert.

3. An older system of footnoting

This system placed reference notes at the bottom of the page on which the quoted or referenced material appeared. This system was troublesome for a number of reasons: first, it required the reader to shift from the text to the bottom of the page, thus interrupting the flow of the reading; second, it was extremely difficult for a typist to allow a precise amount of space at the bottom of a page for anticipated footnotes; and finally, scholars who read research papers tend to be the ones who check footnotes, and they usually know the contributions of authors rather than the precise names of books or articles. Thus, they appreciate the appearance of the author's name in the text rather than at the bottom of the page.

The system advocated here is the one most widely accepted in scholarly writings today. It is also the most commonly accepted system in colleges and universities for research papers.

Bibliography

When writing a bibliography, observe the following details of form:

- Items should be arranged alphabetically according to the last names of authors.

    If the source has more than one author, alphabetize it under the first author's last name. The names of co-authors are written first name first.

- It is not necessary to number the sources in a bibliography.
- Anonymous items such as encyclopedia articles are alphabetized by the first word of their titles, unless the first word is *the*, *a*, or *an*, in which case it is alphabetized according to the second word in the title.
- If an item occupies more than one line, the second line should be indented so that the author's name stands out on the page.
- Type bibliographical entries using single spacing leaving a double space between entries.

Follow the following format when compiling a bibliography:

Books

Kotzwinkle, William, *Dr. Rat: A Wild Novel About the Ultimate Revolt of Mother Nature*, New York: Bantam Books, 1977.

Newspapers and Magazine Articles

"GOP Unveils Tax Relief Ideas," *The Boulder Daily Camera*, March 22, 1979. (no author given)

Attaway, Roy, "A Viking in the Keys," *Motor Boating and Sailing*, April 1979, pp. 67–70 ff. (*ff* means the article is continued later in the magazine.)

Encyclopedias

"United States of America: Racial Composition," *Encyclopaedia Britannica*, vo. 22, Chicago: Encyclopaedia Britannica, Inc., 1966, pp. 18–19.

Interviews

Davis, James S., Interview, Oct. 14, 1981.

A Glossary of Grammatical Terms

Sentence

A sentence is a string of words that makes good sense and is complete. The following strings of words are examples of sentences:

The elephant died.
Drop your packages off at the drugstore.
Every person at the celebration overate.
My dog chased the neighbor's cat into the street.

If a string of words that makes good sense is not complete, it is called a *sentence part*. The following are sentence parts:

On the chair next to the broken window
The carnival manager socked the
The man in the third row from the top of the balcony

Sometimes strings of words make no sense at all. In that case, they are called *non-sentences*. "Dribbled jumped the by and if the man" is a non-sentence.

Sentence Types

Most English sentences are statements or *declarative* sentences. The following are *declarative* sentences:

The book was large and difficult to carry.
Sammy is the nicest cat we've ever had.
The first baseman caught the fly to retire the side.

Another type of sentence is the question or *interrogative* sentence. The following sentences are *interrogative*:

Can you stop and pick me up?
Will John ever grow up?

A third type of English sentence is the command, often called the *imperative* sentence. The following are examples of *imperative* sentences:

Hit the deck.
Please go with me to the movies.
Enter the room quietly and take your places in your assigned seats.

Parts of the Sentence

A sentence consists of a *subject* and *predicate*. The subject is the part of the sentence something is said about; the predicate is the section which says something about the subject.

The Subject

The *subject* normally occurs at the beginning of the sentence. It contains the noun or pronoun which the predicate says something about. That noun or pronoun is called the *simple subject*. The subject is underlined in the following sentences, and the simple subject is enclosed in a box.

The boy *ran fast.*

The boy *who lives in the house next to mine ran fast.*

We *noticed the boy who lives in the house next to mine running down the street.*

Sometimes the subject is not at the beginning of the sentence.

Everywhere there was laughter.

The Predicate

The *predicate* usually occurs at the end of the sentence. It contains the main verb in the sentence and says something about the subject. In distinguishing between subjects and predicates, it is often useful to identify the verb first. Once that is done, finding the subject is usually quite simple.

In the following sentences the predicates have been underlined and the main verbs enclosed in boxes:

The boy ran *fast.*

The boy who lives in the house next to mine ran *fast.*

We noticed *the boy who lives in the house next to mine running down the street.*

Sometimes the predicate is not at the end of the sentence.

Everywhere there was *laughter.*

The Direct Object

The *direct object* is the noun or pronoun which receives the action of the verb. It is a part of the predicate. The direct objects in the following sentences are in italics:

The boy chased the *dog*. We saw *him*. He was chasing a *cat*.

The Indirect Object

The *indirect object* is a noun or pronoun which comes before the direct object in the sentence. It tells for whom or to whom the action of the verb is being done. Indirect objects in the following sentences are in italics:

Mary gave *Susan* a birthday card.

The donkey threw *Henry* a baseball.

Predicate Adjective

The *predicate adjective* is an adjective in the predicate which tells something about (modifies) the subject, and is joined to it by a linking verb such as the verb *to be*. The predicate adjectives in the following sentences are in italics:

The lake is *quiet* today.

The throat of the fire-eater became *sore* after yesterday's performance.

My mother's health seems *better* after her stay in the hospital.

Predicate Noun or Pronoun

A *predicate noun or pronoun* appears in the predicate. It is the same person or thing as the subject, and is joined to it by a linking verb such as the verb *to be*. The predicate nouns and pronouns in the following sentences are in italics:

My mother is the *Representative* from our congressional district.

Jim was the *candidate* who won the election.

It was the Jones *family* coming up our drive.

The culprit could be *she*.

Parts of Speech

Noun

A noun is the name of a person, place, thing, or idea. Here are some examples of nouns.

Henry gave his *brother* the *apples*.

> *Henry* is a proper noun as all names are. It is the SUBJECT of the sentence. Proper nouns are capitalized.

> *Apples* is a common noun and is the DIRECT OBJECT of the verb; it tells directly what was given.

> *Brother*, another common noun, is the INDIRECT OBJECT of the verb; it tells to whom the apples were given.

Beauty is everywhere.

> *Beauty* is an abstract noun and is the SUBJECT of the sentence.

Pronoun

A pronoun is a word that takes the place of a noun. In one of the preceding sentences, *he* can replace *Henry*, *him* can replace his *brother*, and *them* can replace *apples*.

Verb

A verb is a word which shows action or expresses a state of being.

> When she *is* at home, they *visit* her.

>> *Is* expresses a state of being; it does not describe an action of any kind.
>> *Visit* is an action verb.

Adjective

An adjective is a word used to modify (more fully describe) a noun or pronoun.

> The *full* moon peered over the *Chinese* junks.

>> *Full* is a common adjective modifying the noun *moon*.
>> *Chinese* is a proper adjective modifying the noun *junks*. Since it is proper, it is capitalized.

Adverb

An adverb is a word used to modify (more fully describe) a verb, an adjective, or another adverb.

> The *very* small child ran *extremely quickly*.

>> *Very* is an adverb, modifying the adjective *small*.
>> *Quickly* is an adverb, modifying the verb *ran*.
>> *Extremely* is an adverb, modifying the adverb *quickly*.

Function Words

Most of the words you use fit in the above five classes of words (parts of speech). These are called *content* words; they carry the majority of the meaning in sentences. Since certain pronouns replace and carry the content of nouns, they are *content* words.

Of course, content words aren't the only classes of words you use in speaking and writing English. Other words are called *function* words. They connect the content words according to the patterns of the English language. They include:

Pronouns

Sometimes pronouns are used to connect two sentences together and form one.

The man lives in Korea.

We met the man today.   (whom)

The man *whom* we met today lives in Korea.

Preposition

Words that connect nouns or pronouns to the rest of the sentence are called *prepositions*. The noun or pronoun is called the *object of the preposition*.

A friend *of* mine lives *in* Canada.

Conjunction

A *conjunction* is a word that connects two parts of a sentence. If the conjunction connects two parts that are similar in structure, it is called a *coordinating* conjunction.

Mary *and* Jim like ice cream, *but* I don't.

And connects two words. *But* connects two sentences.

If the conjunction connects two parts that are different in structure, it is called a *subordinating* conjunction.

Jeremy continued to fight *until* the bell rang.

Until connects a sentence (independent clause) with an adverb clause (dependent clause).

Articles

The, a, and *an* are articles. They always precede a noun and modify it. Thus, they are a kind of adjective. *The* is used when the noun it precedes refers to a specific object or idea.

The man left *the* dream of his boyhood behind.

A or *an* is used when the noun it precedes does not refer to a specific, but rather to a general object or idea.

An elephant can drink *a* gallon of water in seconds.

A and *an* refer to any or all elephants and to any and all gallons of water.

Interjection

An *interjection* is an exclamation that has no grammatical connection with the rest of the sentence. Many times interjections are used to show strong feeling. The following are examples of interjections:

Oh! Oh! There's a mouse in the house.

Please! Don't you know this is a library?

Alas, poor Yorick; I knew him well. (Shakespeare, *Hamlet*)

Multiple Classes

Words that you use in speaking or writing can fall into any number of the previous classes. For example, the word *up* can be used in the following sentences:

Preposition: The men's room is down the hall, *up* the stairs, and to the right.

Verb: Our neighbors *upped* the price of their house $3,000 last week.

Noun: "*Up*" was written on every sign around the hall.

Adjective: The *up* escalator stopped while we were between floors.

Adverb: Anyone going *up*?

The Prepositional Phrase

The *prepositional phrase* is a string of words which begins with a preposition and ends with a noun or pronoun. The noun or pronoun which ends the phrase is called the object of the preposition. The prepositional phrases in the following sentences are in italics:

The girl *with the baseball glove* is my sister.

My sister is the one *with the baseball glove*.

In the afternoon, we went *to the beach*.

On the other hand, we knew the burglar in the house would take the television set *near the family room*, the silverware *from the buffet*, and the coin collection *on my dresser*.

Prepositional phrases may be either adjectival (modifying a noun or pronoun) or adverbial (modifying a verb, adjective, or adverb).

The Clause

The Independent Clause

An *independent clause* is a string of words which could stand alone as a sentence. It is complete and makes good sense by itself, but it is a sentence that is connected to another independent clause or to a dependent clause. The following are examples of independent clauses:

I met a classmate, and *we went to the cafe for a soda*.

The man whom I expected to meet *wasn't there*.

I met a classmate whom I haven't seen in five years.

Dependent Clause

A *dependent clause* is not a complete string of words. It cannot stand alone as a sentence. The dependent clauses in the sentences below are in italics:

I met a classmate *whom I haven't seen in five years*.
The man *whom I expected to meet* wasn't there.

Verb Tense

Present tense verbs indicate action which is taking place at the present time:

The group *is going* to the film.
The singer also *plays* piano.
Ann *does play* the violin well.

Past tense verbs indicate action which took place at a previous time:

The group *went* to the film last period.   (past)
The birds *have returned* from the South.   (present perfect)
The rock band *had finished performing* when the star *appeared*.   (past perfect and past)

Future tense verbs indicate action which will take place at some time in the future:

The group *will go* to the film.   (future)
They *will have left* by the time you arrive.   (future perfect)

Voice of Verbs

Active Voice

The *active voice* verb makes the subject the chief actor, as in the following examples:

The dog chased the cat.
Henry ate his food quickly.
Sarah carried the whole load of firewood.

Passive Voice

The *passive voice* verb places the actor in the predicate, as in the following examples:

The cat was chased by the dog.
The food was eaten quickly by Henry.
The whole load of firewood was carried by Sarah.

Sometimes the passive voice is used when the actor is unknown:

The silver *was stolen*.

An error *has been found* in the ballot count.

Number of Verbs

Verbs may be either *singular* or *plural*. Singular verbs go with singular subjects as in the following sentences:

John (singular) chases (singular) deer out of the family garden nearly every night.

The students (plural) visit (plural) a neighboring school each year.

The book (singular) lies (singular) open on the desk.

Grammatical Relationships

Coordination

Coordination means that two equal things are connected in some way. The following sentences show coordinate relationships between elements:

The *boy* and his *father* walked to school.   (coordinate subjects)

The cat *lapped* the milk and *dripped* it on the floor.   (coordinate verbs)

The teacher thanked *Sandy* and *Martin*.   (coordinate direct objects)

The lady gave *him* and *me* candy bars.   (coordinate indirect objects)

Grandma spoiled Jim, and *Grandpa told her not to*.   (coordinate independent clauses)

They went *over the river* and *through the woods*.   (coordinate prepositional phrases)

The shark was *huge* and *ugly*.   (coordinate predicate adjectives)

Subordination

Subordination means that two unequal things are connected in some way. These sentences show subordination of one element to another:

When I get tired, I find it hard to get to sleep.   (dependent clause followed by an independent clause)

My teacher, *who has been teaching for ten years*, is an expert on language.   (dependent clause connected to an independent clause)

Modification

Modification means that a word, phrase, or clause makes the meaning of another element of the sentence more specific. The following sentences illustrate modification:

> The *big* cat walked *quietly*.   (*Big* tells something about cat; *quietly* tells something about how the cat walked)
>
> The man with the heavy coat left the movie.   (*With the heavy coat* tells which man left.)
>
> In the beginning of the film, the hero finds a horse.   (*In the beginning of the film* tells when the hero finds the horse; it gives a time element to the verb, *finds.*)

Pronoun Antecedent

An antecedent is the word which a pronoun replaces. The following paragraph illustrates the relationship of pronouns and their antecedents:

> Father turned on the news to watch the weather forecast. He (father) said that it (the forecast) warned of a major storm on its (the storm's) way. "Too bad," he (father) mumbled. "Looks like my (father's) golf match will be cancelled."

Pronoun Reference

Sometimes it is not clear what the antecedent of a pronoun is. For example, in the following sentence a reader could misunderstand the meaning because of an *ambiguous reference*.

> The soldiers fought with the invaders until they were nearly destroyed.

Who was nearly destroyed? The soldiers? The invaders? Because the reader cannot be sure of the antecedent of the pronoun *they*, this sentence should be rewritten so that the antecedent is absolutely clear. Placing the pronoun very close to its antecedent usually eliminates the possibility of confusion.

THE BUSINESS LETTER

A business letter should include the following elements. Their numbers may be identified on the sample letter which appears on the facing page.

1. The Heading includes the street address; the city, state, and ZIP code; and the date. Always abbreviate the name of the state, since the recipient of your letter may write back to you, and he or she will want to use your return address on the envelope. The U.S. Post Office asks that names of states be abbreviated on envelopes to make sorting easier.

2. The Inside Address should be identical to the address on the envelope in which you send the letter. It should contain the name and address of the company or person to whom you are writing.

3. The Salutation will always include the name of the person included in the inside address. However, if you are writing to a company, not a specific individual, you have a small problem. Avoid the salutation, *Gentlemen.* That assumes an all-male company, something that almost never exists. If you address someone by title in the inside address (Executive Director, for example), you might write, *Dear Executive Director* or *Dear Director.* If you are writing to a firm and have no idea what area your letter should be directed to, simply wirte, *To Whom It May Concern* as your salutation. That is a bit formal, but if you are quite indefinite about the company, it may be best to be a bit formal in your whole letter. Whenever possible, include a specific name in your saluation.

4. The Body of the letter contains the message you wish to send. It should be clear and concise; it should reflect a business-like tone.

5. The Closing will normally be something like *Sincerely;* however, closings such as *Very truly yours, Respectfully,* and *Sincerely yours* are each appropriate. Capitalize only the first word of the closing.

6. The Signature should appear immediately below the closing, with the full name of the writer typed below it. Generally, one should leave four spaces between the closing and the typed name of the writer.

7. The Envelope should be addressed exactly as is the letter. The return address should be identical to the heading, except that the date is not included; the address should be identical to the letter's inside address.

The following is a list of U.S. Postal Service abbreviations for the fifty states, the District of Columbia, and the several trust territories of the United States. Use of these abbreviations speeds handling of the mail.

Alabama	AL	Nebraska	NB
Alaska	AK	Nevada	NV
Arizona	AZ	New Hampshire	NH
Arkansas	AR	New Jersey	NJ
California	CA	New Mexico	NM
Colorado	CO	New York	NY
Connecticut	CT	North Carolina	NC
Delaware	DE	North Dakota	ND
District of Columbia	DC	Ohio	OH
Florida	FL	Oklahoma	OK
Georgia	GA	Oregon	OR
Guam	GU	Pennsylvania	PA
Hawaii	HI	Puerto Rico	PR
Idaho	ID		
Illinois	IL		
Indiana	IN	Rhode Island	RI
Iowa	IA	South Carolina	SC
Kansas	KS	South DAkota	SD
Kentucky	KY	Tennessee	TN
Louisiana	LA	Texas	TX
Maine	ME	Utah	UT
Maryland	MD	Vermont	VT
Massachusetts	MA	Virgin Islands	VI
Michigan	MI	Virginia	VA
Minnesota	MN	Washington	WA
Mississippi	MS	West Virginia	WV
Missouri	MO	Wisconsin	WI
Montana	MT	Wyoming	WY

287 Beacon Street
①——→Boston, MA 02215
January 3, 198–

②

Director of Public Relations
Denver Museum of Natural History
1295 Colfax Avenue
Denver, CO 80209

④

Dear Director:←——③

    Please send me a copy of your bulletin "Artifacts
of the Plains Indians of Colorado." I am enclosing a
money order for $3.50 which should cover the cost of
the publication. If there is a fee for handling and
mailing, please bill me.

    I would appreciate your prompt handling of this
request. I am writing a paper on the Plains Indians
and need the bulletin immediately.

⑤——→Sincerely,

⑥——→ *Aaron Smith*

        Aaron Smith

⑦

Aaron Smith
287 Beacon Street
Boston, MA 02215

        Director of Public Relations
        Denver Museum of Natural History
        1295 Colfax Avenue
        Denver, CO 80209

A BRIEF GRAMMAR

Sentences

Most English sentences have subjects and predicates, and English speakers naturally expect to hear subjects and predicates when they hear the language spoken. Should a subject be omitted, they automatically supply one. For example, in this sentence

Get out of here!

The English speaker probably understands something like, "*You* get out of here."

The sentences below have been marked with a slash (/) to show the division between subject and predicate. The subject is in the first part of the sentence and the predicate in the last under normal circumstances.

Some dogs / have nasty habits.
No two dogs / behave in exactly the same way.
All dogs, including the so-called barkless hounds, / have voices.
(You) / Watch out!

Elements of the Sentence

There are three basic elements of the English sentence: the simple subject, the simple predicate or verb, and the complement.

Simple subject	Simple predicate or verb	Complement
Dogs	*like*	*humans.*
Newspapers	*spread*	the *news.*
The *pioneers*	*founded*	*Valley City.*
The *school*	*is*	*large.*
Henry	*seems*	*ill.*

A complement is not always necessary to complete the sentence's message; thus, some sentences do not have complements. The following sentences have no complements.

subject	verb
Most *dogs*	*bark.*
Susan	*is thinking.*

Word order.   The order in which words appear in an English sentence is very important in determining meaning. Read the following sentences to see how important word order is.

The lion ate Henry.
Henry ate the lion.

Simple subject.   The simple subject is the main *noun* or *pronoun* in the subject. Simple subjects are italicized in the following sentences.

The *man* with the heavy coat   /   is my father.
The vigorous young *colt*   /   is the son of the winner of the race.
He   /   ate the cookies.

Simple predicate.   The simple predicate is the main *verb* in the complete predicate. Sometimes the simple predicate contains more than one word. Simple predicates are italicized in the following sentences.

The man with the heavy coat   /   *is* my father.
The vigorous young colt   /   *is* the son of the winner of the race
He   /   *ate* the cookies.

Transitive verb.   Transitive verbs are simple predicates which take direct objects as their complements. Transitive verbs are italicized in the following sentences.

Henry *chased* the intruder.
The caterpillar *made* a cocoon.

Direct object.   The direct object is the most common complement. It receives the action of the verb. Direct objects are italicized in the following sentences.

Henry chased the *intruder*.
The caterpillar made a *cocoon*.

Indirect object.   The indirect object is a special complement which may appear only when a direct object is present. It indicates the person or thing for whom or to whom something is done. The indirect objects in the following sentences are italicized.

Sally gave a book.   Carrie showed her stamp collection.

Sally gave *Sandy* a book.   Carrie showed *Jim* her stamp collection.

<u>Object complement.</u>   The indirect object always precedes the direct object; the object complement follows it. In the following sentences, the object complement is italicized.

The voters elected Maria *treasurer*.

The results made Sam a former *politician*.

The couple kept their marriage a *secret* for ten days.

<u>Linking verbs.</u>   Linking verbs connect the subject with certain kinds of complements. Linking verbs are words such as am, are, is, were, was, be, being, been, seem, appear, become, smell, and taste. Linking verbs are italicized in the following sentences.

Marv *became* a dragon for the school play.

Sherril *is* the main character.

The play *is* really good.

The leading character *must be* terribly ambitious.

<u>Predicate noun.</u>   Predicate nouns are complements which follow linking verbs. The predicate nouns in the following sentences are italicized.

Marv became a *dragon* for the school play.

Sherril is the main *character*.

<u>Predicate adjective.</u>   Predicate adjectives are complements which also follow linking verbs. The predicate adjectives in the following sentences are italicized.

The play is really *good*.

The leading character must be terribly *ambitious*.

Basic Sentence Patterns

There are six basic sentence patterns in English. These patterns are the common ones, those which every native speaker of English understands naturally. These patterns reflect the order in which the elements of the sentence appear; thus, they contribute much to meaning.

<u>Subject, Verb, Direct Object Pattern.</u>   This pattern is the most common of the sentence structures in English. In it; the subject acts

through the transitive verb on the direct object. The following sentences illustrate this pattern.

subject	verb	direct object
Our *dog*	*ate*	the *cake.*
He	*chased*	the neighbor's *cat.*

Subject, Verb Pattern. This pattern has no complements. The verb is called an *intransitive complete verb* because it is complete, not requiring complements. The following sentences illustrate this pattern.

subject	verb
Dogs	*bark.*
Birds	*fly.*
Henry	*sits* in the garden every night.

Subject, Linking Verb, Predicate Noun Pattern. In this pattern, the noun after the linking verb means the same as the subject. The following sentences illustrate this pattern.

subject	linking verb	predicate noun
The Mississippi	*is*	a *river.*
Elephants	*can be*	good *workers.*

Subject, Linking Verb, Predicate Adjective Pattern. In this pattern is much like the Subject, Linking Verb, Predicate Noun pattern except that the word in the predicate is an adjective. It tells something about the subject, rather than being another word for it. The following sentences are examples of this pattern.

subject	linking verb	predicate adjective
Candice	*is*	*ill* today.
Little *brothers*	*can be*	*troublesome.*
Defensive *backs*	usually *are*	strong *runners.*

Subject, Verb, Indirect Object, Direct Object Pattern. This pattern introduces a receiver of the direct object. The following sentences illustrate this pattern.

subject	verb	indirect object	direct object
Consuela	*gave*	her *family*	the *money.*
Mary's *mother*	*showed*	*everyone*	her baby *pictures.*
The *pitcher*	*threw*	the second *baseman*	the *ball.*

Notice that each of these sentences can be rewritten to place the indirect object in a prepositional phrase following the direct object.

subject	*verb*	direct object	phrase
Consuela	*gave*	the *money*	to her family.
Mary's *mother*	*showed*	her baby *pictures*	to everyone.
The *pitcher*	*threw*	the *ball*	to the second base-man.

Subject, Verb, Direct Object, Object Complement Pattern.   This pattern is the least common of those listed. The object complement follows the direct object and is a noun which means the same as the direct object. The following sentences illustrate this pattern.

subject	verb	direct object	object complement
The *couple*	*named*	their *baby*	*Harrington Spencer III.*
The *class*	*elected*	*Dennis*	*treasurer.*

Notice that in each instance you can connect the direct object and the object complement with "is." (Their baby *is* Harrington Spencer, III. Dennis *is* treasurer.)

Variations on the Sentence Patterns

There are a number of variations on the basic sentence patterns. These variations usually involve a shifting of the elements of the sentence, the addition of words, or the omission of words.

Questions.   Basic patterns are formed into questions in several ways. Notice the basic patterns below and the ways in which they have been changed to make questions.

Subject, Verb, Direct Object Pattern
Our dog ate the cake.
Did our dog eat the cake?

Subject, Verb Pattern
Dogs bark.
Do dogs bark?

Subject, Linking Verb, Predicate Noun Pattern.
The Mississippi is a river.
Is the Mississippi a river?

Subject, Linking Verb, Predicate Adjective Pattern
Candice is ill today.
Is Candice ill today?

Subject, Verb, Indirect Object, Direct Object Pattern
Consuela gave her family the money.
Did Consuela give her family the money?

Subject, Verb, Direct Object, Object Complement Pattern
The couple named their baby Harrington Spencer III.
Did the douple name their baby Harrington Spencer III?

Negatives.   The following examples illustrate some of the many ways that negatives may be made in English.

Samantha has slept much this week.	(positive statement)
Samantha hasn't slept much this week.	(negative through *n't*)
Samantha has not slept much this week.	(negative through *not*)
Samantha needs sleep.	(positive statement)
Samantha needs no sleep.	(negative through *no*)
Samantha needs little sleep.	(negative by diminution)
Samantha needs hardly any sleep.	(negative by diminution)
Samantha needs scarely any sleep.	(negative by diminution)
Samantha is kind.	(positive statement)
Samantha is unkind.	(negative by prefix)
Samantha is not kind.	(negative through *not*)

There are many other ways to form the negative in English; they usually involve shifting meaning by using different words.

Commands or Requests.   Requests and commands normally do not have directly stated subjects. English speakers usually understand the subject, however, even when it is unstated. If there is any question about the identity of the person to whom the command or request is directed, the listener normally asks the speaker to name the subject. The following are examples of requests and commands.

Please polish the car this morning.
Close the door when you leave.
Hit the deck!

<u>Passive Voice.</u>   Only Subject, Verb, Direct Object patterns may be changed to passive voice. This operation permits the Direct Object to function as the Subject of the sentence. In the examples below, the first sentence is in active voice; the second is in passive voice.

Active: The alligator ate the duck.
Passive: The duck was eaten by the alligator.
Active: The president opened the meeting with a bang of her gavel.
Passive: The meeting was opened by the president with a bang of her gavel.

Sentence Expansion

English would be a rather unexciting language if its speakers could only use the six basic sentence patterns without embellishment. In actual practice, one might think of the basic sentence patterns as a kind of framework on which the sentences of the language are formed. As one adds to that framework, the language fills out just as a building might take shape around its wooden or metal framework.

<u>Modification.</u>   One of the most common ways to expand sentences is through modification. Look at the following ways in which modification may take place in sentences.

<u>Single-word Modifiers.</u>   Words that modify (more fully explain or describe) nouns are called *adjectives*. Look at the following sentence-combining problems to see how basic sentence patterns are expanded through the addition of adjectives.

Basic sentence: The car blocked the street.
Add modifiers from: The car was <u>dirty.</u>
                       The car was <u>old.</u>
                       The street was <u>busy.</u>

<u>Expanded sentence:</u>   The *dirty old* car blocked the *busy* street. *Dirty, old,* and *busy* are adjectives. *Dirty* and *old* modify *car* (they tell us more about *car*); *busy* modifies *street.*

Words that modify verbs, adjectives, or other adverbs are called *adverbs.* The adverbs in the following sentences appear in italics. Notice how they make the meaning of the verb more specific by explaining *how, when,* or *under what conditions.*

I won *easily.*   (explains how I won)
I won *yesterday.*   (tells when I won)
I won *handily.*   (tells under what conditions I won)

Notice how easily adverbs may be moved around the sentence.

Yesterday I won the golf tournament.

I won the golf tournament *yesterday*.

I *easily* won the golf tournament.

I won the golf tournament *easily*.

Immediately I felt better.

I *immediately* felt better.

I felt better *immediately*.

In all modification, the basic sentence pattern remains. Adjectives and adverbs are added to make the meaning of the sentence more precise.

<u>Phrase Modifiers.</u>   Phrases (groups of words usually beginning with prepositions such as *of, in, between, among,* or *with*) that modify nouns are called *adjective phrases.* The adjective phrases in the following sentences are printed in italics.

The girl *in the car* shouted.

They built a cabin *in the mountains*.

The dog bit the man *with torn pants*.

The house *between the oaks* is ours.

The blade *of the knife* is very sharp.

We love our little house *among the pines*.

Phrases that modify verbs, adjectives, or adverbs are called *adverb phrases.* As with single-word adverbs, they often tell *how, when,* or *under what conditions.* They also may be placed in many different parts of the sentence. Adverb phrases in the following sentences are italicized.

We eat breakfast *in the morning*.

We eat breakfast *in five minutes*.

We eat breakfast *in the kitchen*.

We eat breakfast *with our friends*.

We eat breakfast *with Grandma's old silver*.

Notice how easily adverb phrases can be shifted to different places in the sentence.

In the morning, we eat breakfast.

We eat breakfast *in the morning*.

There is little change in meaning when adverb phrases are shifted within sentences. Emphasis, however, changes a good deal. In the examples above, the first sentence (In the morning, we eat breakfast.) suggests that you will tell a listener what you do at other times of the day in later sentences. We might expect you to say, "Then, we have lunch at noon," or something like that in your second sentence.

The second example suggests something else could follow, although not necessarily so. One might follow "We eat breakfast in the morning" with "Some people sleep so long they have to wait until noon for their breakfast."

<u>Participial phrases</u> are phrases that begin with participles (verb forms) and modify nouns. The participial phrases in the following sentences have been printed in italics.

Going full speed, the biker collided with a telephone pole.

A little boy *carrying a large bag* slipped on the ice.

The man *sitting there* is my uncle.

<u>Clause Modifiers.</u> Clauses are groups of words that have subjects and predicates. Those that can stand by themselves, without the addition or deletion of words or phrases, are the same as sentences. They are called *independent clauses*. Those that cannot stand by themselves but must be included in the context of a sentence are called *dependent clauses*. It is the dependent clause which can serve as a modifier.

<u>Adjective clauses</u> are dependent clauses that modify nouns. Look at the following sentence-combining problem which produces an adjective clause.

Base sentence:	Vandals destroyed the house
Add modifier:	Vandals lived in our neighborhood (who)
Expanded Sentence:	Vandals who lived in our neighborhood de-stroyed the house.

Notice how "who lived in our neighborhood," a dependent clause, modifies the noun *vandals*.

Adjective clauses usually follow the noun they modify, just as adjective phrases do.

<u>Adverb clauses</u> are dependent clauses that modify verbs, adjectives, or adverbs. The following example illustrates the formation of an adverb clause.

Add modifier:	A storm had raged throughout the night. (After)

Basic sentence: We woke up to a yard full of fallen trees.

Expanded sentence: <u>After a storm had raged throughout the night,</u> we woke up to a yard full of fallen trees.

Or   We woke up to a yard full of fallen trees <u>after a storm had raged throughout the night.</u>

Adverb clauses begin with *subordinating conjunctions,* words such as *after, when, until, because,* and *if.* Adjective clauses begin with relative pronouns—*who, which,* and *that.*

<u>Joining.</u>   Basic sentence patterns can be joined together quite simply. The simplest way is through the use of a *coordinating conjunction* (*and, but, or,* or *nor*).

I like apples.

My sister likes plums.   (, but)

Result: I like apples, but my sister likes plums.

Two sentences may also be joined by using a semi-colon (;), thus avoiding the use of the coordinating conjunction.

I like apples.

My sister likes plums.   (;)

Result: I like apples; my sister likes plums.

Sentences that have similar subjects may be joined by stating the subject only once and incorporating the remaining words into the new sentence.

The angry elephant jerked the rope off the stake.

,   The angry elephant turned toward the stands.   (,)

, and   The angry elephant charged at the surprised spectators.   (, and)

Result: The angry elephant jerked the rope off the stake, turned towards the stands, and charged the surprised spectators.

Sentences that have similar predicates may be joined by stating the different subjects and then stating the predicate only once.

Jim checked his watch.

,   Charlie checked his watch.   (,)

, and   Kevin checked his watch.   (, and)

Result: Jim, Charlie, and Kevin checked their watches.

Words

Nouns

Nouns are naming words; they normally name persons, places, or things.

Kinds of nouns

<u>Concrete nouns</u> name things that can be observed with one or more of the senses. Words such as table, city, apple, and girl are concrete nouns.

<u>Abstract nouns</u> name things that usually cannot be observed with the senses. Words such as hostility, love, anxiety, and concern are abstract nouns.

<u>Proper nouns</u> include all nouns that specifically name people, places, or things. Words such as Sandra, Mt. McKinley, Broadway Avenue, and *The Washington Post* are proper nouns.

<u>Common nouns</u> include all nouns not included in the category of proper nouns.

<u>Collective nouns</u> are common nouns that refer to groups or collections of persons, places, or things. Examples are crowd, gathering, and family.

Functions of nouns.

<u>Subject of a sentence.</u>   Nouns are commonly used as simple subjects of sentences. The nouns used in this way are printed in italics in the sentences which follow.

> The *man* is nearly seven feet tall.
> Whether we like it or not, that *team* is going to win.

<u>Direct Object of a verb.</u>   Examples of nouns used in this way follow:

> Thoreau wrote *essays* in the nineteenth century.
> The jury made a *decision*.

<u>Predicate Noun.</u>   Examples of nouns used in this way follow.

> Texas is the largest *state*.
> The overcharge was really a *tax*.

<u>Indirect Object.</u>   Nouns used in this way appear in the following sentences.

> The French offered *the United States* soldiers.
> Henry gave *Lucy* a locket.

Objective Complement. Nouns used in this way appear in the following sentences.

The judge appointed him *bailiff*.

The people elected him *chairman*.

Object of a Preposition. The examples that follow are prepositional phrases (a preposition followed by a noun or pronoun, together with any modifiers). Nouns acting as objects of prepositions are printed in italics.

in the *house*

near an open *field*

outside the *law*

Possessive. Singular nouns show possession as in the following examples.

Henry's automobile

Carolina's apples

the *law's* variety

the *crowd's* anger

Forming plurals of nouns.

The following rules may be helpful in determining the plural forms of nouns.

Most nouns form their plurals by adding *s*. Some notable exceptions are listed in the following items.

1. Nouns which end in *s*, *z*, *x*, *ch*, and *sh* form their plurals by adding *es*.

   Examples   lens, lenses; fox, foxes; wrench, wrenches; wish, wishes.

2. Most nouns ending in *f* or *fe* change the *f* to *v* and add *s* or *es*.

   Examples: knife, knives; calf, calves.

3. Some nouns have similar singular and plural forms.

   Examples: deer, sheep.

4. Hyphenated compound nouns (nouns which contain more than one word) usually form their plurals by making the first part of the word plural.

   Examples: Secretaries-of-State, mothers-in-law.

5. Nouns ending in *y* preceded by a consonant change *y* to *i* and add *es* to form the plural.

   Examples: fairy, fairies; cherry, cherries; spy, spies.

6. Nouns ending in *y* preceded by a vowel form their plurals by adding *s*.
   Examples: monkey, monkeys; alley, alleys.
7. Some nouns form their plurals by changing the entire word.
   Examples: man, men; woman, women; mouse, mice.
8. Nouns ending in *o* preceded by a vowel form their plurals by adding *s*.
   Examples: radio, radios; studio, studios.
9. Nouns ending in *o* preceded by a consonant form their plurals by adding *es*.
   Examples: potato, potatoes; hero, heroes. There are several exceptions to this rule, however. Some are: piano, pianos; solo, solos; soprano, sopranos.
10. Nouns with Greek roots ending in *-sis* form their plurals by changing the i to *e*.
    Examples: analysis, analyses; hypothesis, hypotheses.
11. Some nouns keep their foreign forms.
    Examples: datum, data.

Pronouns

Pronouns are words used in place of nouns. They may be classified as personal, relative, demonstrative, reflexive, or indefinite.

Personal pronouns refer to persons. They are classified according to person, case, and number. The following chart illustrates this classification.

	First person Singular	First person Plural	Second person Singular	Second person Plural	Third person Singular	Third person Plural
Nominative Case	I	we	you	you	he, she, it	they
Objective Case	me	us	you	you	him, her, it	them
Possessive Case	my, mine	our, ours	your, yours	your, yours	his, her, its, her	their, theirs

Nominative case is used for subjects and predicate pronouns. Possessive case is used whenever ownership is expressed. Objective case is used for direct objects, indirect objects, and objects of prepositions.

Relative pronouns take the places of nouns as well as joining dependent clauses to the remainder of sentences. The relative pronouns are *who, which, what, that,* and *whom.* Examples of the use of relative pronouns in sentences are as follows:

The fellow *whom* I saw in the store is following us.
Those *who* step forward will get $8,000.

Demonstrative pronouns point out some definite person, place, or thing.

Examples: *This* scarf is mine, *that* one is yours.
These seats are taken; *those* are not.

Reflexive pronouns are formed by adding *self* or *selves* to the personal pronouns. They may be used in the following ways.

Direct object: He likes *himself* too much.
Indirect object: He bought *himself* a candy bar.
Predicate pronoun: The ducks are not *themselves* this morning.
Object of a preposition: Play by *yourself* for a while.

Indefinite pronouns are words like none, something, nothing, anything, and everything. They do not require antecedents, since they stand for things that are non-specific.

Verbs

The verb is the chief function word in the predicate. It establishes a connection between the subject and the complements that follow, or it serves to complete the sentence's action.

Transitive verbs are verbs that express action and that take direct objects. The following sentences contain transitive verbs (printed in italics).

Karl *hit* the fence.
While we all looked on, Daphne *tied* the score.

Each of the above sentences is in the *active voice,* that is, the direct object receives the action (expressed by the verb) of the subject.

The *passive voice,* on the other hand, involves shuffling the sentence around. The following are the same sentences expressed in passive voice.

The fence *was hit* by Karl.
While we all looked on, the score *was tied* by Daphne.

<u>Intransitive verbs</u> either show no action at all or limit their action to the subject. The following sentences illustrate the *intransitive complete verb*.

> The dogs *are barking* tonight.
>
> The pianist certainly *plays* well.

Contrast the last sentence with this same verb used as a transitive verb. Note the presence of the direct object in the changed sentence.

> The pianist certainly plays *Bach* well.
>
> *Bach* is the direct object in the sentence; thus the verb *plays* is now transitive.

<u>Intransitive linking verbs</u> connect the subject to either a predicate adjective or a predicate noun or pronoun. Linking verbs are usually forms of the verb *be* (*is, are, was, been,* etc.), although others such as *seems, became, appear, feel, smell, taste,* and *sound* may also be used. The following sentences illustrate the use of the intransitive linking verb.

> *Henry is* certainly a good basketball *player.* (*Henry* and *player* are connected by the linking verb *is.*)
>
> *Henry seems better* today. (*Henry* and the adjective *better* are connected by the linking verb *seems.*)
>
> The previously tame *tiger became* a *monster* in thirty seconds. (The subject, *tiger,* and the predicate noun, *monster,* are connected by the linking verb, *became.*)

<u>Forms of Verbs</u>

Verbs take two forms, regular and irregular. One of the reasons children or persons just learning English make errors such as "I holded the puppy" is that they are attempting to make the verb *hold* a regular verb. If it were regular, one would say, "I am holding the puppy," "I holded the puppy," "I have holded the puppy," and "I will hold the puppy." As you can see, when the same thing is done with a truly regular verb ("I am carrying the puppy," "I carried the puppy," "I have carried the puppy," and "I will carry the puppy"), *hold* is *not* a regular verb.

<u>Regular verbs</u> have four forms. The first, called the *infinitive form,* is the basic word from which all forms are created. The second is the *singular* form; it is used with singular subjects. Its regular form is made by adding -*s* or -*es* to the infinitive form. The third is the *past* form, used to express action which has occured in the past. Its form is created by adding -*ed* to the infinitive. The final form is the *present participle* form, made by adding -*ing* to the infinitive.

The following table shows the four basic forms of regular verbs.

infinitive	singular	past	present participle
carry	carries	carried	carrying
stop	stops	stopped	stopping
walk	walks	walked	walking
move	moves	moved	moving
hiss	hisses	hissed	hissing

Note the irregularities in spelling. Rules governing the spelling of regular verb forms are stated above. However, exceptions include the following.

1. When the infinitive form ends in *y* preceded by a consonant, as in *carry*, the *y* is changed to *i* and -*ed* is added to form the past.   (carried)
2. When the infinitive form ends in *s*, *x*, *ch*, or *sh*, as in *hiss*, add -*es* rather than the normal -*s*.   (hisses)
3. When the infinitive form ends in *e* as in *move*, add only -*d* to form the past and drop the *e* when adding -*ing* to form the present participle.   (moved, moving)
4. When the infinitive is only one syllable and it ends with a consonant preceded by a single vowel, as in *stop*, double the final consonant when adding -*ed* and -*ing*.   (stopped, stopping)

Irregular verbs do not appear to make their forms according to any systematic formula as do regular verbs. The following list illustrates the considerable number of irregular verbs. It also shows how common they are in ordinary usage.

infinitive	singular	plural	past	past participle	present participle
be	is, am	are	was, were	been	being
begin	begins	begin	began	begun	beginning
bite	bites	bite	bit	bitten	biting
choose	chooses	choose	chose	chosen	choosing
do	does	do	did	done	doing
feel	feels	feel	felt	felt	feeling
forget	forgets	forget	forgot	forgotten	forgetting
freeze	freezes	freeze	forze	frozen	freezing
get	gets	get	got	gotten	getting
have	has	have	had	had	having

infinitive	singular	plural	past	past participle	present participle
hold	holds	hold	held	held	holding
know	knows	know	knew	known	knowing
lie (recline)	lie	lie	lay	lain	lying
write	writes	write	wrote	written	writing
swim	swims	swim	swam	swum	swimming
go	goes	go	went	gone	going
make	makes	make	made	made	making
run	runs	run	ran	run	running
say	says	say	said	said	saying
sit	sits	sit	sat	sat	sitting
hurt	hurts	hurt	hurt	hurt	hurting
teach	teaches	teach	taught	taught	teaching
wear	wears	wear	wore	worn	wearing
thrust	thrusts	thrust	thrust	thrust	thrusting
think	thinks	think	thought	thought	thinking

Functions of verb forms

The infinitive form is used in the present tense and with the pronouns *I* and *you*. It may also be used with helping verbs such as *can, may, should, could, shall,* and *will.*

> I *will begin* at the beginning.
> I *feel* as good as new.
> The man *will choose* the fabric for the uniforms.

The singular form is used with singular nouns and certain pronouns, in the present tense.

> The detective *knows* the truth.
> She *swims* well enough to win the tournament.
> Horace *runs* the forty in twenty-seconds.

The plural form is used with plural subjects to express present tense.

> The members of the class always *forget* to close the door.
> They *hold* their new puppies so carefully.

The past form indicates past tense with either singular or plural subjects.

> He *chose* to go skiing.
> They *chose* to go skiing.

The past participle form uses the helping verb *had*, as well as related forms such as *should have, must have, might have, could have, should have,* and *will have.*

We *had begun* our trip by eight o'clock.
We *should have felt* relieved to be getting out of there.
We *had run* as far and as fast as we could.
We *could have worn* warmer clothes.

The present participle form uses helping verbs such as *am, is, are, was,* and *were.* It expresses action which is continuing, is anticipated, or had been happening.

The champion *is swimming* around the pool.
The children *were freezing* to death.
I *am getting* out of here.
They *are holding* the puppy.

Adjectives

Adjectives modify nouns in one of two ways; 1. they describe the noun or 2. they limit it.

Descriptive adjectives are the more common type, and are reflected in the following sentences.

The *tired old* man straightened his *aching* back and smiled.
It was a *solid* victory, and the team was *happy.*

In the second sentence, the adjective *happy* is a predicate adjective. It modifies the subject, *team*, just as if the sentence had begun, "The happy team . . ."

Limiting adjectives are of three types.
1. Numeral adjectives show how many or in what order things are considered.

There are *three* types of limiting adjectives.
The *first* item concerns the condition of the classroom.
2. Demonstrative adjectives indicate "which one" or point out specifics.

This book should have been returned to the library.
Both criminals were guilty.
3. Indefinite adjectives express an indefiniteness about a noun. They serve a writer by permitting the expression of a non-specific quantity or quality.

Some students want the lunchroom closed.
However, *many* want it to remain open.

All descriptive adjectives and some limiting adjectives have the potential for expressing comparison. The table below illustrates this quality.

adjective base	comparative form	superlative form
old	older	oldest
young	younger	youngest
fat	fatter	fattest
kind	kinder	kindest

Adjectives of one syllable normally form their comparative and superlative forms by adding *-er* for the comparative and *-est* for the superlative. However, those with two or more syllables often form their comparatives by adding the words *more* or *less* the words *most* or *least* being used for the superlative form.

adjective base	comparative form	superlative form
dependable	more dependable	most dependable
careful	more careful	most careful
foolish	less foolish	least foolish
careless	less careless	least careless

Some adjectives form their comparatives and superlatives on irregular bases. Following are some examples.

adjective base	comparative form	superlative form
good	better	best
bad	worse	worst
many	more	most
little	less	least

The comparative form of an adjective is used when one is comparing two things.

My father is *older* than yours.

That runner is certainly *faster* today than the last time I saw her.

I am even *more tired* today than I was yesterday.

The superlative is used when comparing more than two things.

My father is the *oldest* person in the room.

That time must be the *fastest* she has attained.

I am the *most tired* today that I have ever been.

Adverbs

Adverbs, like adjectives, modify other words. Adverbs modify verbs, adjectives, and adverbs. They can help a writer express time, place, manner, degree, and cause.

Time is expressed by adverbs such as *now* and *today* for present; *soon* and *tomorrow* for future; *before* and *yesterday* for past. Duration of time is shown by the adverbs *always* and *never*; frequency is shown by adverbs such as *frequently* and *sometimes*.

Place is expressed by adverbs such as *above* for position; *forward* for motion toward; *away* for motion from.

Manner is expressed by adverbs such as *quickly, slowly, better,* and *worse.*

Degree is expressed by adverbs such as *little, more, very,* and *almost.*

Cause is expressed by adverbs such as *consequently, then,* and *why.*

The following examples illustrate adverbs used in these ways.
Today we're going to the country.   (present time)
Soon we'll go to the country.   (future time)
Yesterday we went to the country.   (past time)
We're *always* going to the country.   (duration)
Sometimes we go to the country.   (frequency)
The picture is *above* your favorite.   (position)
Move the picture *forward* just a bit.   (motion toward)
Get that cat *away* from me!   (motion from)
Let's get this over *quickly*.   (manner)
Move it just a *little* to the right.   (degree)
If we don't want to get fired, *then* we'll have to work harder.   (cause)

Many adverbs end in *-ly*, and are easy to identify. However, some adjectives also end in *-ly*, thus creating a problem. Also, there are many adverbs which do not end in that suffix.

It is probably best to think of adverbs as answering questions like "When?", "Where?", "How long?", "How often?" and "How much?" Look at the following sentences.
adjective   We all need *daily* bread.
adverb   We all need bread *daily*.

Note how *daily* in the first sentence modifies bread. It functions as *wheat* in *wheat bread*. In the second sentence, however, *daily* functions as an adverb in that it answers the question, "when?" Therefore, it modifies the verb *need*. It tells the reader when the bread is needed.

Some adverbs which are commonly used but which do not end in *-ly* are the following.

almost	here	never	straight
already	instead	now	then
back	late	often	there

Prepositions

Prepositions are used with a noun or pronoun to make a phrase called a prepositional phrase. Such a phrase acts as an adjective or adverb in a sentence.

The following is a list of commonly used prepositions.

about	at	but (except)	into	through
above	before	by	near	to
across	behind	down	of	toward
after	below	during	on	under
against	beneath	for	out	underneath
along	beside	from	outside	until
among	between	in	over	up
around	beyond	inside	past	with

The following sentences illustrate the use of prepositions.

The man *with the Western hat* is a singer.   (adjective phrase)

We always eat *on Grandma's best china*.   (adverb phrase)

The rope *around the tree* keeps insects *from the leaves*.   (adjective phrase; adverb phrase)

INDEX

Abbreviations, H-27–28
Abstract, H-50
Active voice, H-9–10, 69
Address
  inside, 284
  return, 265, 284
Adjective, H-66
  predicate, H-65
  proper, H-33, 66
Adjective phrase, H-16
Adverb, H-66
Adverb clause, 35
Adverb phrase, H-16
Agreement
  pronoun-antecedent, H-5–6, 71
  subject-verb, 251–253; H-7–8
Anecdote, 189, 212, 213–214
Antecedent, 319–322; H-5–6, 71
Apostrophe, 319; 23–24
  for omission of letters, H-25
  with plurals, H-24, 47
  for possession, H-23–24
Appendix, H-51
Appositives, H-17
Articles, H-34, 67
Author's style, 238

Beginnings, 28–29, 100–101
  for a research report, 187–190, 193
Bibliography, 192–193; H-51, 61, 62
Bibliography card, H-54–55, 56
Body, of a letter, 265, 284
Book reviews, 232–256
  criticism in, 245–246
  editing, 254–255
  publishing, 255–256
  writing, 247–251
Brackets, H-27
Brand names, H-32
Business letters, 259–262, 280–285;
  H-28
  form of, 283–285

Calendar custom, 291–292
Capitalization, 98; H-31–35
  in poetry, 155–158
  of proper adjectives, H-33
  of proper nouns, H-35, 65
Card catalogue, 170, 171–174
Characters
  in book reviews, 236–237
  in a play, 314–315
Childhood memories, 22–25
Cinquain, 145–149
Clauses, H-68
  in apposition, H-17, 18
  adverb, 35
  dependent, H-16, 69
  independent, H-15, 21, 22, 68
  introductory, H-17
  nonrestrictive, H–18
  punctuation with, 51
  subordinate, H-8, 11
Closing, of a letter, 265, 284
Collage, 94–97
Collective noun, H-8
Colon, H-21–22
Comma, H-13–20
  in certain conventional situations,
    H-20
  with introductory items, 51, 76;
    H-17
  with items that interrupt sentences,
    H-17–20
  with pairs and items, H-15–16
  with quotations, 99
  in a series, 41; H-13
Commands, H-27, 63
Comparison, in poetry, 115–121, 133–
  139
Complete sentence, H-12
Compound noun, H-47
Compound number, H-26
Compound subject, H-7
Conclusion, in a research paper, H-59

Concrete poetry, 149–154
Conjunctions, H-67
    combining sentences with, H-11, 15
    coordinating, H-67
    subordinating, 35–36; H-67
Content footnotes, H-61
Content words, H-66
Conundrum, 299
Coordinating conjunction, H-67
Coordination, H-70
Copyright page, 250
Criticism, in book reviews, 245–246

Dash, H-25
Dates, H-20
Declarative sentence, H-63
Degrees and titles, H-20
Dependent clause, H-16, 69
Description, 188
    in poetry, 124–217
Descriptive words, 40–42
Details, selecting, 38–40
Dialogue, in a play, 323–324
Direct address, nouns of, H-19
Direct object, H-5, 64, 65
Direct quotations, 97–100; H-20
Discovery draft, 166, 183–184, 250–251

Editing, 15, 29–30, 254–255
Ellipses, H-29
Enclosures, in a letter, 284
Encyclopedia, 170, 174–177
Endings, 101–102
Exclamation point, H-28

Family, 201–227
    anecdotes, 212–214
    extended, 214–216
    and folklore, 290–291
    single-parent, 219–223
    traditional, 204–208, 217–219
    values, 208–209
Feelings, writing about, 3–15
Fiction, 238
Film reviews, 229–232

Folklore, 289–307
    personalization of, 315–316
Footnotes, H-61
Fragments, H-11–12
    phrase, H-11–12
    subordinate clause, H-12
Free writing, 4
Friendly letter, 262–279; H-20
    form, 265
    voice in, 268–269
Function words, H-66
Future tense, H-69

Ghost stories, 309–326
Greeting, 265, 284; H-20
Greeting cards, 266–268

Haiku, 144–145
Heading card, H-54
Headings, in a research paper, H-59
Home remedies, 294, 295
Hook, 100–101
Hyphen, H-25–26

I, you, 253
ie or *ei,* H-44
Illustrations, for a research paper,
    H-50, 51, 60
Imperative sentence, H-10, 63
Independent clause, H-68
    colons with, H-22
    commas with, H-15
    semicolons with, H-21
Indirect object, H-6, 65
Indirect question, H-28
Inside address, 284
Interjection, H-67
Interrogative sentence, H-63
Interviews, 93, 178
    by folklorists, 294
    note-taking in, 91–92
    questions to avoid, 88–91
Introduction, H-50
Introductory words, H-17
it, 322

Italics (underlining), H-35
its, it's 319

Key words, 92, 169–170

Legends, 302–306
Letters
of appeal, 275–279
of attack, 269–271
business, 259–262, 280–285; H-28
of complaint, 280–285
friendly, 262–279; H-20
of praise, 263–265
punctuating, H-20, 28
Library, 171–179
lie, lay, H-38–39
like, as, 118–120

Material culture, 289–290
Metaphor, 133–139
Mnemonic techniques, H-43
Modification, H-71
Modifiers
commas with, H-14–15
placement of, H-10

Names, H-20, 32
Narrator, in a play, 313–314, 315, 325
Negative criticism, 245–246
Nonrestrictive words, H-18–19
Note cards, H-56–57
Note-taking, H-53–57
for a book review, 236
in interviews, 91–92
Noun phrase, H-16
Nouns, H-65
collective, H-8
compound, H-47
of direct address, H-19
plurals, H-46
predicate, H-65
proper, H-32, 65·
Numbers, H-32
commas in, H-60
compound, H-26

expression of, H-59–60
plural, H-47

Object
direct, H-5, 64, 65
indirect, H-6, 65
of preposition, H-6, 67, 68
Older people, 81–104
Opinion, 67–75
Oral lore, 289–290, 292, 296–297
Outline
for a research paper, H-53, 57, 58
reviewing the, H-57

Paragraphing, 85–87
Paragraphs
concluding, H-59
for quoted material, H-30
in a research paper, H-58–59
Parentheses, H-26–27
Parenthetical expressions, H-19, 27
Participles, H-9
Parts of speech, H-65–67
Passive voice, H-9–10, 69–70
Past participle, H-9
Past tense, H-9, 69
agreement with, H-7
Perfect participle, H-9
Period, H-27–28
Personal letter. *See* Friendly letter; Letters
Personification, 133–139
Persuasion, 53–59
language of, 67–68
Phrase fragment, H-11–12
Phrases
adjective, H-16
adverb, H-16
in apposition, H-17
for emphasis, H-20
introductory, H-17
nonrestrictive, H-18–19
noun, H-16
prepositional, H-68
verb, H-16

Plays, 311–326
    dialogue in, 323–324
    scripting, 313–317
    stage directions in, 325–326
Plot, 237
Plurals
    apostrophe with, H-24
    forming, H-46–47
    of nouns, H-46
    of verbs, 252; H-70
Poetry
    capitalization with, 155–158; H-31
    comparisons in, 115–121, 133–139
    concrete, 149–154
    description in, 124–217
    form, 130–133, 138–319, 155–158
    punctuation with, 155–158; H-30
    reading, 108–111
    writing, 113–127; 139–145
Poets, 107–110, 124, 129–130
Possession
    using apostrophes, H-23
    pronouns, 318, 319; H-6
Predicate, H-64
Predicate adjective, H-65
Predicate noun, H-65
Predicate pronoun, H-65
    agreement with H-5
Prefixes, H-44
Preposition, H-67
    object of, H-6, 67, 68
Prepositional phrase, H-68
Present participle, H-9
Present tense, H-9, 69
Pronouns, 317–322; H-66
    agreement with antecedents, 319–322; H-5–6, 7–8, 71
    possessive, 318, 319
    predicate, H-5, 65
    reference of, H-71
    relative, H-8
    as subject, H-7–8
Pronunciation, 297–298
Proofing, 15, 30
Proper adjective, H-33, 66

Proper nouns, H-32, 65
Pun, 297
Punctuation, in poetry, 155–158
Punctuation marks
    apostrophe, H-23–24, 25, 47
    brackets, H-27
    colon, H-21–22
    comma, 41, 51, 76, 99; H-13–20
    dash, H-25
    ellipses, H-29
    exclamation point, H-28
    hyphen, H-25–26
    parentheses, H-26–27
    period, H-27–28
    question mark, H-28–29, 30
    quotation marks, 98–100, 190–101; H-28, 29–31
    semicolon, H-21, 29

Question mark, H-28, 29, 30
Questions
    for beginnings, 190
    embedded, H-19
    indirect, H-28
    in interviews, 88–91
Quotation marks, 98–100, 190–191; H-28, 29–31
    single, H-31
Quotations
    for beginnings, 188–189
    direct, 97–100; H-20
    for endings, 101–102
    extensive, H-31
    footnoting, H-61
    from interviews, 97
    from printed materials, 190–191, 193, 250
    punctuation with, 99
Quotation stems, 98–100

Readers' Guide to Periodical Literature, 171, 178
References
    in bibliography, H-51, 61
    footnoting, H-61

Relative pronoun, H-8
Research paper, 163–196; H-48–62
   beginnings for, 187–190, 193
   choosing a topic, 166–169; H-51–52
   conventions, H-59–62
   language in, 186–187
   limiting the topic, H-52–53
   planning, 165–166
   parts of, H-49–51
   resources, 164, 170–179, 193
   revising, 193–194
   sharing, 194–196
   taking notes, H-53–57
   writing, 183–184; H-57–59
Return address, 265, 284
Reviewing
   books, 232–256
   films, 229–232
Revision, 15, 193–194
Rhyme, 109–111
Riddles, 299–302
rise, raise, H-39
Run-ons, H-11

Salutation. *See* Greeting
Semicolon, H-21, 29
Sensory writing, 33–43
Sentence(s), 20–21
   complete, H-12
   fragments, H-11–12
   non-, 20–21; H-63
   parts of, H-64–65
   types of, H-63
Sentence-combining, 26–27, 50–51,
     68–69, 273–274; H-11
   descriptive words, 40–42
   paragraphing, 85–87
   subordinating conjunctions, 35–36
Sentence part, 20–21; H-63
Series, comma in a, 41; H-13
Setting, in a play, 315
Sexist language, 186–187
Similes, 118–121
Simple subject, H-64
sit, set, H-39

Social folk custom, 289–298
Spelling
   frequently misspelled words,
     H-40–42
   mnemonic techniques, H-43
   rules, H-44–47
   visualizing, H-43
Stage directions, 325–326
Statements, H-27, 28
Stereotypes, 82–83
Storytelling, 17–30
Subject, 251; H-64, 65
   agreement with, 251–253; H-5, 7–8
   collective noun as, H-8
   compound, H-7
   placement of, H-18
   plural, H-8
   pronoun as, H-5, 7–8
   simple, H-64
   singular, H-8
   of subordinate clause, H-8
Subordinate clause, H-8, 11
Subordinate clause fragment, H-12
Subordinating conjunctions, 35–36;
     H-67
Subordination, H-70
Suffixes, H-44–45
Summary, H-50
Superstition, 293–294, 295
Syllabication, H-25–26

Table of contents, H-50, 58
Television, 47–61, 63–76, 222–223
Thesis statement, H-57–58
Title(s)
   of persons, H-20, 34
   for a research paper, H-53
   of works, 191; H-30, 34
Title page, 249, 250; H-49
Topic(s)
   choosing a, 166–169; H-51–52
   limiting the, H-52–53
   for an outline, H-54, 57, 58
   for a research paper 166–169;
     H-51–53

Underlining (italics), H-35

Verb phrases, H-16
Verbs, 251; H-66
   agreement of, 251–253; H-7–8
   number of, 252; H-70
   strong, 13–14
   voice of, H-69–70
Verb tense, H-69
   correct use of, H-9
   future, H-69
   past, H-7, 9, 69
   present, H-9, 69
Visualizing, spelling aid, H-43
Vocabulary. *See* Word Bank

Voice, of verbs, H-69–70
   active, H-9–10, 69
   passive, H-9–10, 69–70
Voice, in writing, 268–269

Word Bank, 72–73, 103–104, 179–180,
   306–307
   family, 223–225
Words
   commonly confused, H-36–39
   definitions of, 103
   descriptive, 40–42
   of foreign origin, H-47
   frequently misspelled, H-40–42
   weak, 67–68
Writer's Notebook, 34

Art Credits

Susan Avishai: pages 205, 288; *Robin Cline: pages 228, 272, 316; Leslie Evans: pages 2, 12, 54, 308; Donna Rae Hirt: pages 32, 43, 128, 258; *George Hughes: pages 40, 282; *Larry Johnson: pages 62, 95, 106, 215, 321; Charles Joslin: pages 86, 144; Kathy Parkinson: pages 23, 200; Alfred Ramage: page 207; David Rose: pages 16, 18, 67; *Ron Rudat: pages 162, 240, 303; Jim Steinberg: pages 80, 182; *Joe Veno: pages 46, 65, 209, 267, 297, 298. *Represented by Gwen Goldstein.

Photo Credits

Page 74: Stock Boston, Inc., Michael Hayman; page 116: Stock Boston, Inc., Jack Prelutsky; page 122: Stock Boston, Inc., Ira Kirschenbaum; page 135: Jeoboam, Inc., Evan Johnson; page 157: Peter Arnold, Inc., Werner H. Müller; page 177: Culver Pictures, Inc.; page 189: Hale Observatories; page 230: *Movie Star News*